GISELA KONOPKA

the Institution

A MODERN CHALLENGE

Association Press

New York

Association Press, 291 Broadway, New York, N.Y. 10007

Revised edition, 1970

Standard Book Number: 8096-1777-3

Library of Congress Catalog Card Number: 54-5837

Printed in the United States of America

Group Work in the Institution

A MODERN CHALLENGE

Group Work in

Foreword by **FRITZ REDL**

To My Husband

FOREWORD

With this book by Gisela Konopka the whole group work field proudly emerges from its past confusion in approaching the institutional issue, and also from its role as a prestige step-child in the field of the social sciences. Its mere appearance at this time marks a decisive step forward in the maturation process of a whole scientific discipline, where promising stops and performance begins.

This is the first real, experience-based textbook on institutional issues for the group worker's training. It is perhaps of even greater value to institutions because, also for the first time, they will find a specific spelling-out of the present state of goals and methods of group work as it can apply to the institutional field, so they can know just what they are buying.

And it's about time we stopped "awakening" to "what is really needed in the institutional field," and began to produce it. By "we," I do not mean the institutions and those who work in them. (True, it would be a fascinating task to depict the institutional field's gradual awakening to the point where it began to demand from us what we had thought we had to urge it to accept. But it would be too long a story for these short lines.)

By "we," I do mean those who aspire to represent professional knowledge, thought and skills in the field of human engineering, or what we might term the behavior sciences in general.

Yes, we are all of us equally to blame. We psychiatrists, social workers and so forth have too long been merely complaining about the scandalous neglect of the institutional field. All of us at one time or another have indulged in a search for printable adjectives to describe the shortsightedness and incredible lack of interest shown by the public toward institutions. Yet until not too long ago, we ourselves to a pitiful degree indulged in confused thinking.

So let us cease this criticism of others and, for a change, begin to assess our own errors. Needless to say, much of this assessment will be somewhat exaggerated and oversimplified in order to make a sharp point in a narrow space, and will have many exceptions of which certainly the reader is one.

From 1936 on, the development of the professionals' attitude in the human behavior sciences toward the institutional problem seems to me to divide into three phases. (I have to begin with 1936 since that was the year I landed on these hospitable shores, and up to then I hadn't known a thing about all this.)

Phase I: I would like to call it the "that's just too bad" period. The attitude held during it could best be described in this way: "Not that we want to blame any one *person* or *group* of people—banish the thought. But there is no doubt that institutions are something awful, and there really shouldn't be such a thing. Of course, there is nothing one can do about this, except hope that eventually every child will have his foster home to live in and his psychoanalyst to go to; and all old folks will live, not in the same building of course, but in a separate little cottage on the same estate-grounds with their children's families; and of course there shouldn't be any slums, and poverty ought to be taken care of. In the meantime—let's get away from placing people in institutions and let's forget about how hopeless it would be to try and change them or to educate those who work in them, benighted fools that they are."

This line dominated thinking through 1936, especially in psychiatric and case work circles. The idea of putting a child or adolescent into anything but a foster home seemed unthinkable. In fact, I noticed at cocktail parties that my eagerness to find out what institutions in the United States were like, almost caused a kind of embarrassment, and at best was considered a somewhat backward interest. I am sure only the fact that I came from Vienna and therefore obviously had a guarantee ticket of psychiatric sophistication in my vest pocket, saved me from being suspected of naïveté or backwardness myself. By the way, even at that time, August Aichhorn's *Wayward Youth* was still considered a wonderful book—it seems people felt quite safe in believing it would promise to remain just that.

Phase II: "Let's throw the poor suckers a crumb from the tables of the rich. Some of them might even deserve it." This has nothing to do with the economic situation. The shame of our financial listlessness toward the needs of the "people nobody wants" I won't even mention today. I mean by "our tables of the rich," our fields of specialization, our special knowledge and technique, our stockpile in the fields of psychiatry, psychology and child development, of sociology, anthropology and so forth, and of course especially of social work and all the so-called "helping professions."

The main line of thought dominating this phase in our development looked somewhat like this: "You know, it isn't really true that all institutions are bad, and maybe some of the people could benefit from some good, institutional care. In fact, some of the workers there are nice guys and deserve a better break. I can't understand how they can bear working under such conditions anyway. If only they weren't so benighted, the poor souls, and had more training and knowledge. Then at least we could prevent some of the damage that is being done the inmates.

"Of course, one couldn't really expect to have all institutional workers trained. To begin with, most of them wouldn't even be eligible for graduate university credits. Some of them are too old to take classes. They might even think of demanding a living wage if they suddenly found themselves in the class of trained professionals. Then where would we be? So let's try and pick a few, send them to a university, bring them back after they get their degrees so we can show there is a professionally trained worker in this institution now.

"Let's buy some time off a psychiatrist, and instead of his seeing the kids—there are too many for him to go the rounds anyway—let's make him talk to the housemothers every once in a while about psychiatry. It would have to be very elementary of course.

"And let's get the case worker to explain to the houseparents why Bobby's thumbsucking is related to earlier childhood experiences, but of course let's be sure we pick those experiences which they can accept without shock, or without becoming prejudiced against Bobby in the process."

In short, we wanted to implement a concept of general enlightenment without looking at what institutions really are and should be, without considering what institutional workers in their varying functions really have to face and need to know. We watered down and sprinkled around a few of the less precious morsels from the tables of Freud, Rank, Adler, Dewey, Margaret Mead or what have you. This became a most conscience-acquiescing pastime among those of us whose job it is to train.

Phase III: This is just beginning. And let's be frank and admit that we have been pushed into it by the institution people themselves. All of a sudden we began to notice an amazing reversal taking place among them. For years when we tried to talk about anything but discipline we were called dumb theorists. We were used to having our insights into human behavior ridiculed as that much sissy stuff, to having our demand that scientific thought be applied to the diagnosing of a child's or a cottage's problem dragged in the mud of contempt for "fancy, academic nonsense that does a grass roots worker no possible good."

All of a sudden (the word "sudden" must be taken in historical perspective) the tables seemed to be reversed. The institution people began to cry for "trained workers." Even obviously reality-wise administrators began to shock their boards with insistence on budgets for special services, interest in decently protected work loads, and to offer one's staff in-service training became an obvious must, if one wanted to keep them.

All this was quite a shock. We were so used to being martyrs and preachers in the desert that it was something to adjust to the idea of filling a realistic demand for specific training setups.

The theme of this Phase III, therefore, runs something like this: "Listen, pals, you want us to train people for your institutions. Maybe we better learn something about those institutions and what it feels like to be part of your team before we even pretend to know just how to train?"

It was on this basis that the human behavior sciences really began to penetrate into institutional thinking. These efforts of course took a wide variety of directions.

Some of us concentrated on just going into institutions with our eyes wide open and working there so as to learn before we taught. Others among us started developing smaller institutional living-designs ourselves—camps or so-called "treatment homes." We hoped by clearly defining our goals and by carefully selecting the needs or pathologies of our clients, we might have some of the variables under control, so as to find out just what a "residential life-design" really could do under favorable circumstances. (By the way, notice how these experiments are already establishing their own terminology. Something is happening when "institution" with its inherent smell of large dormitories and toilet-bowl cleanser has given way to the more shrubbery-conscious "residence."

Others among us, again, have tried to focus more on the question of just how we could *produce* the kind of institutional worker that the more enlightened institutions have begun to scream for.

In short, we are now noticing the flaws in our own designs of university curricula. We see the problem of correlating curriculum with institutional life, the need of taking the hurdle of red-tape course requirements which block so many eager learners from getting what they want and must have. We have even become sufficiently ambitious to hope that some day a real institutional curriculum could be designed. This would provide workers with what they actually can use, instead of their having to accept a lot of what they don't need, just because the other discipline happens to be one with provisions for a degree.

Among all the specializations in the applied human behavior sciences, social group work obviously can claim a high affinity with the institution field. In fact, it is easy to understand that the psychiatric social worker, for instance, looking at an average institutional design, might shudder with the thought of what all that might do to the delicate flower of his "transference," or how one ever could get such a widely scattered and huge number of people really "supportive" of his treatment plan for Johnny, who is one four-hundredth of the institution's population. But the group worker, wouldn't he recognize this display of group psychology as the most stimulating sort of challenge? Isn't it one of the most obvious facts about institutional life that it is bound to the limitations as well as the assets of life in a group setting?

It is only fair to our sister professions and to truth, that we admit this was not so. We, in the professional group-work field, were just as dumb and confused as all the other professions on my list. And we, too, went through a long phase of indignant contempt for the "superficiality of mass recreation and regimentation" as though this in itself was typical of institutions as such.

Though recognizing the special structure and task of institutional work, we, too, tried to make the institutional field over "in our own image" before we began, finally, to search out the ways of becoming really useful.

Actually, the group worker had a hard, inner task of his own to fulfill before he could recognize where his responsibility lay, and so begin to cope with it.

Remember the tendency of upper class mobile children in a prejudicial neighborhood to feel threatened by and ashamed of the behavior of their wilder brothers from disorganized slum neighborhoods. It is the same tendency that makes oppressed minority groups, as soon as they reach a haven of comparative security, suddenly develop a prejudice of their own against still lower-status endowed groups of other nationalities, races or creeds. The more you are in the position of the pushed-around, low-status minority, the harder it is to reach out to your brother who is being pushed around. Instead, you're apt to reach out for, and cling to the prestige items typical of the majority group.

In the group worker's battle to win scientific recognition there would naturally be a tendency to strive for and to cling to the attributes of the high-power group for whose status of recognition the group worker strives, rather than openly to join hands and work sympathetically with other rejectees.

Gisela Konopka in this book signals the release of social

group work from this tendency. There is no condescension in her concept of group worker and houseparent as professional partners. This makes for straight thinking and also a refreshing lack of false modesty which so often veils itself under general promises of "how much one's field could contribute," without saying just what this is.

There's another aspect I am underlining right here lest the reader miss it once he falls under the fascination of this exciting book. *Group Work in the Institution* is unique because of its skill in saying simply what in reality is a most complicated affair, and it does so without any watering-down of the real issue. I have never seen this done so artfully before.

Most people when they attempt a nonacademic "tone" will of course avoid too much scientific lingo. They usually end up either giving an impression of straining to reach the level of illiterates, or they actually sell out the ideas they have to communicate as exchange coins in the popularity market.

Much is left out here, much is simplified. It had to be. But nothing is distorted. Where oversimplification is necessary, ample illustrations immediately restore the full complexity of the real issues.

In fact, for many readers, one of Konopka's finest contributions will be her manner of step by step persuading us to accept this full complexity as a reality of life.

By the way, group work wasn't as smart as Gisela Konopka makes it out to be. Much of what she modestly describes as though it were just plain "group work practice" is actually *her contribution* to what it should be, and, with the help of the institutional field's people, is about to become!

FRITZ REDL

CONTENTS

PREFACE

> "To mean something in the world is the deepest hunger of the human soul, deeper than any bodily hunger or thirst, and when a man has lost it he is no longer a man."
> Alan Paton, *The Long View*, Praeger, 1968

> "Now—I am no longer a girl—I am just a delinquent."
> A 15-year-old girl in an institution.

Fourteen years have passed since the original book was written. Times and people change rapidly—is the book still valid? It seems to me it is. We continue having institutions, in fact, often mass institutions which do not help fulfill "the deepest hunger of the human soul" of which Paton speaks. And we still have not given enough recognition to those on the staff who do the most significant work with children and young people—the "counselors" or "house parents." What I tried to do—fourteen years ago—was to translate the demand of real respect for the integrity and dignity of each human being into daily work into those who live in what we call "institutions." I chose to discuss a particular method, not because I considered group work the only important approach, but because of its significance in those settings. It was not a "how-to" book, and should not be so. Its intent is to convey understanding of people in a particular situation and find some way of moving toward, what they and all of us need most, a sense of self-respect so that one can respect others. The book was written at a time when group work was considered inferior, and there was still little appreciation of the great power of the group. This has changed considerably. Many professions have accepted the significance of working with individuals in groups. This is very gratifying to those of us who see the group much as an "atomic power" in human relations—immensely potent for good or bad.

In the past years I have learned more about group work and want to stress two points:

1. It belongs or should belong to any work with human beings—to social work, education, psychiatry, community action and others.

2. It enhances individuals and their relationships to each other only when it is based on and carried through a philosophy of absolute respect for every person. This means honest and open work *with* people, not a manipulation of them.

Group work sometimes sounds simple, but it is difficult to work in a variety of roles with the interplay of people, who all carry in them fear, hate and, hopefully, love for each other. I have tried to update some specifics of my writing, but, generally speaking, I have let it stand. I hope it will continue to help both staff and those served in institutions to find themselves, to enhance mutual aid, and to deal with, as Fritz Redl put it, this "complexity" which is the "reality of life."

Gisela Konopka

INTRODUCTION

Before you start reading the book you will want to know to whom it is directed, why it was written, and what you can expect from it. You can be sure that I cannot be wholly objective about this, especially not about the last. But I will try to answer these questions as honestly as I can.

To whom is this book directed? To all those who are interested in improving life in our institutions, those for children and those for adults. I might say right in the beginning that I will consider more intensively the institutions for children and young people, but will apply much that is said about them also to institutions for adults. One major form of institutions for adults, the hospitals for mentally sick persons, will require a more detailed study of the specific problems of seriously disturbed people.

The book is directed toward both the professional and the lay person working in or interested in institutions. I have a real conviction that this is possible. I believe that anything worth saying can be said in the language of the field and still be clear and understandable to everyone. This means there will be psychological and psychiatric and social work terms, just as a book about chemistry would include chemistry formulas. Yet I hope they will be used so clearly that they will not cover meaning with scientific language.

Why was this book written? This will need a longer answer. One part of it I will postpone to the first chapter, when I will talk about the importance of institutions today and what role they play in our society in the twentieth century—different from what it was at other times. This is the crucial part of the answer.

I am also keeping a promise to the many houseparents or counselors with whom I have worked in innumerable institutes. I found that I usually learned more from them than they probably learned from me. Morris F. Mayer, executive of the Bellefair Institution in Cleveland, talking about houseparents in a speech given in Minnesota, said they are the ones in the "foxholes" of institutional life. I liked this colorful expression. All day they are in the middle of this life full of problems and also enjoyment, but certainly full of responsibility. They see the reality of the situation and deal with it, sometimes right, sometimes wrong, but they are the ones who do the job. I will talk far more about them in the course of this book. Here I want to say only that this book is written largely because of them and their desire to have a book directed toward the whole question of group living with which they are vitally concerned.

I am writing this book because social work is a large profession with many specific aspects and we sometimes get confused about where we belong, which skill we use at what place, and how we use it best. I will talk more specifically about this point in my chapter on social group work; actually, the whole content of the book will deal with the contribution social group work, one specialization in social work, can make to the institutional field. Let me make it clear right here—and I will repeat it at other points—that I in no way contend that social group work is the *only* specialization in social work that has a place in institutions—there certainly is a very distinct place for other methods. Nor do I say that only social work can make a contribution to institutions. The institutional setting must be carried by a whole team of professional people as well as by many others engaged in highly skilled vocations. This book has a specific focus—social group work's contribution to the institutional field—and it hopes to clarify and spell this out—*but it in no way denies the importance of other specialists engaged in this field.*

And finally, this book is written because several people in the social work profession felt strongly that it was overdue. They said that institutional life is group life, that here and there we have clarified what implications this has for our profession, that a few great pioneers have done a wonderful job in presenting specific thoughts about it (I name here only authors such as Aichorn, Bettelheim, Susanne Schulze, Redl and Wineman, Mayer and Burmeister), and that we need now a clear picture of what the role of the social group worker in institutional life must be, and this in many different institutional settings. Special recognition for the "push" toward writing must be given to Harleigh Trecker and Rose Terlin, who had very convincing arguments against my reluctance to add to the literature on the subject. If their expectations are fulfilled only to a very small extent I will be satisfied to know that it is not "just another book."

But, finally, this book is written because of a compelling drive in the author. Social work is concerned with needs—with the needs of children to grow up naturally and happily and capable of standing the normal frustrations of everyday life; with the needs of teen-agers to learn about values in our society and intelligently find their own way through conflicting choices and demands; with the needs of adults who want their groups to enrich the life of our society or with the needs of adults who have come to some difficulties they cannot solve alone—everywhere where there are specific needs, social workers will try to use their knowledge and their understanding and their deep art to be helpful. The people in institutions are usually the ones with the greatest needs. Whatever the institution is, it is not the place where the otherwise capable young person or adult would be if there were not a serious difficulty in his life, be it death or sickness, delinquency or crime, or family strife. He is, in our culture, taken out of the regular stream of life, and so we need to do our very best to help him re-enter this stream, capable, proud, and whole again. Or if we deal with chronic illness, then our aim must be to make him as capable and as happy as possible and useful to others in the institutional surroundings. This book is written because of a dedication to those who need us most.

And finally, what can you expect from the book? In the last analysis, you can answer this only after you read it. It is not a compilation of facts and not a historical presentation. I will try, as sharply as possible, to present our modern concept of social group work and its relationship to institutions as they now exist. I am limiting myself largely to the situation in the United States today. You will find record material illustrating practice of the social group worker in institutional life. For the houseparent some of the chapters relating to specific living situations and a tentative outline for simple recording might be especially helpful. I will try to spell out the team relationship with other professional personnel related to the institution.

I would like to summarize what this book can be by borrowing from Erik H. Erikson's foreword to his *Childhood and Society*:

. . . this is and must be a subjective book, a conceptual itinerary. There is no attempt at being representative in quotations or systematic in references. On the whole, little is gained from an effort to reinforce vague meanings with quotations of vaguely similar meaning from other contexts.[1]

[1] Erik H. Erikson, *Childhood and Society* (New York: Norton, 1950), pp. 12-13.

Group Work in the Institution

A MODERN CHALLENGE

1. INSTITUTIONS IN MODERN SOCIETY

Every one of us thinking of institutions has a different mental picture. It depends on our experience or inexperience, both general and institutional, and even on the era in which we were born or in which we received our professional training.

In one of the many institutions that I visited in Germany after the war a twelve-year-old boy stepped forward and with an angry scornful look on his face challenged me, "What are you coming here for? Why do you look at us? What use is all this visiting?" I could see beneath his anger the desperate loneliness, the feeling of hurt, and the wonderful courage to stand up and challenge a stranger who had come with some symbols of authority. And I felt the great weight of this question, because it challenged our own motives. So I tried to give the answer, hoping that I would not rationalize but would be able to convey to him our real concern.

I said that I had come because we all know that there are many young people in institutions in his country as well as in the United States and many other countries. That we realize that the institution becomes their whole life for a long time, and we know that it should be made as helpful as possible, and yet we all know that we are not doing our best. So some of us visit many such places, talk to the staffs, talk to the boys and girls, and slowly form a picture not only of what there is but of all the hopes and feelings that are enclosed in these places to find how we can do a better job. We are not coming to snoop or to criticize, but we are coming to learn, from him and his friends, and maybe help in return.

He looked rather surprised, because he was not very used to being taken seriously by an adult, but his eyes softened and he said that he certainly would like to talk to me and he did have some ideas. Later he also said in a warm and serious way that he hoped some day I would really tell some of the things I learned in seeing so many institutions and talking to so many people. In some way, therefore, I am keeping a promise, not only to this one youngster, but to many in all the places I saw, and often I am using their thinking. They are the ones mostly concerned and they can see many parts that no one who has not lived through it can see the same way.

When I worked with teen-agers we often played a game to test our prejudices. We called out different nationalities and asked for free association. It is also a good game for adults. I did the same with the word "institutions" and let the pictures arise in my mind. What do they show?

I hear a bell ring and see boys marching in straight lines to get their dinner, looking all alike with guarded faces. . . .

I see a new girl in an institution for delinquents look out of a window and see other girls laughing and calling to each other, and I hear her surprised voice saying, "My, this is not so bad. This is more like a home." . . .

I see stairs waxed and polished like mirrors and children walking carefully on them, anxious not to scratch them, and looking frightened and forlorn. . . .

I see a battered playroom with an old record player and children laughingly running around and singing at the top of their voices, undisturbed by the visitor. . . .

I see a seventeen-year-old girl brought in by police, a white bitter face, and I see her put into solitary confinement (a runaway). . . .

I see another girl, disheveled, also a runaway, whose same sullen look changes to deep astonishment at the housemother's, "My, you must be tired out—let's get a bath and some rest, and we can talk things over whenever you want, or you can talk to your caseworker, if you prefer that." . . .

I see youngsters lined up in the morning to get their work orders, and I see a group of boys with a staff member, sitting in a circle studying together what needs to be done and planning how to do it.

FROM OUT OF THE PAST

You can see that my free association brings forth many contradictory pictures, and we will find today many different kinds of practice in institutions. This results not only from the specific philosophy of the superintendent or board or sponsoring organization of an institution but from the historical development of our dealing with dependent people. Right now we are in the middle of a controversy about our correctional institutions for adults, for instance, while there is much less disagreement about institutions for dependent children. But in the beginning of social services, controversy about this particular field would have been just as vehement.

In earlier times almost all dependency was treated in a punishing way. Let us not forget that the Elizabethan Poor Laws represented progress in terms of taking care of the dependent, but incorporated the thinking of the times that dependency was based on individual guilt. The poor, the drunkards, the mentally sick, the dependents, the criminals, the unmarried mothers, the children born out of wedlock were indiscriminately looked upon as guilty and most institutional care was not differentiated. For a long time institutional philosophy was based on two principles: protection of society, and punishment for behavior that would threaten society. Living in the twentieth century we can look with disdain on such "inhuman" attitudes, but it seems to me we should try to understand the historical point of view.

The thinking about institutions and the people served by them had to be based on the problems and the scientific knowledge available at those times. The basic philosophy of "Help thy neighbor" was considered even then, but little was known about the capacity of the human being to grow and change or the effective means of bringing this about. There were also severe social problems growing out of far less advanced medical knowledge. Death in childbirth was high and the orphaned population, therefore, was great. Sickness struck with heavier impact, especially during times of a real epidemic. That meant an increase of homeless children and dependent adults. There was also not yet any knowledge about the cause and treatment of mental illness and no understanding of factors contributing to delinquency and criminality. We have to realize that better treatment of human problems rests not exclusively on a more humanitarian attitude but also on more scientific knowledge.

CHANGING PATTERNS

The first improvement in institutional treatment was related to dependent children because the attitude toward them was much less punishing than toward the adult, who seemed to be responsible for his behavior. We saw a separation of children from adults in institutions before we saw the sorting out of any other problem. Even in children's institutions, though, a strong punitive attitude was kept alive.

Not much later the handicapped, the blind, the deaf, the mentally deficient, and finally the crippled were separated from other problems and more educational institutions for them were established. I think everybody reading this knows about the courageous fight of Dorothea Dix to establish separate institutions for the mentally sick. (Her long campaign reached its peak in the 1840's and 1850's.) Even in our times one group of sick people, the epileptics, is often still kept in institutions with the mentally sick, though their sickness is a completely different one and though they are often intelligent, capable, rational human beings.

Much more difficult was a change of attitude toward those who were violating the codes of society. The purpose of institutions for unmarried mothers was for a long time exclusively to separate them from their children so that the chilren should not learn the "bad ways" of their mothers, and somewhat later to "reform" the girl who had borne a child out of wedlock.

The juvenile offender was for a long time treated as a criminal. He was not separated from adult criminals in jails and workhouses until separate institutions for the juvenile delinquent were established. As for the adult offender, we are still almost completely in the stage of protecting society from them and punishing them, though there is a great deal stirring in this field.

It is interesting to see how in the course of history small parts of the institutional field were selected for improvement, then stood still while others got the attention. Probably the field that gained first from better knowledge of human behavior was the treatment of juvenile offenders. The Child Guidance Movement, growing out of an interest in this subject, made first use of the team approach of psychiatry, psychology, and social work. Unfortunately progress was confined almost exclusively to treatment outside the institution while inside the institution little was done for a long time.

Actually, with our better understanding of the dynamics of human behavior and of how much the social environment and intimate family relationships mean to people went a severe neglect of institutional life on the part of professional people. The pendulum, as so often happens in history, swung far to the other side. While for a long time every dependent child had been put into an institution regardless of his individual needs, suddenly social workers disregarded institutional placement completely. It was progress that we saw the need of every child to grow up in a healthy family. But along with this went a blindness towards the child who could not adjust in a boarding home, and we see now the disastrous results of a long history of continuously changing boarding homes for some children. Claudeline Lewis, in her article "Selective Intake and Placement in a Children's Institution," [1] tells about a child who had gone through five foster homes. The caseworker finally suggested to her placement in an institution where she could be part of a group and find out why she was so unhappy. The girl's relieved reply was, "That should have happened to me about three foster homes back!"

The foster home program, the individualization of the child or the young person in trouble, has greatly contributed to improved treatment of children, but we begin to see now that not all children can be treated in individual homes and that the same careful thinking has to go not only into the placement in institutions but into institution life itself.

Since this book will deal with institutional placement, we will not here go into all the criteria for intake. I will say only that we know that the child who is greatly disturbed can usually not be handled in a foster home or group situation, because

---

[1] Susanne Schulze, ed., *Creative Group Living in a Children's Institution* (New York: Association Press, 1951), p. 147.

of his acting out and disturbing behavior, and also because he cannot accept the close, new relationship with a foster family. What the child needs, at least for some time, is a secure, accepting group environment where he can be somewhat selective in the kind of adult to whom he wants to relate—the housefather, the housemother, the cook, the gardener, the caseworker, the group worker—whomever he chooses. Also, the disturbed child needs a setting that can offer professional services not always available in a private home or in every community.

Institutions will be needed, too, for the young person or the adult who has violated the law if the causes for this behavior cannot be handled in his family environment. Probation and parole have given us the opportunity to treat the offender in the community whenever this is possible. Yet in many cases institutional placement is the only possible help because of difficult home relationships.[2]

The person who is sick, mentally or otherwise, will often have to be treated in an institution because of the professional services available and because of the need to protect society from contagion or violence.

With the increased life span of our population, we will continue to need institutions for the aged and the chronically ill.

THE PURPOSE IS TREATMENT

It is clear that the main purpose of institutional placement today is *treatment*. It is foolish to say that there is not also the purpose of custody, as for instance in the case of the offender or the sick person, but the main purpose is treatment.

What does this mean? And how is it accomplished?

There is hardly an institution any more which will not say that its purpose is treatment. The purpose and function of

---

[2] In this day I hardly dare use the term "institution." What I mean is *group communities*, not mass institutions.

one of the large training schools, for instance, is given as help for

maladjusted boys who because of conduct and behavior are found on the basis of individual study to be in need of special treatment and training. The purpose shall be to prepare these boys so that they may function as normal, adequate individuals according to their capacities and abilities.[3]

The Child Welfare League of America in 1952 published a descriptive study of children's institutions called *Residential Treatment of Emotionally Disturbed Children.* In this study residential treatment is described as

the development of a total approach to therapy. Individual psychotherapy with the child and his parents, a therapeutically designed living experience and remedial education are all seen as parts of a whole.[4]

This definition clearly puts emphasis on the total approach of therapy.

Though treatment as a goal is accepted by almost everybody in the institutional field, we see one major fallacy looming large: the use of treatment as a "gadget" attached to a small part of institutional life, but not permeating the total living situation. Let me be very clear on what I mean by this. Recently I was told proudly by a person working in an institution that they have greatly changed their approach to children because they now have a part-time psychiatrist who will be available two hours a week. The interesting point was that it was not even determined for what he would be available, whether for direct treatment of children or for consultation. It was sufficient for the staff to feel that they now are going

---

[3] "General Report, Minnesota State Training School for Boys," p. 6.
[4] Joseph H. Reid, Helen R. Hagan, *Residential Treatment of Emotionally Disturbed Children* (New York: Child Welfare League of America, 1952), p. v.

along with the "modern trend in treatment" by having the two-hour services of a psychiatrist.

Maybe this case sounds exaggerated, but we have numerous examples of emphasis being placed on employing a caseworker, psychiatrist, or psychologist, and assuming that treatment was in this way guaranteed. I have seen institutions where the main role of the caseworker was to be the shoulder on which the youngster could cry about the poor treatment he was receiving; or the caseworker had to be the recipient of a great deal of expressed hostility, not only because of the basic problems that the youngster brought with him but also because of the restricting atmosphere of the institution. In such a setting the child was not only confused about the roles of adults, but unhappy relationships between the staff of the institution and the caseworker resulted too. The caseworker continually played the role of the good mother while the staff members who had to take care of the day-by-day situations were looked upon as the bad mothers.

I learned of an institution with a high reputation for its approach to therapy where participation in recreational activities was still looked upon as a reward for good behavior instead of another tool in treatment. Youngsters in such institutions learn very easily that they can play the clinical team against the rest of the institution as they might play father against mother in a divided family.

Actually, the home in which treatment is only an attached gadget is at points more disastrous than the home that shows consistency in all its approaches. *The most important part of treatment in any institutional setting is the mental hygiene climate of the whole living situation.* Other services are extremely important and must not be neglected, but institutional treatment has its core in the group living situation. I cannot say it more colorfully than Fritz Redl expressed it in a general session of a state-wide Institute of Children's Institutions in Chicago, March 7-8, 1949:

Let's beware of fancy stuff. In the last three years I have been running into reformatories of 3000 children. And they are always asking me how to use group therapy. Right now we have fancy stuff called "group therapy." We talk to them about the problems of life and we have group therapy. First of all, you have to have a healthy and reasonably designed happy group life, even when you have children who are disturbed, to say nothing of the children who are not disturbed. The way they live with each other, the type of rules and regulations they have are a more essential part of the total diet of the youngster in the institution. I am not against group therapy. I am not talking myself out of my favorite hobby, but these other things are more essential to the basic problem.[5]

THE TREATMENT TEAM

I repeat that additional clinical professional services to those dealing directly with group living are certainly important. *The team approach is essential for institutions.* This has been said very often, but, recently, those dealing directly with the group living situation, the houseparents, are many times not really accepted as part of the team. Actually, they are "the hub of the wheel," as Morris F. Mayer has called them. In one of my following chapters I hope to point out some ways in which they can be made part of the team.

In many institutions, strangely enough, the administrator actually is not looked upon as a member of the team and he does not look upon himself as such. He thinks he can delegate the responsibility for treatment to a group of outside experts. It is my contention that this is impossible. The adminis-

[5] "Report of Illinois State Institute of Children's Institutions, 1949," pp. 17-18.

trator of an institution will set the climate found in the institution. His dealing with his own staff, with the youngsters or the adults given into his care, and with the community around them makes treatment possible or impossible. This is not a book on administration, but I want to make it clear that administration cannot be separated from the content of the purpose for which the institution is created. Only the administrator who has a basic philosophy, conviction, and knowledge regarding the treatment purposes of his institution can create the kind of atmosphere conducive to the fulfillment of this purpose.

GROUP LIVING AS TREATMENT

We have used the words "group climate" and "group living" already quite frequently in relation to the institutional setting. When institutions changed from the idea of pure custody to that of treatment they originally thought of themselves as replacements for family life. They were convinced of the necessity and the therapeutic value of a happy family relationship and they thought to reproduce it in an institutional setting. No question this was a great step forward compared with the impersonal, regimented, unindividualized, large custodial institution. The idea of institutions as family units had occurred because we had learned about the importance of close family life and its psychological meaning to the development of every human being.

The added knowledge that human beings are also strongly influenced by group associations other than the family has been comparatively recent. Even newer and not yet completely clarified is our knowledge of the impact of group associations and their negative as well as positive influence. When we realized that there is a choice not only between an imitation of family living and mass education but that a third possibility is individualization in group associations, we could look differently at the institution and use its unique group living reality in treatment. The movement from the imitation of family settings to the consciously guided use of the group living situation is, therefore, not a change in basic philosophy, but a more truthful acceptance of reality and better knowledge of group interaction. Actually, the child or youngster knows that the institution cannot offer the same situation as a real family. I do not need to go into the obvious differences between family and institution, but I would like to point out some of the basic psychological differences. A child in his own family, for instance, knows that his parents are "stuck with him." He knows that even if he behaves quite badly the family feels still responsible for him. The child in the institution knows that this is not the case. He knows that he can be removed.

There certainly are very different relations between a parent and a child than there are between a professional person working with a child, even if this person is warmer, kinder, more accepting than any parent ever can be. I am not saying the one is better than the other, but there is a different kind of relationship. It lies in the simple fact that child and houseparent or counselor (we have not yet found the right term) usually do not know each other from the child's infancy on. Very often it is this aspect of the relationship that allows for treatment in the institution. There is less strong emotional impact from the beginning. There can be strong emotional relationships for therapy purposes, but they can be kept in line because of the conscious and disciplined use of self in the institutional personnel. Group constellation has not been brought about by the accident of birth but can be consciously arranged according to the therapy needs of the individual coming to the institution.

Susanne Schulze has pioneered in making clear what institutional living can offer:

> The unique function of the institution is to provide group living to children in need of this experience, group living of a nature which it alone has to offer. This stand is taken with the assumption that while the institution will make its major contribution through its peculiar characteristics, its personnel will at the same time be alert to, and skillful in incorporating, any aspects of family living that can be reconciled with its primary function.[6]

This same thinking is also applicable to institutions for adults. In the hospital or correctional field for adults we have not tried to imitate the family setting, but we have done very little to use the group relations to bring about desirable changes. Thinking in this direction is quite recent. Before I go into this, though, I think we have to clarify the purpose of our treatment in institutions, the final goal towards which we are striving.

The final purpose of any work with people, whether they are healthy or sick, young or old, is to help them use as many of their capacities as possible so that they are themselves happy and can contribute to society as a whole. The fact-finding report of the mid-century White House Conference on Children and Youth is concerned with the healthy development of personality and the factors involved in it. The report, therefore, had to clarify what we mean by "the healthy development of personality." I am quoting from the introduction:

> It will be noted that in this report the expression "healthy personality" has been substituted for the National Committee's phrase "individual happiness and responsible citizenship." In this substitution there are various implications.

[6] Schulze, *op. cit.*, p. 4.

First and most obviously, we imply that to be happy and responsible is to be healthy in personality. If so unscientific a statement can be allowed at all, it is surely only if the emphasis is on the "and." Many people are apparently happy without being particularly responsible as citizens, and perhaps without being healthy in personality. Many are responsible citizens but clearly far from happy—and certainly not healthy, as their stomach ulcers and even suicide attest. What we desire in these days of strain and crisis is that young people shall have both of these qualities, so that, among other things, they may produce a social order in which the chance for happiness will be greatly improved.

In stating the matter this way we imply, too, that happiness is something other than a lighthearted, frivolous pleasure in one's own well-being. The happiness that characterizes a healthy personality, the happiness that endures in spite of the individual's and society's vicissitudes, is made of sterner stuff. It is an equanimity indicative of personal integrity. It encompasses the possibility of both anger and tears.[7]

The last purpose, therefore, of all education or treatment in our culture is related to our democratic way of life, that is, to have people who can constructively participate in the building of better human relationships. Everybody entering an institution has experienced some difficulty and our goal is often quite far removed. We have in our institutions problems ranging from the child who has had the traumatic experience of the breaking down of family relationships, through death, sickness, or other difficulties, to the person who has a mental breakdown, or the one who has offended the laws of society, to finally the one who has just grown old and has not the resources in his own family for staying with them. The problems are, therefore, very different and have to be handled in different ways. Yet the goal is always the same. On the way

[7] *Personality in the Making* (New York: Harper, 1952), pp. xvii, xviii.

to achieving it we have to use many means of treatment: physical medicine, individual psychotherapy, casework, group work, education, and many other means that can be used in the daily living situation.

You might object and say that in many cases damage so great is already done that the final goal of a healthy personality cannot be reached. As far as our present knowledge goes this is certainly true. In certain cases the protective goal of institutional placement will overweigh all the others. Yet science has improved remarkably in the last decades and we have seen the limits of treatment widened considerably. There was a time when we would think of the placement of the physically handicapped only in terms of custody and, a little later, of training in a very limited sense. Today, with modern methods of medicine and education as well as better understanding of the emotional components of physical handicaps, we see no limit any more in helping a blind or deaf or crippled person to become self-supporting and a valuable member of our society.

While only a short time ago mental sickness meant an end to normal living, we know now that in many cases we can restore a person to full capacity. We have not yet learned enough about why certain disturbances are expressed by antisocial behavior and appear, therefore, in the form of delinquency or crime, but in continued study there is no reason why we cannot learn more about this too and, therefore, stretch the limits of treatment farther still.

We have seen in recent years that our image of the aged was wrong and that one *can* teach "an old dog new tricks." We have learned that, given all-round treatment, homes can restore to quite capable personalities aged persons who acted like seniles. We have every right to hope that with more knowledge and improved treatment methods, even those who now seem beyond reach can be helped.

RETURN TO COMMUNITY

It has been proved in many years of studies in human behavior that we *learn best by gratification,* even if learning in itself carries at points some pain. The baby learns better how to use the bottle when the mother gently and gradually withdraws the breast and when she still provides the comfort of the loving arms—and the adult will more easily accept the curtailment of a pleasure when life offers other satisfactions. Everyone in our institutions has gone through some severe deprivation, some hurt. Being in an institution means being singled out from the normal part of life in our culture which is based on family relationships. It always means deprivation in one form or another, even if it might mean improvement in housing or in food supply or even in kind acceptance. Treatment, therefore, will have to overcome unhappiness, distrust, and hate. It is often feared that this knowledge will lead to "sentimental coddling" of those who "do not deserve it" and they will like institutional life so much that they will not want to leave. All of us who have worked in institutions know that this fear is completely unfounded. Being in an institution always means necessary conformity to rules based on the large number of people present, and this is hard for most people. In addition to that, it always means not being part of the general stream of life, which is a basic need in all human beings. It always means some restriction of freedom.

We know that there will be ambivalence about leaving an institution in many cases, even if the stay was not too pleasant, because of the fear of the unknown and the protective environment that the institution offers. It is actually the test of successful treatment in institutions to help the person to want to leave and to be able to adjust to outside life.

For a long time efforts in institutional work had been directed towards making the child or the adult as conforming as possible to the institution's demand. This kind of training has led to the person's being incapable of adjusting to outside life more than has the so-called "coddling." I remember an eighteen-year-old girl who had lived practically all her life in institutional care (something that fortunately today hardly happens). This young girl was so afraid of living outside of the institution that she had developed severe neurotic symptoms mainly for the purpose of not being sent into the unknown world. I also remember a young man who had left a training school with high recommendation for his conforming behavior who was unable to initiate any activity after his release and who was actually yearning to go back to the institutional setting where he would be told what to do every day. It was not an especially kind experience that he had had, but a too protective one that had stifled his capacity to stand on his own feet. An understanding treatment would have left him with more initiative.

Some regret in leaving an institution is something we will want, because it shows that the person was able to make a positive relationship and that he can continue to make a satisfying adjustment. Experience in an institution must open the way to happy community relationships. An adult friend of mine who has made great contributions to a scientific field and who has established a wonderful family told me with great fondness of his experience in the institution in which he was placed for several years. I have never forgotten when he said that they had always made him feel that he was just as good as any other child and they had let him choose his profession. No higher recommendation than the achievements of this man in his adult years could be given an institution. The test of good institutional work will always be whether the individual who was placed in it can successfully and happily get along in the outside world. The test does not lie in conformity inside the institution.

We need to find ways of determining whether an individual will get along well on the outside while he is still in the institution. We will discuss some of this in the chapters dealing with specific settings.

2. SOCIAL GROUP WORK—SCIENCE AND ART

A group of young adults who have great difficulties in relation to a physical illness with which they are afflicted had their second meeting with the social group worker. Painful experiences in their social relationships had been related and one of the young men had opened up and told the group about his desperate feelings of inadequacy. At the end of the meeting he looked at the others and said almost dreamily, "It is strange. I talked several times to a psychiatrist but it took me twelve meetings to find out what I had in common with him while I could open up to you the very first time."

A fourteen-year-old stood trembling before the juvenile court judge. "I would never have done it," he blurted out, "but all the others did it and they would laugh at me if I would not join." And looking at the skinny undersized boy, you knew how much status with his contemporaries must mean to him.

A discussion with some young girls soon to be released from a training school: "Look," said the pretty seventeen-year-old, "do you think they will allow us to meet after we are out of here? Truthfully, I will be able to go straight better that way, because otherwise I am so terribly alone." And there was fear in her eyes.

A club of the aged had a party. One of the older women

got up with tears in her eyes and said, "I was ready to just lie on my bed all day and give up and wait until I die when this young man came and asked me to join the club. It seems foolish, but I want to live now for a long time. I am no more alone."

HUMAN BEINGS CANNOT STAND ALONE

All these expressions show with what the social group worker is working. It is one of the strongest and deepest emotional powers in human life, the feeling of belonging, of security, of safety, of realizing that one can contribute to others, that one is "somebody." Human beings cannot stand all alone. The group is not just one other aspect of human life, but it is life blood itself because it represents the belonging to humanity. Nothing great or important has been achieved in this world by a person alone. The great achievements, sometimes damaging and sometimes helpful, have always come about through associations of human beings with other human beings. When man was completely alone or felt completely alone, he either perished in desperate loneliness or took his own life, or he began to hate the rest of humanity and to want to destroy it. I do not want to be misunderstood. I believe in the great strength, the capacity, and the power of the individual, but just because of this I know how much *belonging* and *being a part* and *contributing* mean to the individual.

There has been justified criticism of a trend in recent years to set the group above individual development and demand conformity, in this way killing the creativity of the individual. I am speaking about the opposite: I am speaking about group life that gives the individual security and nourishment so that he can fulfill his greatest promise while helping others to fulfill theirs too. I am aware that the group can lend its strength to destructive as well as constructive purposes, but we must realize that it is one of the greatest powers in human life. To deal with such a power is no easy task. Social group work, in dealing with it, has taken on at least as responsible a task as the engineer who is working with dynamite. Because of this work with complicated and powerful human emotions, the group worker has to become a disciplined professional person and must use all the knowledge available in modern science.

SOCIAL GROUP WORK—SCIENCE AND ART

Social group work, like all social work, is based on science and is an art in practice. The group worker must be able not only to learn theoretically about people but to use this learning in a helping way. To be able to do this a person needs a basic capacity as well as dedication to human beings, to their weakness and to their strength. He needs scientific training and he needs continued exercise of the use of his knowledge. If we want to know what contribution a person can make to a field, it is helpful to know what he has learned. I would want to know whether a person had learned the mechanics of watchmaking and the way the gears fit together before I gave him a precious watch to be repaired. The most precious things in the world are human beings, and we do not want to give them into the hands of somebody who has not learned what makes them tick. In institutional work we are dealing with human beings who have experienced some form of breakdown, and it is important to have the repair work done by somebody who has pertinent skill and knowledge.

What then is the present-day education of the social group worker? He has had four years of college education, usually with an emphasis on social sciences including psychology, and two years of professional education in a graduate School of Social Work. He was accepted in the latter not only because of a good academic record, showing that he had intelligence to deal with theoretical problems, but also because of the indication of a real desire to help people, a warmth toward and an acceptance of all kinds of people regardless of their origin or their difficulties or the way they look. He must have shown flexibility in the approach to different situations. He had taken part, either as a participant or as a worker in community endeavors which helped to enrich the life of people and which were related to the whole problem of human relations. These were some of the qualities which the School of Social Work was looking for in the applicant.

His interest in people must be based on a concern for the other fellow, and not on a desire to use people for his own purposes. We sometimes see imaginative and gifted young people who will use a group either to further their own interests or will manipulate it in the direction they most enjoy. Behind this is not a deep and genuine respect for the other human being but merely a self-seeking that expresses itself in something that looks like service on the outside.

All social work is based on the conception of the human being as a whole; physical, emotional, and mental processes cannot be separated. He can and does grow and change. He is influenced by his environment and he in turn influences environment.

Social work serves as a helper in human relations.

The service of the professional social worker is recognized as an enabling process by which the person, the group or the community is helped to identify needs, to clarify goals and to resolve personal and social problems.[1]

The social worker's work is based on a conviction of the dignity of each human being and his right to develop all his

[1] Ernest Hollis and Alice L. Taylor, *Social Work Education in the United States* (New York: Columbia University, 1951).

capacities and use them for his own satisfaction as well as his responsibility to use them for making a contribution to society and to not harm others.

Social work moves toward this goal by helping the individual to adjust to difficulties as well as by helping to change the environment if it interferes with the development of the individual. The social worker's role is, therefore, always the dual one of therapist and reformer.

Social work has developed special methods to fulfill its goal, the major ones today being case work, group work, and community organization.

In 1947, Harleigh Trecker defined group work as "one way of giving service or help to individuals and to some degree social group work is used in all social practice. Primarily it is a specialized method of providing growth opportunities for individuals and groups in the functional settings of social work, recreation and education."

In the course of time, social group work has become more identified with the profession of social work but has widened its function. The question arises whether it belongs to a great variety of professions related to interactional work.

The present definition, as it appears in my book, *Social Group Work: A Helping Process*, is "social group work is a method of social work which helps individuals enhance their social functioning through purposeful group experiences and to cope more effectively with their personal, group, or community problems."

PROFESSIONAL EDUCATION

To achieve competence in the methods and to learn how to contribute to increased knowledge regarding human relations, social conditions, and how to work with them, professional education in social work consists of the following areas for *all* social work students, regardless of specialization.

1. *Understanding the dynamics of individual behavior.*

He learns about the changing life cycle, what different needs are at different times in life, how human beings try to fulfill them, and what they do when they are thwarted.

He learns about the influence of family and how early life has a great deal to do with the way an adult acts. But he also must learn that this does not mean predetermination of all behavior and that at any time of life we can learn to change, even though childhood is an important influence.

He will begin to understand, for instance, why a child who shows good native intelligence cannot learn when the weight of insecurity is lying heavily on him. He will understand why Johnny, just recently placed in an institution, not knowing how long he will be there or whether he will be placed in a foster home, not knowing whether father is beating up mother again tonight, being afraid that they will completely forget him—why this Johnny seems to have lost all his capacity of learning and is "dumb" in school.

He will learn that eneuresis does not occur because the child willfully wets his bed. He will take it as a symptom of either a physical illness or, if this is not the case, of some emotional disturbance. He will see whether the little bed-wetter is perhaps in a group that makes him feel especially lonely or whether the big boy is so filled with hostility but also with fear that he can express it only unconsciously in this way.

He will understand how size can sometimes lead to real difficulties and why the little fellow always gets into the biggest fight because he somehow thinks that he is not as good as the others.

2. *Social policy and the history of the settings in which social work is practiced.*

Most social work is carried out in agencies established by the community to serve needs which cannot be served by organizations working for a profit. The agencies are established by groups of citizens for the purpose of service. Whether in private or public agencies, the social worker is responsible to a smaller or larger part of the population. This includes the need to understand the organization and development of such agencies and to realize their changing philosophy.

3. *Understanding of principles of administration.*

Administration everywhere is the effective way of dealing with human beings to achieve a determined goal. Sometimes the human being is forgotten in the process and the mimeographing machine becomes the only tool for communication. In agencies, where the spirit of humanity is the lifeblood, a live administration becomes a necessity.

4. *Understanding of principles of community organization.*

Improvement of the environment requires support from enlightened citizens. However, they have many other concerns and it is the expert's task to let them be informed about the needs of the community and help them to organize the needed action. In many communities, for instance, young people are still held in jail because no detention facilities are available. The social worker must be able to let the citizens see how grave this problem is and help them alter a situation which is not only illegal but exceedingly damaging to our youngsters.

5. *Understanding principles of research.*

Not every social worker will become a full-time research worker. Yet every one must be informed about the possibilities of research and be able to contribute from practice to such a project.

Social work curricula change with changing needs in society and with new knowledge. Today, the social worker will learn more about environmental factors that influence human behavior. He learns more about the variety of cultures and subcultures. His education also stresses serious urban and rural problems and the tasks of policy making.

I would like to consider this in more detail so that we may clearly see its application to the institutional setting.[2]

INDIVIDUAL AND GROUP IN THE LIFE CYCLE

The infant does not yet relate to a group. He needs the one-to-one relationship, the close tie with one loving person. (The adult whose difficulties go back to this period will be more in need of individual therapy than of group treatment. It is important for the group worker to know where the limitations of his work lie.)

Young children begin to enjoy the group, even outside the family, though still quite content with themselves. When you see them playing in a group they are actually playing "alone together."

The eight- and ten-year-olds search actively for group relations outside the family. Father and mother are still very important to them, yet they try their wings with outside friendship groups. They change friends frequently, but they need to have them. The group worker is to them at times father and mother, but he is also hero and beloved image (and we will see in institutions the same feeling towards housefather and housemother). They cling to him and they want him. The adult means a great deal to them.

---

[2] See also Gertrude Wilson and Gladys Ryland, *Social Group Work Practice* (New York: Houghton Mifflin, 1949), Chap. 2.

Adolescence is the age of which Grace Coyle once said, "Adolescence runs in groups." Here the powerful stuff of group relations really begins to show itself. I will not go into a detailed description of adolescence, since there is a great deal written about it.[3] Group workers who, in informal educational agencies, work a great deal with adolescents gain much special knowledge about them. They realize that it is an age at which occurs a whole reappraisal of values and that association with a group and with an adult other than the parent is extremely important.

Adolescence is often presented as the age of revolt. This is very true, because the young person feels that he wants to become independent of his own childhood, which is symbolized in his parents. But adolescence is also an age of anxiety, when he is not quite sure what it will mean to grow up, when many pressures come to bear upon him through physical forces inside himself as well as through forces from outside. Strong group association and clinging to his contemporaries is very often the only safety the adolescent finds at this moment. If the group worker does not understand all the turbulence in these youngsters, he will miss one of the greatest opportunities of helping with anxieties, hopes, new values, with emerging attitudes and a whole life philosophy.

It has sometimes frightened me to see how youth workers or youth counselors in our institutions consider it sufficient to work with adolescents on a superficial activity basis. They must have never heard the cry for help that is very often hidden in the giggling, the pushing, the handing around of dirty pictures, or the sullen defiance. One of my friends recently had a visit from a young man whom she did not recognize until he introduced himself, saying, "Remember the guy in camp who made all that trouble? You were the only one

[3] See Irene Jocelyn, *The Adolescent and His World* (New York: Family Service Association of America, 1952).

who made me feel as if I were somebody and you did not kick me out. You also did not make me feel as if I were a dope when I told you about my wish to become an engineer." This young man felt that the person who had listened to him then instead of only seeing his difficult behavior had greatly influenced his life.

Adolescence is the time of life where one also wants the feeling of strength that comes with group association, the strength that actually has built our society. It is through group associations that decisions are made and carried out. And in adolescence one wants to use this power of decision-making, not only alone but as a group. I remember a girls' training school in which material for clothing was always given to the girls. At one time the staff workers decided to ask the girls' council how it would like to distribute the material. There was an amazing group discussion regarding the needs of different girls, their appearance, and these things were thoughtfully measured against the available material. Actually, the final distribution was not so different from that which the staff had made previously. Yet the group climate was considerably changed and the pride that the girls felt in having accomplished the distribution by themselves was not only great but very constructive.

While group associations in adolescence are all-important, they also continue throughout life, but not with such intensity. The group association of the adolescent is so much the anchor to which he holds that it usually comprises his whole emotional being. In young adulthood group associations become less all-inclusive and take their place as only one part of life, offering an opportunity to test ideas, develop new thoughts, move into actions, and help in finding a mate. This knowledge will be helpful in the institutional setting. We sometimes seem to forget, when we see them in correctional institutions, that we have there adults with all the normal human needs. Actually, they are in an enforced group situation, and if we consider their general group needs we can make this situation far more constructive.

Later adulthood often finds a great deal of satisfaction not only in the newly established family group but also in community groups that afford outlet for activity as well as the need for status. The adult who finds himself alone and perhaps an outsider in the community will need special encouragement to become part of such groups, because what we call "the loss of self-respect" really means the absence of status in one's community.

For a long time we thought that the old person wanted to sit in a rocking chair and was perfectly satisfied to be alone with his memories. Yet the recent focus of our attention on older people has shown us clearly that this was a great fallacy. Loneliness and the feeling of futility can be especially strong in the aged, particularly in a culture where they do not retain much meaning for their own family. There is no point in trying to return to former patterns or to imitate cultures that give the aged a great deal of status in their own families. In our culture it will be our responsibility to give the aged sufficient outlet for their capacities, energies, and need to contribute to the whole flow of life by allowing them to participate in group associations just as they have done when they were younger.

A group worker placed in a home for the aged described the dead and impersonal atmosphere that she found in the beginning. People living in the same room did not even know each other's names. Though the wish for group association was there, help was needed to bring it out and make it active. The description of the same boarding home ten weeks later sounded completely different. The residents had, for instance, started a newspaper and through the work on the paper as well as the items related in it they began to know each other and to appreciate their companions and themselves. One older man said, "I thought I belonged on the ash heap. I will dare anybody now to throw me there." To me that means just as much as saving a human life.

DYNAMICS OF GROUP RELATIONS (THE GROUP PROCESS)

There are forces in a group that go on whether anybody observes them or works with them or not, just as the law of gravity exists whether we drop a stone or we don't. Research into the behavior of small groups has taught us much about these forces.

We see that the pattern of a group grows out of the forces of acceptance and rejection that work in it. Every individual carries in him a great power, the power to like and to dislike, to love and to hate, and this flow of energies is mutual in a group, though we must realize that it is not the same for each member. Johnny might be very fond of Jim, but this does not mean that Jim will like Johnny. Susan can be friends only with Emily; the two are constantly together. Edith is always by herself; nobody cares about her. Garry is an isolate too, but they hate him. Out of this pattern grows the picture of the group.

We know that this acceptance and rejection pattern is not related only to individual likes and dislikes, but is also strongly related to the purpose of the group. If the group purpose is, for instance, to win a football game, the most accepted person will be the good football player, even if he is not the best liked one. The group worker must be very conscious of the purpose of a group (sometimes openly expressed, sometimes not even quite consciously known to the members themselves), so that he may better understand the rejection and acceptance pattern than if he does not know the goal. In institutional settings, for instance, acceptance and rejection is most closely related to liking and disliking and will have a great deal to do with the way the individual behaves in a living situation. Helen Jennings, in her book *Leadership and Isolation*,[4] has given a lively picture of these patterns in institutional settings. If we observe them carefully we will see the development of subgroups and leadership and the rejected or neglected isolate.

If a patient comes to a physician and complains about severe backaches, the physician will check the whole body, every part of it, to find the cause. He will also ask the patient for a history of the symptoms. Only by doing all this will he be able to establish a diagnosis. If the group worker wants to help a group, he will have to know about the individuals, but he will also have to take the whole body of the group, check on all parts of it, understand the mechanism working in it, and only then can he make a diagnosis and decide on treatment.

To me it is one of the frightful failures in working with groups (including institutional group settings) that too often this careful diagnosis is not made because the diagnostician knows only about one part, the individual. The isolate in the group, for instance, cannot be helped if we know only about himself, his family background, his inner emotional difficulties. Do not misunderstand me! They have to be known. Yet it also has to be known what the goal and the mores of the group are, and what the group constellation is.

Johnny, for example, is a rejected isolate. Nobody in his cottage wants to have anything to do with him. He is continually kicked around by the others. What is there in the group constellation that does this to Johnny? We know that he is quite a boastful youngster who is very insecure and is hiding this by playing the "big shot." He came to the institution because he was the leader of a gang that stole small

[4] New York: Longmans, Green, 2nd ed., 1950.

articles in five and ten cent stores. Outside the institution Johnny showed leadership capacity; how did he become an isolate here?

It so happens that this cottage group had been comparatively stable for quite a while prior to Johnny's arrival and the youngsters in the group had established a working relationship with each other. Johnny's entrance—as very often the entrance of a newcomer may be—was in itself a disturbing element. The group had felt comparatively comfortable in their relationships and they did not want to be disturbed in them. In addition to this, the boy who had developed as an indigenous leader of this group had a very similar behavior pattern to Johnny's. He too expressed his basic fear of adults through open defiance of them and he felt his situation threatened by the newcomer. Because of his influence on the others, he could keep Johnny from being accepted and becoming a threat to his leadership. We see, therefore, that Johnny's being an isolate has its root in two factors of the group situation:

1. He was a newcomer in an already quite well-established group.

2. He was a potential rival to the indigenous leader.

Having made this diagnosis, we can now direct help not only towards Johnny's own inner problems but also towards the situation in which he finds himself. There might be some group discussion regarding the boys' responsibility toward a newcomer, helping them remember how it felt when they first came in. Some help might be given to the leader of the group to let him see that Johnny's doing something in the group will not interfere with his position, and we might help Johnny to work with this indigenous leader instead of against him. In such a situation we see clearly the importance of knowing the dynamics of grouping as well as the dynamics of the individual.

Knowledge of subgroups is an important one. Every group develops subgroups and this is a normal and healthy process. One cannot expect people to have equally strong relationships with all members if a group goes beyond a certain number. Sometimes houseparents are quite concerned about this fact and wonder whether they have failed to establish an *esprit de corps* if subgroups develop. They can be reassured that this is not harmful. The difficulty arises only if walls around the subgroups mount considerably and we have actual cliques. The clique does not allow a member to move into another subgroup and usually there is strong hostility among the different cliques. This really will interrupt general group life, and it lies within the skill of the group worker to see this coming and to prevent it, or, if it has developed, to find ways of overcoming it.

Understanding of the development of leadership is important. For far too long a time leadership was looked upon as something people are born with and which they possess for the rest of their lives. But we have learned that leadership grows out of the group process, though it is also related to personality. Leadership means that the members of the group are willing to accept the suggestions of a person and act according to them. Constructive leadership in a democratic society will mean that this person is concerned with bringing out the capacities of all the members and is willing to put their needs and the purpose of the group before his own interests. Destructive leadership will mean a ruthless search for power in which the needs of the leader are fulfilled beyond those of everyone else and where no participation is encouraged. In between those two there are many degrees.

All forms of leadership are found in our groups, and it is important that the worker learn to diagnose them, their meaning to the leader himself, the other members of the group, their own healthy development, and their relationship with the community around them. The worker's skill will lie in the use of this diagnosis to encourage where it is constructive, to help effect a change where it is destructive, and to give every member in the group the opportunity to take on leadership functions if this is helpful to them.

One of the most important aspects of group process is the development of bond, the feeling of belonging. Actually, it is the factor that makes a group into a group and not just a mass of loosely related people. When we look at cottage groups or subgroups in our institutions we will have to see whether there is a bond, whether it is strong or weak, and what kind of a bond it is. It could be that there is actually no bond, that youngsters do not relate to each other at all, that there is no feeling of commonness. It could be that there is a strong bond, but that it is one of hate, directed against the institution and against everything that comes from it; or it could be a bond that helps the fearful newcomer to relate easily to the group and to the purpose of the institution. Again we see that the assessment of every aspect of the group process is very important in helping with treatment.

SKILL IN PRACTICE

Use of Program

One part of translating knowledge of individuals and groups into practice is the *use of program as a tool in group relationships*. There are still many people who think group work is equivalent to activities or recreation simply because the group worker frequently uses the same tools as in recreation. It is as if we should say that the surgeon is a butcher because he uses a knife and cuts into flesh, or that the caseworker is a talker because he uses only words. The use of activities as a tool is a great art, and we will return to it in other parts of this book. The more activities the group worker knows and the more program skills he has, the better. This way he has in his hands a wealth of material and can intelligently relate them to human needs. He will understand the meaning that certain activities have to certain age groups or emotional stages. He will be alert to what effect they might have on certain group constellations and on certain individuals.

There is yet a great amount of research to be done about this. In numerous papers Fritz Redl has given a real impetus to thinking about this very important area. A study done by Paul Gump at Wayne University, Detroit, Michigan, on the emotional connotation of specific children's games has added some knowledge. Yet, what group workers at present know about this has come mainly from experience. It is an area that has been woefully neglected and its poor use can only be compared with the way drugs have been used indiscriminately in noncompetent hands.

Two mistakes are commonly made: (1) A use of program activities without any regard for underlying individual or group needs, and (2) a superior disdain of all program activities and, therefore, a monotony in approach to group life. The group worker must make a sharp and discriminate use of program activities and yet have a capacity to do without them, if necessary.

Referral to Community Resources

It is not enough to know other agencies in the health, welfare, or recreational field in order to be of service to the group member. It needs special skill to help a child or an adult to accept those services which may give rise to anxiety. The group worker must be able to evaluate services in relation to each individual's needs. Susan and Olga might both be of the same age, and might both need group services outside the institution, yet Susan will profit only by a service which is highly individualized in its group approach, while Olga can mix in with anybody and will enjoy mass activities.

This knowledge and skill in referral will be indispensable in institutions in making them part of the community or in helping residents leaving an institution find the necessary group relationships.

Supervision of Volunteers and Untrained Personnel

Group workers usually practice in settings where direct work with the group is not always carried by the social group worker himself but by volunteers. A great deal of study in the second year of graduate work is related to the way he can transmit clinical knowledge as well as knowledge about group behavior into lay language and how he can most effectively teach this. He learns about individual supervision as well as about the use of group discussions and staff meetings to transmit some of this knowledge. It is taught not only academically but also in field work under supervision. In discussing specific institutional settings we will see how this aspect of training in social group work can be especially helpful.

SUPERVISED FIELD WORK

Supervised field work is the method by which the social group worker learns how to translate his knowledge into practice. How is this carried out?

For centuries vocations and professions have supplemented theoretical learning with either apprenticeship or laboratory work. Social work too started out with apprenticeship, which means placing the learning person in a given agency to learn by practice. Today supervised field work is based on a very different approach. Like an intern in a hospital, the worker is practicing his profession in the field. He writes an account of his observations and his work and on the basis of these "process records" he has weekly conferences with his field instructor. The field instructor is something like an individual tutor to the student. The focus of the field instructor conferences is twofold:

1. Relating practice to the theory learned in the classroom.
2. Helping the student himself to become a disciplined professional person.

The latter objective includes necessarily a deepened self-knowledge. For instance, one student has in the beginning great difficulty in working with adolescents. Superficially this could be handled either by suggesting that he not work again with adolescents or by making it clear to him that he will have to work with all age groups and, therefore, will have to force himself to do this. The skilled field instructor, however, will begin to explore with the student the reasons he has such difficulty in working with adolescents. They may find that the student still feels guilty about the way he behaved as an adolescent and he does not want to see this repeated in others. In the student's being helped to understand his own adolescent needs and to distinguish between himself and those with whom he is working, he is being enabled to do his work.

One student placed in an institution showed real capacity and warmth in his work with youngsters, but was extremely annoyed when parents came for a visit and was not able to use those contacts constructively. Yet in theory he had learned that working with parents is important and that we cannot, either in our thinking or in our work, separate the helping process for children from the one for parents. In his supervisory conferences the field instructor helped the student to think through why he felt so punishing towards the parents. It developed that he had been a very dependent youngster and still felt very resentful that he had been kept in that role for so long.

Another second-year graduate student was extremely critical

of the institution staff and he rationalized this by saying that one must expect high standards of performance from professional people. It took considerable time to get at this student's great insecurity in wanting to be a capable professional worker and, therefore, his fear of any failure he saw in others.

I remember one student in social group work who in spite of a real sensitivity to people which could be seen in her writing about them tried to stay away from any emotional problem when it was expressed in the group. She was consequently not helpful to the members of her group. It was learned that she herself had once been badly hurt when she gave her confidence to somebody who should have been in a helping position but did not help, and this was the reason for her own rejection of the helping role.

There are probably very few people in any society who do not have some struggle about accepting authority. Yet in all institutional work the capacity to accept and deal with this constructively is essential. Every institutional setting will demand an understanding of the use of limitations. The correctional institution will, in addition to this, demand an understanding of the need of society to protect itself and, therefore, to use authority in a harsher sense than has to be used in an institution directed exclusively toward treatment.

One of the graduate students working in a settlement house had to do a great deal of work with a gang of fourteen-year-old boys. He did very helpful and sensible work with them. At one time police arrived during the meeting and had to arrest one of the boys. The student was extremely disturbed and though he covered his feelings quite well during the incident he expressed considerable hostility against all "cops" in his supervisory conference. It needed far more than one conference to help this student see the important position that the police play in society as well as to work with his own feelings of rebellion based on many childhood experiences in a tough neighborhood. He had to learn what his role should be if he really wanted to be helpful to the youngster with whom he was concerned. He learned to see that the outlet of natural adolescent rebellion did not have to be delinquent behavior if he, as the group worker, took on the constructive role and helped the youngster to express his feelings of bitterness and defiance directly, verbally, or in a group program, instead of violating the law. Yet he would have been unable to move toward this if he had not been helped to understand the angry and hurt young boy he had himself been.

This kind of field instruction does not present a form of psychoanalysis, but it does present an understanding of oneself in relation to the work that has to be done. At times this is painful, but in the hands of a kind and supporting supervisor who is not using this to make the student feel that he is incapable all around, it becomes a real learning process. The student is helped also to see where his true strength lies so that he may capably and with confidence enter the demanding profession of social work. The student begins to learn about his own feelings, not for the sake of himself, but for the people with whom he is working. In looking at himself he will learn how difficult learning can be for people, how all of us struggle with resistances against new learning or new demands, how it is not easy to accept authority, and how all of us have different ways of dealing with life's problems.

Field work, therefore, will help to relate theory to practice. In Bertha Reynolds' words, "The sensitivity of the layman raised to the 'Nth degree' is the result of professional education." Deeper understanding, greater knowledge, and constant critical analysis of one's own work can not lead to intellectual dishonesty but must lead to a deeper humility, a greater understanding of how much we have still to learn, and a growing freedom from any tendency to let one's own needs interfere with those of the other person.

One of the beginning students in social group work said she was quite puzzled about what we meant when we said that a social worker should "involve" herself in the helping process. She thought this contradicted the idea of not using people for our own purposes. There was real understanding in her eyes and an obvious feeling of relief when she learned that "involvement" means to be completely available to the person or the group with whom we are dealing. She said, "They must understand and I must really feel that I am there for *them* completely and I must understand their problems the way they seem to *them*." It is by this attitude that the professional worker will become really helpful.

I want to summarize what the social group worker gains in his professional education: he intensifies and clarifies a *basic philosophy* which shows respect for *all* human beings and their capacity to grow and change. It also must include a deep conviction of the responsibility to use his helping profession ethically and skillfully according to the best of his knowledge.

He gains *knowledge in*
   Individual dynamics (normal and pathological);
   Dynamics of group behavior (normal and pathological);
   Social policy;
   Understanding of administrative principles;
   Knowledge of community resources and community organization.

He develops *skill in*
   Direct work with groups;
   Supervision of lay staff and volunteers;
   Diagnosis of individual and group behavior;
   Recording, summarizing, and analyzing group process and individual material;
   Referral to other agencies or other professional people.

He develops *some skill in*
  Casework, counseling, community development.

He develops an *attitude of*
  Professional discipline and integrity;
  Respect for and appreciation of the contribution of
    others in his place of work;
  An inquiring mind;
  Flexibility in the use of principles and tools;
  Freedom and creativity in the use of himself.

OBJECTIVES OF SOCIAL GROUP WORK

Social group work is a method of helping people in the group situations so basic to all human beings.

Not all groups need a social group worker. The worker enters where the individual in the group or the group as a whole or both need professional help to fulfill their own purposes and to become a constructive part of society. Many groups, just as many individuals, will be perfectly capable of carrying out their programs by themselves and will not need professional help. The social group worker, as part of a helping profession, will be used and should be available wherever help is needed.

We will find the group worker helping normal child and adolescent groups with the growing-up process that cannot be achieved completely unaided. There certainly are other institutions that are helping with this, such as family, church, and school. In the church and school settings the group work method should be used far more than it is today. There is a trend in this direction. The group worker's role in relation to youth groups is always a helping one and not a purely recreational one.

This distinction has to be made clearly. Recreation is a very important and vital part of life, but not all aspects of recreation must necessarily be carried on by social group workers. Some forms of recreation are individual occupations and others are carried on in mass activities which do not demand interpersonal involvement. There are forms of recreation where the group worker is essential. His role is always in the area of human relationships. He will work where individualization is necessary and possible, where interpersonal relationships have to be dealt with, which means in youth groups, treatment groups, gangs, adult groups where there is a need to improve cultural, religious, or racial relationships, groups that need help with understanding their own problems, and groups that need help in working toward the improvement of community services.

What are some of the objectives of the group work method?

1. *Individualization.* Group work is not "group thinking" in the derogatory sense. It does not aim at conformity, but on the contrary it helps the individual to free himself while being helped to interact with his fellow man.

2. *Development of a sense of belonging.* Loneliness is one of the deepest despairs of mankind. Suicides can almost always be traced back to the feeling of abandonment. The loneliness of people in our modern society, in cities filled with people, is frightening. It is not something that can be helped by just meeting people. It is a deep inner need that can be helped only by developing an emotional maturity in the individual himself and giving him the kind of associations that have real meaning. A young and attractive woman with two small children and a kind husband said in a small group meeting, "I am usually so lonely I just shudder. I love my children and my husband, but I am afraid because there seems nothing else." It would be foolish to think that this person could be helped just by continuing in a group. The sense of belonging can only come when we understand far better her needs and her concern.

3. *A basic development of the capacity to participate.* Participation is one of our basic democratic concepts. Edward Lindemann once said, "In a democracy nobody needs to agree, but everybody must participate." A democracy cannot live without the individual participation of every human being, but participation is not something that comes by itself. We have often presented it exclusively as something pleasurable, something that everybody wants and feels hurt by its being withdrawn. But that is really only one side of the feelings we have about participation. The *Trägheit des Herzens* (laziness of the heart), as the German philosopher and poet Schiller called it, is the other side of our feelings about participation. Surely we want it. But we like it if we do not have to make the effort and if some decisions are made for us. The skilled and sensitive group worker will accept this ambivalence and work toward overcoming it through positive experiences. This again leads to greater freedom of the individual and to a form of self-discipline by overcoming his dependency tendencies. It also means guaranteeing the lifeblood of democracy.

4. *Increase of the capacity to contribute to decisions on grounds of rational thinking and through group deliberation.* Again this is something that is not easily learned. We have seen this clearly in the many cases of mass hysteria in our society where decisions were not made on grounds of rational thinking and we see it in many of our groups, children and adults alike, where the word of one person carries the decision. In work with a delinquent gang in one of our large cities, the group worker saw the beginning change in the gang's relationship to the rest of society when individuals in this group began to speak up about some of the issues instead of letting Joe, the gangleader, make all the decisions alone. The first steps of the decision-making process in this group were handled simply by physical violence. The gangleader and his followers beat up those who dissented, but the group worker saw dis-

sention as the first step in this process of decision-making. The next step was no more physical violence but a mechanical counting of votes, until finally one day almost triumphantly the record showed a real group discussion which ended in a decision on grounds of argument.

5. *Increased respect for differences among people.* Groups have difficulties in achieving unity and a feeling of belonging and they will try to achieve this easily by demanding complete conformity from the individuals in their group or by choosing their members so that only people of the same kind can belong. We find these groups often in our society, yet if we want humanity to learn to live together peacefully and constructively we will have to help them to accept differences among people, not as a liability but as something that makes life richer and more interesting. In institutional work we see very often the formation of harsh cliques because of the fear of the already insecure individual to associate with anybody different.

6. *Development of a warm and accepting social climate.* This is the most intangible and yet the basis for any constructive work where several people meet together. Eva Burmeister has described this beautifully when she says in her article, "Social Climate in the Institution," that one can

feel the tone of a children's home as soon as one enters the front door. There is something in the air, in the noises, smells, sounds, space, color, light, the movement and expressions on the faces of the children and staff, that tells the whole story.[5]

Constructive group climate frees its members to give to others and to accept from them in a free interplay of human personalities.

The major *tools* of the social group worker are:

[5] Susanne Schulze, ed., *Creative Group Living in a Children's Institution* (New York: Association Press, 1951), p. 35.

1. *The conscious and disciplined use of himself.* This does not mean a cold and only observing kind of behavior. It means knowledge of himself and the best way he can help others within the framework of his own strength and limitations.

2. *The verbal interaction between himself and between members.*

3. *The discriminate use of program activities related to the needs of the individual and the group.*

4. *Interaction among the group members themselves.*

THE GROUP WORKER IN THE INSTITUTION

It seems strange that social group work did not relate much earlier to the institutional field. It can only be explained historically by the neglect with which social work as a whole treated institutions. When the basic purpose of institutional life was established as treatment, it became clear that social group work was especially capable of helping with the whole group living process. August Aichorn, who first saw the treatment value of institutional life, said in his book, *Wayward Youth:* "Specific educational methods are far less important than an attitude which brings the child into contact with reality," and at another point, "this matter of grouping is of first importance." Since the 1940's, group work's contribution to the institutional field has been better understood. The National Conference on Prevention and Control of Juvenile Delinquency called together in Washington, D.C., in November, 1946, expressed this quite clearly.

Group work services should be provided for those apprehended for delinquent behavior, for those in institutions for detention, and for long term treatment of juvenile delinquency.[6]

Young people need experiences through which their elemental

[6] "Case Work-Group Work," p. 38.

desire for friendship, recognition, adventure and creative expression may be realized. Juveniles living in institutions share these same interests with all youths. In addition because they are separated from family and neighborhood groupings they have increased need for informal relationships with others. . . .[7]

As early as the 1950's, lecturing on the history of correctional institutions at the University of Minnesota, Professor Richard Guilford pointed out that the adult offender too needs to relearn his relationships to other people and that he is placed in a group situation which should be used to prepare him for life outside the prison. He pointed out to the class that there was yet very little experience in this but that the social group worker's contribution will lie in this area.

Morris F. Mayer has crystallized his thinking through a long period of experience in his large children's institution at Bellefaire by summarizing:

The group living process has become an important treatment tool in itself, and as such, combined with the casework process, the education, the medical and psychiatric care, represents a therapeutic channel through which the child develops into a stronger personality.[8]

The group worker in an institution cannot be used only in a part of the institutional setting, as, e.g., in its recreational aspect. His knowledge must permeate the whole group living situation; he must bring to bear on the institution his understanding of the dynamics of group behavior just as the case worker and psychiatrist have brought to the institution their basic understanding of individual treatment. Practically, this will mean that *the social group worker will take on a special helping role towards the houseparent or counselor*, since they

[7] "Report on Institutional Treatment of Juvenile Delinquents, 1946," p. 30.
[8] Morris F. Mayer, "The Houseparents and the Group Living Process," Schulze, *op. cit.*, p. 97.

are directly related to the group living process. It will be a different role according to the different function of the institution as well as to the personnel who are employed. I will try in the chapters relating to different institutions to spell out this function of the group worker in each specific setting.

Another basic function of the social group worker in any institutional setting will be to *work directly with formed selected groups on some specific problem of the group,* as, for instance, discharge from the institution, intake into the institution, special behavior problems, or problems around emotional needs that cannot be handled in the day-to-day group living situation.

The group worker's role will be *to supervise and coordinate special services* which are not carried by the houseparents but which relate to the group living experience. I am thinking of such services as recreational mass activities, special interest groups, and some educational endeavors. It is important that they are coordinated from the point of view of social relationships as well as of treatment for the individual, so that in them the treatment focus is maintained. If, for instance, it becomes clear that a cottage group is under great tension, it will be important that the social group worker transmit this to the one in charge of recreational activity so that he knows not to start a competitive ball game on this day. Or he will let him know that Susan just had a very upsetting letter from her family and will not be able to take any failure in a game. Coordination of knowledge in the group atmosphere as well as individual needs will be of immense help to the staff in those activities.

The group worker should be *responsible for referral to recreational and group association resources in the community.*

He should *work with volunteers, if the institution uses them.*

He should *work with groups of relatives of institutional residents.*

In the preceding chapter I have presented the knowledge and skill the social group worker brings with him, the basic objectives of social group work, and a broad outline of the function of the group worker in relation to group living in institutions. The picture will gain color and life when we consider next practice as we see it today and as we hope to improve it in the future.

3. SOCIAL GROUP WORK IN CHIL-DREN'S INSTITUTIONS

WHO ARE THE CHILDREN?

Talking to parents about children, Kahlil Gibran in *The Prophet* says:

You may give them your love but not your thoughts,
For they have their own thoughts.
You may house their bodies but not their souls,
For their souls dwell in the house of tomorrow, which you cannot
    visit, not even in your dreams.
You may strive to be like them, but seek not to make them like
    you.
For life goes not backward nor tarries with yesterday.
You are the bows from which your children as living arrows are
    sent forth.[1]

And Mrs. Macauley speaks to her young adolescent son when she has heard him cry at night:

I know that sobbing. . . . I have heard it before. It is not yours. It is not any man's. It is the whole world's. Having known the world's grief, you are now on your way, so of course all the mis-

[1] Printed with the permission of the publisher, Alfred A. Knopf, Inc. Copyright 1923 by Kahlil Gibran. Renewal copyright 1951 by Administrators C.T.A. of Kahlil Gibran Estate and Mary Gibran.

takes are ahead—all the wonderful mistakes that you must and will make. . . . No matter what the mistakes are that you must make, do not be afraid of having made them or of making more of them.[2]

There is a deep demand made on the adult in both of these quotations. He must step into the background and allow this different new human being, the *child*, to become himself. It is hard for any of us to let somebody else be different from ourselves, and it seems hardest on the adult in relation to children, because children can be formed and the wish to form a living human being in our image is very great. How often do we say, "This is best for the child," when we really mean, "This is the way we would like to be, and so he or she should be." I have never forgotten the serious young man who observed a group of adults exclaiming over and over how "cute" the children were, but when the youngsters got more high-spirited they slapped them. He turned to me and said, "You know, they might like children, but they have no respect for them."

Our thinking about children has changed considerably during the centuries. Look at pictures painted in the Middle Ages and see how even the *infant* is portrayed as a little old adult. See in the paintings of the Renaissance how the young child is dressed like the grown-ups, in the stiff robes and walking around in the solemn ways of his elders. People for many centuries have looked at the child as a miniature adult, with the same emotions and capacities of an adult, needing only to be trained. In many ways it was a disgrace to be a child and one had to grow out of it as fast as possible.

The twentieth century, with its increased understanding of the human being, brought a change in the understanding of the child. We learned that they really do not think like an

2 William Saroyan, *The Human Comedy* (New York: Harcourt, Brace, 1945).

adult, yet their thinking and feeling are strong and very real to them. It seems strange that so few adults remember how they felt as children. They will remember that things that seem small to adults, such as dropping a bottle of milk that mother has asked to bring home, can be a tragic event for a child, and not only when one is dealing with a stern mother. It is the feeling of having failed, of having not accomplished a task that one seemed to be able to accomplish. It means little to the adult that the neighbor girls don't care to associate with the little twelve-year-old next door. But it will be a major tragedy in her mind and she may feel abandoned by everybody and reconfirmed in her belief that she isn't worth anything. (This was beautifully presented in the play, *The Member of the Wedding,* by Carson S. McCullers.)

A successful young woman told me about an event that stands out in her mind and that she thinks has greatly influenced her development. When she was three years old a distant cousin visited her family. She greatly admired and loved this cousin, who at about eighteen years of age seemed to the little girl like a fairy prince. She had always felt inferior to her older sister, who was especially gifted and creative. She remembers the moment when her sister was building a beautiful bridge out of blocks which was greatly admired by everybody. She too was standing by admiringly and at the same time very unhappy. At this moment her "prince" lifted her up, set her on his lap, put his arm around her, and while he admired the bridge he also smiled at her and held her close. As an adult she still remembers the feeling of comfort and self-esteem that came to her and how the jealousy she had felt for her sister almost drained out of her. You might think that the emotions of a three-year-old are largely exaggerated in the account of the adult. From observing children I doubt this very much. Yet, even if it were exaggerated, it proves that childhood emotions were at least strong enough to have influenced the future relationship between the sisters and to have helped the little girl gain the self-confidence she was lacking.

Children feel pain and sorrow, joy and happiness, just as strongly as adults, yet very often in different situations. Loneliness is often greater in children than in adults because they are so dependent on others. When one is very small and very dependent security cannot yet be found in oneself or self-chosen relationships or a philosophy of life. Security must come tangibly from human sources and it must be a security that is given freely, not only as a reward for certain kinds of behavior. In the thirteenth century a custom existed in Europe of some churches offering asylum to anybody, whatever crime he had committed. Whenever he entered he was safe and could relieve his conscience in an atmosphere void of retaliation. To the child to whom the demands of life are still new such safety is indispensable, because he will feel guilt even about small events and the fear of retaliation is very strong.

Childhood has been described as a happy stage, and it is certainly happy where a great deal of security is given, but it is especially unhappy where safety is lacking and one stands alone in the face of a world one cannot master. I will never forget little René, who with his mother was fleeing along the roads of France after the German invasion. René was only four years old and while Mother was close to him and protecting him the noise and the strange people were not so frightening, but at one point during the flight he was separated from his mother and around him were strange voices, frightening noises, people he did not know. We will never know what René actually was thinking, but we do know that he arrived a day later with his mother in safety but having lost the ability to speak. For days a usually intelligent chattering little boy sat hunched on a bench unable to utter a sound. I also cannot forget the moment that apparently brought him back to normality: We were sitting in a garden, the mother, René, and myself, and Mother had just hugged him and promised him that we would not leave. We had told René that we understood that he must hate everybody for having left him. Suddenly René jumped up, tore out some beautiful flowers, stamped on them, and began a wild race around the grounds, screaming animal sounds without real words. Only hunters who have seen wounded animals fighting pain and death can imagine how this looked. Probably at this moment René lived through again all the terror of abandonment, all his feelings of fear and hate for what had been done to him. If we had interrupted we probably would not have helped. His mother called to him softly saying that she too had been terribly frightened when she had lost him and at this moment René flung himself at her, burst into tears, and spoke his first word.

Perhaps it is in such dramatic moments that we adults get a glimpse into the depths of feeling of children, yet those glimpses are few and children—as all human beings—do not show all their feelings on the surface. We can live beside them for many years not knowing what they think or fear. If we respect them for what they are and give them security they will be able to work out those feelings by themselves and a strong capable adult will emerge.

We must not forget that the children in our institutions are not the ones who have lived in security nor the ones who can easily trust the world and themselves. They are all little Renés, but for different reasons. The sweet little orphan who has "only" experienced the death of parents hardly exists any more in our institutions. In all institutions in the United States only 3 per cent of the children placed in them are orphans. With our increased foster-home and boarding-home and adoption program the child that is not too damaged will usually be placed in a family situation. We have in our institutions children who come with deep scars because of the break in their security. (At this moment I am not speaking about educational institutions, which I will discuss in another chapter.) The problems behind them range from perhaps long-time illness in the family to badly divided homes, severe neglect, and actual abandonment.

What trust can a youngster have in the adult world when for years he has lived through the experience of his father arriving home only sporadically and whenever he was home they all, including his mother, were afraid of him. Jerry told me quite coolly how he had boarded up the windows every night and nailed wood across the door so that his father couldn't get in. Jerry had taken over the protection of his family the only way he knew, and that was by keeping out the person they could not handle. But with this act Jerry had symbolized an attitude he carried for a long time that said "Keep Out" to every adult who wanted to come close to him.

Susan had solved this problem in another way by just "keeping herself out." Susan had lived through constant quarrels and finally had witnessed a mutual stabbing between her parents. Susan was a sweet little girl of eleven years, quiet and aloof. She would comply with what was asked of her, but she would not really relate to anybody. She would sit and daydream, removed from a reality much too painful to live in. It took months and months of extreme patience to even live with Susan. The housemother sometimes was almost in tears because she had arranged some event that all the other girls enjoyed, but Susan would continue her icy resistance.

Why should children trust promises when they have experienced over and over again promises not being kept? Why should they trust kindness when it sometimes has been used just to lure them into a relationship that was painfully misused? Why should they get along with other children when they have learned that the only law for keeping afloat in a mass of hostile battling human beings is to get as much for oneself as one can? Why should they accept rules when their experience is that rules are made by those with power and without sense? Why should they be orderly when inside them is chaos and nothing around them seems to matter? Why should they make an effort to participate in any decisions if they have learned that they get pushed around anyhow? Why should they take care of property when they never have had the feeling that anything that belonged to them was important to others or respected by them?

We are expecting a great deal of children in our institutions or of children anywhere who have not yet felt that there was any sense in the demands made on them.

If you are a houseparent you will shake your head at this moment and say, "Well, do you mean that we should just let them do what they want to?" I certainly do not mean this, but I want all of us who are working with them to understand with what we are working. No carpenter will start using tools before he knows the material he is working with. He will use different tools or the same tools differently when he is working with oak or with maple. Fritz Redl once said, "Children are at least as complicated as a piece of wood." [3] We must know who they are and with what they come before we can deal with them. We too often have our tools ready, the same kind for everybody, and we are surprised when the wood splits or cracks or breaks altogether. It is the deep understanding of the child with whom we work, a scientific knowledge of the tools that we are using, and a warm dedication to the healing profession that is demanded of the worker in a children's institution.

[3] Fritz Redl and George V. Sheviakoff, *Discipline for Today's Children and Youth* (Washington, D. C.: National Education Association, 1944), p. 63.

Studies reveal that where foster home programs are highly developed, the residue of children in institutions represent the most damaged children who could not use a home atmosphere constructively.[4]

It is the most damaged child that we will find in our institutions. Damage does not always occur in the same degree for the same reasons or show the same symptoms. A great deal of research will have to be done regarding the question of what kind and what degree of damaged child needs institutional care and which one would profit more from family care. The way it appears in practice is that the child who is showing his disturbance through especially acting-out behavior, such as stealing, swearing, sex play, and defiance, is the child that usually has the greatest difficulty being placed in a foster home. A family which has to live with its neighbors has trouble accepting a child with this kind of disturbing behavior. The children who express their unhappiness through extreme withdrawal usually manage to live through a few foster homes until they become so unsatisfactory to the foster parents that they too have to leave and become part of the institutional population.

Our institutions for adolescents will show a somewhat different picture than the ones for younger children. The adolescent in our institutions who is not delinquent is very often either an exceptionally disturbed youngster close to being mentally sick, or he is not especially disturbed but does not want to start at this time in life a too close relationship with a new family. We will therefore find some institutions for adolescents where the population is much closer to the one in a mental hospital, while others offer group living to adolescents whose behavior is comparatively undisturbed.

[4] Norman V. Lourie and Rena Schulman, "The Role of the Residential Staff in Residential Treatment," A. J. *Orthopsychiatry*, XXII, No. 4 (October, 1952), p. 800.

GROUP LIVING AS PART OF TREATMENT

Children's institutions are not places in which a child is kept only to be fed, clothed, and perhaps given a few treatment interviews. The most important part of treatment lies in the daily group living situation with all other resources, such as case work, psychotherapy, school teaching, etc., as much available as possible. All those services must make a coordinated effort in the interest of the child.

I will talk here about the children's institution as we see it mostly in this country. With the kind of population that we have in our institutions, it seems tragic to me that we still have to distinguish between so-called treatment homes and other homes. Actually, every children's institution today must be a treatment home, perhaps with the single exception of the receiving homes that can give only short-term treatment. Yet in using the expression "short-term treatment," I do not really except them either. With our greater interest in institutional work it will be only a short time before we will distinguish only between treatment homes that come up to the expected standards and those that do not, rather than between those that give treatment and those that do not. We expect in a good treatment home the services of caseworkers who will fulfill the child's need for individual treatment as well as keeping him related to his own home or to a foster home into which he might go. A good treatment home will also include the services of a psychiatrist who can deal with the especially disturbed child and who can give consultation. I will not deal here with those special services, but only with the group treatment aspects of the children's institution. Let us see what the group environment means to the child who is entering an institution.

The Newcomer

What does it mean to enter a new group? Numerous studies have been made by social group workers regarding this. Anthropologists have been interested in the way newcomers are treated in different cultures. Let us look at what it means being a newcomer in our institutions, first from the point of view of the newcomer himself and then from the point of view of the group which he enters. The newcomer is a common phenomenon in institutional life, since it is not a stable community with long-term inhabitants, but is built on the premise that there will be new people all the time. The impact of this is strong on the child who enters this new community as well as on the institutional group. The houseparent dealing with this fact must be very conscious of it.

Before entering an institution the child is filled with questions about it and about himself in relation to it. He wonders how those people will be to whom he is responsible. He wonders about the adults he will meet. Will they beat him, will they be kind to him, will they let him get away with anything?

He wonders about the place itself, about its routines, how it looks, how he will sleep, how he will eat? He does not only wonder but he is afraid. All of us are somewhat afraid of new experiences, but if this experience is a result of a long chain of unhappy events and confused feelings it becomes even more frightening.

And the child greatly wonders what his relation to his group will be. He doesn't know those kids. Will he be able to beat them up or will they beat him up? Will they laugh at him? Are they all friends and he is the only new one? With whom will he have to sleep? He wonders what his status will be, what their mores are, how he will stand up in relation to them. He doesn't think it in those words, but these are the questions he has in mind. Very often we haven't realized how difficult it really is being a newcomer.

One of our graduate students, a capable young adult, described in a paper how he as a seventeen-year-old went to a university away from home and had to live in a dormitory. Unfortunately he arrived a few days later than the rest of the boys. At his arrival he discovered that all the beds were taken with the exception of one far in the corner, that only the last place at a table was available for him. He went on to relate how he immediately felt that he was a stranger (though actually the others had been strangers only a few days previously), how he thought that they were talking about him, and how he began showing off in classes a great deal to prove that he knew just as much as they did. He described how this became quite an unhappy time for him and how he made his own life very difficult by feeling this way. It is a perfect description of what it meant being a newcomer and getting no help with those feelings.

The youngster who comes to our institution has even fewer inner resources to deal with this problem and needs the help of the sensitive houseparent and the group he will enter.

And what does the entrance of the newcomer mean to the group? The group as a whole has established some mode of living. The youngsters have begun to know each other. They have overcome some of their fears, they are on the "in" of the institution, but they usually are not completely secure with this situation. This means that they do not like to be disturbed in their equilibrium and the newcomer is somebody who disturbs it. He represents to them again all the fear and uncertainty; he also reminds them of the fact that they are not in an established community. He also may incite some of their feelings of hostility and, being the weaker one because he does not know the place too well, he can easily be put into the role of a scapegoat. On the other hand, he might appeal to their brotherly feeling because of identification with him.

The skilled houseparent will see that for the sake of the newcomer himself as well as the group the entrance into the group is made as helpful and as reassuring as possible. It is very important that the houseparent greet the youngster as somebody who is especially welcome and a wanted member of the community. In some institutions houseparents are not notified when children will enter their cottage or their group and are surprised by the arrival. In permitting this the institutional administration has already defeated the therapeutic purpose. The houseparent cannot be accepting of the newcomer if he himself has not agreed to the addition in the cottage and has not participated in some consideration of whether the newcomer will fit in with the rest of his youngsters. He also cannot plan to be at hand when the new arrival enters.

In addition to the houseparent's trying to make the youngster as comfortable as possible, it is important that he have from the beginning the feeling that his own group will accept him. Here the skill of the houseparent lies in establishing an atmosphere in the group of newcomers being actually fun and not exclusively disturbing. The houseparent can prepare the group for the youngster in advance when he knows who will come. He can have a discussion with the group a day earlier and allow them to bring out feelings of fear and hostility regarding the change in the group situation. He can ask them to help him with making the newcomer more comfortable. Children have an astonishing capacity for compassion if they are approached as reasonable human beings.

In some children's institutions each cottage has established a rotating welcome committee of two or three youngsters who will see the newcomer after he has been seen by the houseparent, show him around the place, and make him feel welcome. In discussion with the youngsters themselves, quite imaginative devices have been found to help the group and the new boy or girl to overcome their initial difficulties. I think of small favors made by the group which were put beside the plate of the newcomer at his first meal, or a quiet evening discussion in which the others told him a little about themselves, that way allowing him to tell also about himself. The housemother was present and helped along so that the newcomer did not feel pressed into revealing what he did not want to reveal.

Individualization

One has become a member of the group, and the living with people who are not one's brothers and sisters and with adults who are not one's parents has begun. It means not only eating and sleeping and working with them, but relating to them, being liked or disliked by them. Will this life perpetuate in the child the feeling of loneliness or will it help him to gain some confidence in the world?

The child has to struggle with rules established by the institution and with rules that grow out of the community of children. He will find friends and lose friends. Life continues on another plane than it was where one came from, but it is still life with its difficulties and its joys and its being part of human relationships. It is the houseparent or the counselor who is in the middle of all these problems. In the treatment institution the houseparent must be able to individualize the youngsters in the group as well as to establish a satisfying group life.

In numerous institutes I have caught a sigh of despair from houseparents when the word "individualization" fell. And when we became better acquainted with each other the houseparents complained that they were expected to be psychiatrists and treat each child individually without considering that this was humanly impossible as well as actually not helpful to the other children. I think the reason for this feeling of despair on the part of houseparents is the poor job that we social workers have done in explaining what we mean by individualizing. The knowledge of the group worker and the way he individualizes in the group is especially applicable to the work the houseparent has to do. Individualizing does not mean that he should sit down alone with the youngster or treat him without any relationship to the others around him. Individualizing in the group means that the houseparent understands and sees the particular youngster as a unique individual different from everyone else, that he gives him the feeling that he is someone special and important, that he allows him choices so that he can be an individual, but also that he expects him to become part of a living group.

Let us see practically what this means. One houseparent felt very strongly that it is helpful to children to settle their own conflicts and, therefore, kept out of the children's quarrels, even when they all turned on one of the youngsters in the group. This had worked well in the case of Emily, who did not want adult interference in her behalf and who spit back with plenty of energy and fire when she was attacked. The housemother was quite puzzled, though, when a month later the cottage was in an uproar after they had turned against Ilse, a girl who had made life very unpleasant for the group by her continued refusal to participate in any kind of routine duties.

In the supervisory interview the social group worker recorded:

We discussed the situation in the cottage and in order to focus on the individual I pointed out that a girl like Emily apparently could hold her own if refused or turned on by the rest of the group. However, a girl like Ilse, despite her mature stature, was still a child and that it would be quite damaging when all the children turned against her like that at this time.

In the following discussion, the housemother realized that basically her idea of youngsters being able to settle their own differences was not wrong, but for *this particular child* it was not helpful. She could see that this child needed some protection in relation to the rest of the group as well as some insight into the reasons why the group was turning against her. When the housemother realized this, she also understood that this did not mean that she was favoring one youngster beyond the other but that she simply was relating to the specific and different needs of each child.

In many discussions with houseparents the fear is brought out that individualization will mean playing favorites, and that the youngsters will resent this. There is no question that in group situations, and especially where the group situation is related to a dependent status, people will be very sensitive about whether they are treated justly and equally. Yet on numerous occasions it could be seen that the children understood very well if one of their contemporaries needed more attention from the adult than they themselves. One houseparent who had just started working in the institutional field told with great surprise and pleasure that she had realized that one of the children needed an exceptional amount of affection compared with others. She had not wanted to play into this because she feared the others would resent it, but she also knew that this child suffered because of the lack of demonstrative affection. One evening one little boy had called to her and had whispered to her that he thought she should sit for awhile with Bob because he felt so lonely and cried until late at night. Actually the children did not resent this special comfort she gave to Bob, but on the contrary expected this of her and seemed to feel reassured by her doing it for him, knowing that she would give them the same attention if they needed it.

Certainly this does not always work out so easily. In an institution for adolescent girls a meeting was called by the social group worker on the staff because the hostility of all the older girls had been increasingly focused on Gertrude. There had been arguments and finally a physical fight among them. In this case the staff decided that the situation should be handled in a group discussion. Quoting from the record:

I (the group worker) opened the discussion by saying that we were meeting tonight to talk over the difficulties they seemed to be having in getting along together. Perhaps by talking things over we could get together some ideas of how to make living together more pleasant. Anna, quickly followed by Fanny and Theresa, loudly and in a very hostile excited manner reiterated a series of incidents for which they were mad at Gertrude. The incidents mostly concerned Gertrude's "getting away with things" without being disciplined by staff members—taking a shower at 3 A.M., seeing her boy friend on the sly, getting out of various work duties. Edith spoke with bitterness about the fact that Gertrude had an outside job for which she was paid and none of the others had this privilege. Joan complained loudly about Gertrude's swearing in front of the younger girls. Nancy's manner was very hostile as she echoed other's complaints but she remained more silent. Much was said about Gertrude's being "PC" (privileged character).

We see here that special privileges can be resented even if they may be part of the treatment plan. It is interesting to follow this record a step further and to see how the worker was dealing more with the feelings of the girls and the need to understand Gertrude than defending privileges she might have.

The girls vented this hostility for several minutes. . . . Gertrude sat silently for some time and then began to make some efforts at defense. At first the girls laughed when Gertrude spoke up. At one point Anna ran to the window and pretended to throw up. I insisted that she sit down. Gradually Gertrude verbalized that she was wrong in certain instances but that she could not change her ways if the girls did not give her a chance. I asked the girls if this made sense to them—that it would take effort and acceptance on their part as well as Gertrude's if things were to go more smoothly. At this point they were still unaccepting of this. The initial outburst of hostility though was beginning to calm. The original complaints kept recurring but more calmly. I introduced some interpretation in the matter of the reason for Gertrude's having an outside job and the girls accepted this for the most part. Fanny expressed an interest in wanting to do something about the situation. Theresa followed along with this idea, but at intervals went back to isolated complaining. Edith talked about how she had been mad about some of the things that had happened, but she had never really had any trouble with Gertrude. About this time Joan started crying and said that her caseworker had told her that learning to get along with others was part of growing up and she wanted so badly to do this.

The meeting continued quite emotionally, some of the girls staying hostile, others saying in a sincere way that they would like to try to get along with Gertrude.

Gertrude said that she realized she had almost always had her own way with her folks, and if she was told she couldn't do something she could always get away with it behind her father's back and that kind of thing had become a habit. Edith told her not to go blaming all of this on her folks—after all, the rest of them didn't have perfect folks either and they had plenty of problems because of it. I suggested that Edith had brought up an important point—that all of them had certain problems—that some of the things we had been talking about tonight were Gertrude's problems while the rest of them had other kinds of problems— but whatever they were it helped to have others understand them and help them work them out. In the emotional atmosphere of this meeting this point seemed to give the girls a bond which included Gertrude.

We can see here how hostility created by something that looked to the others like special privileges could be handled in group discussion that allowed for a free expression of hostility as well as giving some interpretation for the reasons of different treatment. Actually, the group worker did not dwell on this point but helped the girls to realize far more their own problems in relation to others. This excerpt of the record also shows how the group worker can supplement and help the houseparent in this exceedingly difficult task of individualization.

Among distrustful and unhappy youngsters the feelings of jealousy are very strong. They have experienced rejection. Their longing for love and acceptance makes them suspect that everyone else may be loved, only *they* are left out. They see favoritism in every movement, and often misinterpret the most friendly approaches. A preadolescent complained that everybody looked at her on the playground or in the dining room. It took a long time before she could accept the truth of the housemother's response, "Has it ever occurred to you that they do this because you are really very beautiful?"

Houseparents still have to struggle with each new group over those feelings of distrust and jealousy. *Uniform* treatment will not overcome it. Reasonable individualized treatment will help the children to learn that love is not a pie that loses through division, but is a power that grows greater, the more there are to be loved. If they learn this, they will be able to see the other's problems as well as their own.

Establishing of Relationships

There is no treatment process without a conscious and working relationship. Houseparents have often asked what is meant by this. As one of them expressed it, "Does it mean that they must like us always? I cannot make them like me." This certainly is not what is meant by "relationship." What is meant is the development of a mutual trust. It cannot come first from the child. The child is the one who has been hurt and the child, therefore, cannot be the giving one. The giving of trust and of genuine acceptance must come first from the houseparent. This is not always easy in view of some of the very difficult children with whom the houseparent has to deal. It is not easy if there is no initial response on the part of the child. Yet the basic attitude of the houseparent toward the child must be one of honest appreciation, in spite of everything the child might do or say. This does not mean that the houseparent is supposed to like everything the child does, but he must learn to give him the feeling that he is accepted as he is with all his difficulties and that the houseparent is there to help him.

Such an attitude cannot be acquired or practiced without the houseparent knowing something of the basic difficulties of the child. His building up of a relationship must be different according to the different dynamics of behavior in each child. If Susan has experienced severe rejection on the part of several foster mothers, she might be very suspicious towards any woman and an establishment of relationship by being especially affectionate might only increase her suspicion. Perhaps the houseparent will be most helpful to Susan if she lets her feel free to show hostility towards the adult and make her first positive relationship with other girls in the group, letting her see that she cares but is not intruding on her.

The establishment of relationship with Grace might be a

very different one. Grace has also experienced rejection, but not in a hostile aggressive form as Susan has experienced it. She has lived through cold indifference. She too is filled with distrust, but at the same time with a terrible craving for affection and the continued need to be reassured of this affection. Relationship with Grace has to be established by the housemother's giving her the affection she needs so badly.

We can see in these two examples that it is indispensable for the housemother to know something about the background and the problems of the girls if she wants to be helpful to them. This puts on the houseparent the grave responsibility of using such material confidentially and exclusively for the helping purpose. If we realize the houseparents' contribution as an essential one to treatment of the children, we must not hesitate to supply them with the necessary tools to fulfill this task. They in turn must accept professional discipline for themselves.

Relationship is not established on the grounds of a false and sugary kind of attitude. Children have a sixth sense in knowing whether an adult means what he says. They very quickly see through pretense and become very resistant.

Relationship also is established only if the adult is willing to give something of himself in the sense that the child will get to know him. In some so-called treatment institutions I have seen an effort on the part of the staff to stay as impersonal as possible, assuming that this would help the treatment process and—in my opinion—falsely translating some of the attitude of the psychoanalyst to the group situation. Even psychoanalysis has in recent years recognized that the analyst cannot always be the impersonal observer he was in the earlier form of psychoanalysis.

In the living situation we have dynamics working that are completely different from the ones in psychoanalysis. In the treatment situation of the daily life we do not want to use, for instance, transference,[5] and therefore we would want the child to see the houseparent in as real a way as possible. That does not exclude the child's sometimes looking at the houseparent as someone different than he really is and making the bad or good father or mother out of him. Yet in no way must the houseparent play into this by putting on an impersonal front and not showing himself as the real person he is. Children resent pretense and the phoney. Adolescents especially are very sensitive to anything artificial. They themselves will sometimes transform the houseparent into a hero or an angel. Crushes are not always easy to bear, yet it is important that the houseparent show his real self even during those periods when the youngster distorts his image of him. Houseparents can establish a relationship when they themselves are colorful individuals, not when they pretend to be someone in a white starched uniform. It is interesting to observe that in the wards of mental hospitals for children in recent years even the nurses are asked not to wear their uniforms so that the children can feel that they are real people.

Relationship means a mutual understanding that one can be free with the other, that one can be oneself in the presence of the other person and that the other person cares about the way one is. In an institution for twelve-year-old boys a housemother felt that she had established a good relationship with the boys and there was quite a warm feeling between them. She came in some agitation to her supervisory conference because on Sunday morning the boys had acted up with great hostility and had told her several times that they wished she were not around. She wondered whether her relationship to the boys had broken down. The group worker, who was the cottage parents' supervisor, pointed out to her that this had

---

[5] The word transference is used in different ways. In treatment it is usually thought of as the patient's close relationship to the therapist, in whom he sees different persons who have played important roles in his life.

been a Sunday on which several of the parents intended to come for a visit and that the children felt quite anxious and full of hostility in relation to this event. They would bottle up this hostility if they had a poor relationship to their cottage mother, but in this case they felt free to show their anxiety and even to project some of their hostility on her. They obviously were not afraid of retaliation and, therefore, gained from this freedom. When the cottage mother understood that actually this negative behavior had meant confidence in her, she could another time handle it with far more sensitivity and understanding.

Relationship, therefore, does not show itself only in a positive way, but it can be gauged by the frankness and the atmosphere between the cottage parent and the group. If a group is very subdued, if orders are always carried out without any back talk, if things run very smoothly on the surface while neurotic symptoms such as eneuresis or thumb sucking or nail biting increase, then we will know that there is not a positive relationship. In one of the institutions I visited, the grounds looked well kept, the youngsters were busy working, and everything seemed to be fine. Then I observed that at the time when a break was announced the twelve-year-old boys began to play the frightening game of "blackout" in which one child holds the other's neck and presses a certain nerve until the other gets the feeling of fainting. We have seen this also outside of institutions and it is always a sign of deep dissatisfaction with reality and only one step away from the use of narcotics. None of the houseparents had observed this, since it was done in great secrecy. It was an obvious symptom of poor relationship.

A thirteen-year-old boy who had been very secretive about his placement in an institution and who after his placement in a foster home tried not to let anyone know that he had been in an institution, wrote a letter to the group worker a few days before he was confirmed. In the letter he asked her to come to his confirmation and to "sit in the front so that I can see you. I don't mind if anyone knows where I got to know *you*." Here is an indication of how relationship had helped the youngster overcome his negative feelings against institutional life.

Relationship is a word that we use in many different ways. There is a relationship between husband and wife, between children and their parents, between teachers and pupils, between friends among each other. The helping relationship is a specific one, one based not on personal likes or dislikes but on the need of the person to be helped and on the role the helper has to play in this process. The relationship between the psychiatrist and the disturbed child will be a different one than the relationship between this child and the houseparent, yet both of them are equally important. In the relationship with the houseparent the child must expect an understanding of his basic needs as well as warm parental feelings. Though houseparents are not a substitute for parents and though we need to find a different name for them, one aspect of their work is the day-to-day care of the needs of the child.

Dealing with Conflict

In every group situation, conflict solving plays an important role. We know that there are several distinct ways of solving conflicts.

1. One person decides what has to be done, in some cases this person being the houseparent, in others one of the domineering members of the group.

2. The group decides by majority rule how the conflict should be solved.

3. The group decides according to discussion and through some form of integration how to end the conflict.

Conflicts arise around personalities and around ideas. In a group living situation, especially in the first stages of getting acquainted, conflicts will mainly be around personalities. It will not be easy for houseparents to deal with this constantly, especially since they want to keep in mind the individual needs. The housemother, for instance, might understand very well that one youngster cannot take too much pressure, but she is in a situation where the pressure is put upon this youngster by the group and they will not accept a different attitude. The housemother, then, will have to decide whether life will become more difficult for this youngster if she protects him or whether his problem is so great that he needs the protection of an adult and this has to be interpreted to the group. It is clear that such conflict situations cannot all be solved in the same way. Each must be solved in relation to the specific situation in the group and to the specific child involved. A basic principle must be, therefore, that the decision be made with full knowledge of the individual and of the group.

If the conflicts are very severe the houseparent will have to consider several possibilities: (1) Is the child misplaced in this group and should he, therefore, be placed in a group that may be less attacking towards his behavior or that will less provoke his behavior? (2) Is there one member of the group that could be especially helpful to this youngster and can the houseparent interpret some of the difficulties to this more accepting youngster so that he can help instead of the adult? (3) Is the behavior of the child so much related to inner conflicts that special casework help is needed and, therefore, more intensive casework interviews are indicated? (4) Does the youngster need some "exercise" in a small group more protected than the living group and, therefore, should be referred to a special group conducted by the social group worker? These are four possibilities that should be open in a good treatment home and should be considered. I realize that the resources are not available in all children's institutions, but I am speaking here about a minimum that I think essential for good work.

It will not be helpful to the children if all conflicts are solved by the houseparent himself or—as is still done very often—conflicts are solved by sending the child to the "front office." This practice seems to me an especially damaging one. It separates limitations from the daily flow of life and creates in the child an added confusion about the sources of control. In normal life control is related to the daily occurrence of mistakes and of our rubbing shoulders with other people and the laws of society. To take these controls away from the person who represents security as well as demands distorts the picture of our world and does not help the child to establish inner controls and solve his conflicts with others as part of the daily flow of life. It has been argued that this method will help the houseparent to be seen as the friendly accepting person involved in "therapy," completely unrelated to punishment. This argument can stand only if we think of therapy as something devoid of limitations and every limitation as a punishment. It has to be said emphatically that limitations, if imposed by a kind and understanding person, will be far more therapeutic than if given by an outside person. They can be accepted by the child as a concern for his welfare if he has established a real friendly relationship with the houseparent.

Conflict solving in the area of ideas demands a skill in discussion method which the houseparent can use informally around an evening table. At this time the houseparent can give an interpretation of behavior that has led to conflict and give permission for free expression of ideas.

Discipline

This always seems the most important subject in discussing institutional life. It often sounds as if we are continually talking about two extreme schools of thought: (1) that there should be no limitations, and therapy means all-out permissiveness, and (2) that one can deal with children only with an iron hand. Both extremes are damaging, and equally damaging. The attitude of the iron fist has been widespread for many years and has resulted in dehumanized children. We have read a great many descriptions about this and we cannot pretend that the condition no longer exists. I myself have seen institutions where a child who came to a meal with dirty hands had to stretch out his hands and get rapped across them. I have seen institutions where discipline was enforced by a completely unnatural way of life, such as, for instance, lining up for every meal, living by the sound of the bell, having to give strict obedience to every command uttered, lying rigidly in bed without saying a word to one's neighbor, being under the continued watchful eye of a houseparent, having only regimented recreational time, and leading in general a life that no adult could take but that was expected of children.

I have also seen an institution that called itself therapeutic because it worked on the idea that "living out" is the best therapy. There was really no protection for the child from being attacked by others or from his own instincts. In one such institution I observed an eleven-year-old boy full of anger approaching the counselor about the big bully who had again beaten up several of them and asking the counselor to do something. The counselor's answer was, "You feel angry at this, don't you?" And he moved coolly along the room. The boy in real rage shouted at him, "This is all that I get from you every time I need you," and then with tears in his eyes he shrugged his shoulders and said, "What's the use?" It was clear that he felt just as abandoned in this situation as he might have felt when his family broke up. In a similar institution a child with a temper tantrum was left completely to his own devices and was simply put into a small empty room in which "he could do anything he wanted to do." There was no understanding of the terrible cruelty of leaving a child alone with his turmoil and feelings in a place where there was no human comfort.

In our present-day thinking we have moved away from the idea of complete permissiveness or punishment for punishment's sake. Our concern must be related to the dynamics of individual behavior as well as the dynamics of the group situation. The houseparent at times will feel frustrated because the group situation will not allow him to give exactly the kind of attention and help he would give if he were alone with the youngster. In fact, the behavior of the youngster is usually not the same in the group as it is in the individual situation. We have to help the houseparent to see that he is not expected to do the same as a person who is in an individual-to-individual relationship to the child and that a specific value lies in handling behavior difficulties in the group situation.

One of the teachers in a rural school tells an amusing story about a little boy who had been especially difficult in class and the teacher finally asked him to stay after school. While they were waiting together, the teacher asked him why he was so much nicer when she was alone with him than he was in the classroom, and he answered, "Why, Miss Smith, you're so much nicer when we're alone too." Behavior difficulties very often arise from the group situation and so there is no point in relating to them only in individual therapy. In fact, the group situation that gives enough freedom of expression offers an invaluable tool for understanding what the problem of the youngster really is. The houseparent is the one who can help the child realize how his behavior brings upon him the wrath of the group and makes difficulties in living together. Limitations will be helpful only if they are related to reality, the demands are not unusually high, and they can be understood by the youngster.

Institutional life always puts some unusual demands on the individual because the living together of so many people requires a greater discipline than in a smaller unit such as the family. Food certainly cannot be served at all times, and yet there are different needs for food with children at different times. (Small treatment institutions can take care of this by providing special snacks at the times children need them.) Living together with people one has not chosen puts a strain on relationships. All these are demands that are unavoidable and part of the "discipline" of institutional life. It is important though to lighten this burden instead of increasing it through added rigidity. It will be very important for the houseparent to learn to relax in the daily living situation and to enforce limitations only where they are of real help to the youngsters.

At the end of a training course for houseparents one of them handed in a paper which I want to reproduce here in full.

I let a peeve grow into a mountain of irritation. I spent my first two years in this work trying to solve the riddle. I did not get results. I got more misbehavior directed at me; until a very simple and obvious truth filtered through.

My peeve was that children straggled into the dining hall late. I impatiently awaited the largest group. We said grace. Three or four latecomers (they were considered really late if they arrived after grace had been said) always had to be reckoned with. I shall proceed to list some of my trials and errors in dealing with the offenders.

Trial 1: "You will go without dessert if you come to the table after grace."

Errors, as they appeared to me: Attitude of latecomers did not become positive. Lateness continued. Many desserts were put in the refrigerator, which seemed a shame, because the little happiness they might have caused was turned into acid. Acid directed toward me, and toward the staff, generally. Getting dessert is not proper motivation for promptness. Further—after thanking God for food, I felt like a horrid vulture taking away desserts from the unhappiest kids.

Trial II: "You will get the job of cleaning the dining hall if you come late."

One feature of this seemed positive. Reasonableness. Latecomers make duty people wait because they hold up the dining hall. Therefore, latecomers do the duty.

Errors, as I saw them: Attitude on part of offenders not positive. They performed poorly, half-heartedly. Ill-set tables. Certain lucky children escaped all duties; unhappiest kids were clearing dining halls three times a day. Still got no results.

Trial III: "You may be served, and then sit on the floor and eat. Those of us on time may enjoy the greater comfort of tables and chairs."

Errors: Latecomers managed to get lots of attention in getting served. They didn't apparently mind the floor after they got wise to the idea that it enabled them to use barbaric manners; besides the area offered convenient places to dispose of unpopular side-dishes. Still no results.

Trial IV: "You shall not come into the dining hall if we have said grace. Remain in the butler's pantry, sitting on the floor. When we have finished eating, you may take all the leftover food to one table and eat there."

Errors, as I saw them: Latecomers increased in numbers. They interrupted our meals by sticking their heads in through the door, asking, "Have you said grace?" They enjoyed each other's company in the butler's pantry. When they ate later no counselor was available to supervise the stragglers' table. Consequently they ate only what they pleased, using the manners of little animals. Results: *Terrible!*

Trial V (A light dawns): "You no longer need to sit in the butler's pantry. If you are late, your place is ready for you. Come in, join the group, say your grace, and eat."

Results: A change in attitude. "We are somebody. We are late, and nobody punishes, or scolds, or deprives. We still eat at the table with linens, and dessert. We get recognition as important people, not attention in negative ways.

Staff relaxes, enjoys children more, because they are putting effort into guiding a pleasing atmosphere. Eating is fun!

Children excuse themselves and leave the table as soon as they are through eating. No waiting for latecomers. Yet anyone may wait if conversation interests them, or if they want to remain until a pal is finished.

The only mention made of slowness is directed at the last child to leave the table—and that may be like this, "John, take your plate and finish eating in the kitchen. I'm not gonna wait all year to do my duty," from the child whose duty it is to clear John's table this time.

How I understand now: It is not important to punish all misbehavior. It is terribly important to give the naughtiest kids the feeling that they are really important persons, and that they have status even though they are naughty. The child bidding for even negative attention can be shown such acceptance that he stops punishing me. Life is pleasing to him, to me, and to the group when people are less punishing.

We see in this instance how the houseparent's attitude changed with her better understanding and how at the same time the results were better. It wasn't that finally no limitations were used but that they became limitations related to "a purposeful way of living," as Morris F. Mayer called it in a paper given at an institute in Minnesota.

Some institutions think that they can handle the discipline problem by letting the children themselves make decisions regarding misbehavior of other children. This is about the same as if we would let hospital patients treat another patient instead of letting the physician do it. Children cannot know all the implications that their actions might have on the other youngster and their basic reasoning is much more primitive and much more related to punishment and reward. Yet, on the other hand, it might be helpful to have them participate in the thinking that goes into making rules relating to institutional life.

In one instance the staff of an institution was still struggling somewhat with the concept of letting the children make the decisions, but realized that they themselves had to be very active in it. This institution served preadolescent children and had established a committee consisting of some of the children whose purpose it was to discuss different problems of the house. The social group worker was working with this group and some houseparents participated in it. In the following quotation from the record, the issue with which the meeting dealt was again being late at the table.

Robert then phrased his suggestion—that if a child came so late that two others had already left the table, the late child could not eat at the table. This seemed to muster some support and there seemed to be some vindictive feeling in some of the statements that were made. Mrs. B. reminded the group that there were sometimes very good reasons why a child needed to be late for meals and asked if it wouldn't be good to allow an exception to be made to the rule when a child had a good excuse. Robert denied this and Dan put the motion to a vote. . . . I then suggested that after we had tried it for two weeks we would review it again at the next meeting and see if we want to keep the rule.

In interpreting this meeting the social group worker pointed out that the children had been more harsh with each other than adults would have been with them. On the other hand this meeting showed that the children felt free to vote against adult opinion and that there was already some progress in decision-making since they let the decision rest on a vote instead of trying to outshout or beat each other up as they would have done previously.

It was important in this instance not to forget the suggestion which had come from the adult and to review this at a later meeting.

The next item to be discussed was the review of the rule made last time covering those who came late to meals. This turned out to be one of the best examples I have seen of children being able to really discuss an issue frankly, understandingly and with tolerance for each other's ideas. Tom got up and in all seriousness announced, "I've decided to do away with the rule." Richie and Allen thought this was a good idea. Joseph brought out the fact that there had been misunderstanding of the rule—he had seen it applied differently from the way it stood in the minutes. Robert seemed not to look beyond this point, perhaps because he had some identification with it because it had been his original motion. He thought the only thing needed was to clarify the rule. Allen thought the rule should be changed to say a late child had to leave the table when the counselor did. Don, up to now sort of withdrawn and resistant to attempts to involve him constructively, said that wouldn't work because the counselor would just stay at the table until everyone was through. (I felt this indicated an attitude on his part that counselors were basically trying to make life easier for the kids—right now he didn't want that done.) At this point I asked what had the rule been made for? Through discussion it was brought out that no one had even thought of it punishing children who were late because they had been out with their workers, at the Y.M. or such like—yet it was pointed out that it had been made "to take care of Fred." I accepted this, but asked the whole group what they thought of the whole group making a rule against one boy like that. I asked if there were any other reasons for making it. Another was that it was to keep kids from loitering. Allen said he didn't think it was fair to make a rule against one kid. Joseph made a motion that this rule be done away with so we could make another. It was passed unanimously. After a little more discussion which seemed to be questioning the real extent of the need for such a rule, I asked if the group thought they'd like to try the next two weeks' period without a rule, then talk about it at the next C.C. meeting. That didn't quite satisfy, and Joseph made another motion, this time that a counselor use his judgment in dealing with youngsters who come late to meals. This also passed unanimously. There was a reminder from Robert that anybody eating late in the dining room got in the way of the floor sweeper—maybe that has happened to him.

We see here that the children were able to change their decisions and this meant real learning. They also gained some insight into their own motivation by finding that they had really wanted to make this rule against one particular youngster. In doing this they began to establish inner self-controls as well as learning how to make a group decision.

Into the question of discipline, almost more than into any other question, enters the feelings of the houseparent, his own experiences, and his reaction to the way he feels about himself. Over and over we will find an argument that the houseparent has to "save face," especially since he is dealing with a group of children and he cannot let them get away with something. Jack Simos, when he was supervisor of houseparents at Bellefaire, collected records of several such situations, for example, the following:

Billy refused to wash the dishes in the morning because "he didn't feel like it." When the cottage parent told him he had to, he said, "Make me do it." Billy came to the institution about four months previous to this incident. He had been involved in stealing. He is one of four children of a very brutal domineering father and a very neurotic mother. Both parents deserted the family at times, but came back.

We can very well imagine how provoked the houseparent must be with a reply, "Make me do it." There are five other pairs of eyes perhaps watching her and wanting to find out what she will do. The first reaction easily will be to show that one is not weak, that one can "make him," to be sure that the children will have respect and that one will not run into the same thing with others. The reaction of a very frightened houseparent might also be to just sigh, shrug shoulders, and say, "what is the use?" in this way showing her weakness.

What sort of thinking do we expect of the houseparent who really wants to be helpful? The main principle is that she must not think of herself at this point. It is not important for the children to look at her as the strong person she might want to be. It is important that they gain what they need from an adult, which is a basic feeling of being wanted, but also the feeling that this adult is strong and cares enough about them so that she will help them to take on responsibilities. So, what will she do?

If she insists, or slaps Billy, she probably will get the dishes washed, but she will be to Billy nothing but a repetition of the domineering father or the neurotic mother with whom he has to put up but whom he does not respect. In the eyes of the other children watching her, she will surely be somebody to reckon with, but more with fear than with love. Knowing Billy's background, the housemother will want to let him feel that he is now in the presence of understanding adults.

She will show this in different ways, according to her own personality, since none of us will do things exactly the same way, but it will lie somewhat in this direction: She might say lightly to Billy that she has no intention of "making him do it"; that she had hoped that today or some other day he would like this place well enough to want to help with the work that has to be done. Sometimes this will startle the boy into doing it right away. At other times he may turn to leave. Does that mean defeat for the housemother? It does not, if she again lets him and the others know that she is understanding about what is going on, perhaps turning to the others and saying that Billy obviously does not feel that this is his home and would one of them like to help him with this? She might suggest that she will wash the dishes herself today, or would somebody be willing to help today and then be free another time when Billy felt more at home with them? In no way is the housemother implying that Billy will never have to do his duty, but she allows him to go his way at this moment. This way she will not have lost face but on the contrary will have let him feel that he is important, but that also the community in which he lives is important and needs to be served.

In almost all training institutes for houseparents somebody gets up and describes how he gained acceptance with the youngsters when he showed them how tough he could be by beating up the toughest guy in a contest of strength. I cannot help always wondering about two things: (1) How much of the meaning of this victory to the housefather was because he needed to prove to himself that he was stronger than the boys (secretly fearing that he really was not), and (2) what would happen if he actually could not defeat the boy?

What does a relationship mean that is based on the proof of physical superiority? Behind this lies an adolescent admiration of the power of muscles and little confidence in one's ability to establish a relationship in any other area. In a group meeting a very aggressive thirteen-year-old boy had snatched the football away from the others and was boasting that he would not return it; the worker should just try to take it away from him. The group worker, a slightly built young woman, smiled and said calmly that she knew she could not take the ball away from him, that he actually was much stronger and much faster than she was. They would very much like to have the ball in order to continue playing, but she would not make the effort to chase after him. The boy was so startled about this frank and calm admission that he suddenly grinned and threw the ball back at her, suggesting that next time "those guys could run after him." The worker had in this case given him recognition for the strength he needed to display to bolster his own ego, but had not lost any of her own effectiveness.

Only a person who himself feels quite secure can act therapeutically. This means that houseparents must acquire this security.

What about limitations when individuals become dangerous to others? We have seen among upset youngsters a great deal of violence, physical and psychological. There is no question that the houseparent is responsible for the safety of the individual in respect to both body and soul. It is a very serious responsibility that weighs heavily on the houseparent. Physical safety has to be considered. Fights among youngsters can often be well fought out among themselves, but if dangerous tools are being used or the rage against each other is mounting too strongly, the houseparent has the responsibility of interfering. He has to understand at this moment that he may not be dealing therapeutically with the attacker, but that he is simply protecting an individual or the group. He cannot let them harm each other or break down the place in which they are living. If he interferes at this point, it is something like "first aid," and he is not yet "healing." He just establishes the possibility of continuing the treatment process. If he is clear about this he will not need to rationalize his interfering action, but will fulfill it the way it must be done.

Very often psychological safety is also involved, sometimes that of the attacker as much as the attacked. In a group of twelve-year-old boys the gang leader showed especially sadistic tendencies and easily got the others to join him in torturing one of the smaller boys by taunting the youngster, though they were not harming him physically. The younger boy had lived under the shadow of two brutal older brothers, and this experience repeated in him an extremely painful situation. There was no question that he had to be protected against these attacks. Yet, they were just as harmful for the chief attacker, who expressed in individual interviews a great deal of guilt because of the pleasure he received from this kind of behavior. If the houseparent had let him go on and had condoned his behavior, he would have felt that the adult really did not understand his inner conflicts and had not helped him establish the inner controls he so sorely needed.

Inner controls develop only when one can feel a deep security and an identification with an adult whom one loves. We have very often acted toward children as if controls can be achieved through asking them to repeat desirable behavior over and over again. If this were true we would not hear adults often say, "You know, I will never touch spinach again because they made me eat it so much as a child." Obviously the repeated demand had only established a dislike of what the parent wanted to achieve. Or we hear an adult say, "I'm always late because we always had to be punctual in our family." Obviously our idea that inner discipline grows out of establishing a behavior pattern cannot be quite true. Another theory on which we act considerably is that discipline grows out of *Verbot*. There is no question that in some ways the *Verbot* limits behavior, and very often quite effectively, but in no way is it proved that it establishes an inner control that will continue when no retaliation is in sight.

A basic achievement of inner controls is reached in comparatively early childhood when the child feels secure and loved by his parents and wants to, like them, follow the rules. When the time comes in adolescence that he feels very independent and does not completely accept the judgment of adults, the process often is interrupted and the youngster will resist certain limitations. Again, if he has felt security and confidence in relation to adults, he will overcome this resistance after a while and develop standards of a kind that make it possible for human beings to live together. It is a deep sense of safety that allows one to apply controls to oneself. *Basically, inner control is the capacity to accept frustration or postponement of gratification of one's wishes.* One can only accept frustration if one sees the sense in it or if one knows that at some time or another gratification will come.

Just recently I observed at a lake a little boy in the water struggling with his rubber innertube. Somehow it had drifted away and the little boy had followed it into the deeper water. Suddenly we saw that he had lost hold. His father, fully dressed, was sitting on the shore. Immediately the father was in the water with all his clothes on and in a few seconds was pulling the child back to safety. When the two came out of the water the father held the trembling boy close to him without showing any of his fear and the child held tight onto him. There was no shouting, no reproach. They sat for a minute in the sun and then the father got up and quietly said that they had better drive home so that he could dry off. The little boy took his hand and nodded.

To me this was a perfect picture of the way safety was established for this little boy, not only in terms of physical safety but because he had learned in this one moment two things: (1) that his father was there if he needed him most and cared more about him than about his clothes, and (2) that he was not scolded or punished, but he could see that he in some way had spoiled a beautiful day by not accepting the limitations imposed on him as a nonswimmer. I am sure that this child had moved toward inner control.

We need to remember that very few of the children in our institutions have such experiences. Most of them have never experienced the safety that comes from adult love and so their controls will be poorly established. If they are older children, we will have to go back in giving them the first taste of security and start on the level of a much younger child before we can expect them to accept the world around them as something that they can trust and themselves as being able to contribute to the trust.

Discipline never really grows out of fear. We will do or not do certain things out of fear, but only when we are sure that our wrongs will be discovered. In a dictator state the citizen will follow the rule out of fear, but he will not really participate and he will willingly and quickly change to other behavior when the dictator weakens. Again, there is no inner discipline established. Many of the children who come to our institutions have known only discipline based on fear. Sometimes the argument is advanced that because of this we have to continue imposing some of the fear because they have not learned to react to anything different. In my opinion this is fallacious thinking, because we would continue the vicious circle.

Without question, it is an unusually difficult task to work with a child who has learned to react only to fear. For quite a while the child will think it weakness if one does not use the same means of discipline to which he is accustomed. There is no help for the houseparent in this difficult task but to examine over and over again what basic needs this child has and to accept those needs as he would accept the fact that a person with high fever cannot go out and work, though we would demand work of the healthy person. At the same time the houseparent certainly will be most helpful when the child can feel in his attitude not weakness but the calm strength of somebody who knows what he is doing and why he does it and is not afraid of the child's erratic and undisciplined behavior. The houseparent will say at this point that this sounds very fine but how can it be handled? Again, we have to look at each specific case, knowing that two basic principles will help us: (1) we must know something about the reason for the child's behavior, and (2) we are responsible for the safety of the child and the group and have to be aware of this even if this at times might not fulfill the inner therapeutic purpose.

One form of the loss of self-discipline that seems to be especially difficult to handle in a group situation is a *temper tantrum*. The temper tantrum is quite normal in the infant, who "wants what he wants when he wants it." If the infant does not get his food immediately, he screams and yells and kicks, and we consider this perfectly natural because the ability to accept frustration and to postpone gratification is something we are not born with but must acquire. Yet this same behavior, if found in an older child or in an adult, shows disturbance and is without question very disturbing to the group around him. To deal with the temper tantrum, we have to understand its meaning. It is a form of behavior that reverts to the state of infancy and is actually an outcry of desperate frustration. At the moment when it occurs the child or the adult has no real control over himself and is almost unaware of reality around him. This "being out of touch with reality" during a temper tantrum is the reason it is so difficult to deal with it. There are time-honored methods of dealing with it, such as throwing water at the child or locking him in an empty room or beating him.

Let us see what these methods really mean. All of them

show that the adult too is frustrated and does not know how to handle the situation. The beating is really the adult throwing a temper tantrum on his own and retaliating in the same way as the child has acted. The only achievement in such a case is that the adult will be relieved of some of his own frustration, but nothing is really done in relation to the child with the temper tantrum. He will stop when he gets exhausted or when the punishment hurts too much, but he will continue seething inside and the temper tantrum will occur at another time. The method of throwing water at the youngster in a tantrum is really nothing but shock treatment. It might bring the youngster back to reality and shock him out of the symptoms of the tantrum. None of the causes will be touched, however, and he will hate the humiliation and increased frustration of standing before others dripping wet, shocked out of something he could not handle in the first place. The locking up allows the youngster to finish his process of rage but might actually prolong it. The person in a tantrum feels abandoned and full of hate. Being alone in a room accentuates the feeling of loneliness and the hate.

We cannot deal with a temper tantrum without trying to gain a great deal of empathy [6] with the person who is in a tantrum. It is really one of the most painful experiences, not only for the onlooker but for the one experiencing it. How do we ourselves feel when something is done to us that we feel is unjust and that we cannot do anything about? We usually are not only angry but we feel a rage mounting. We feel that somehow we have been made incapable of dealing with our own fate; we feel like somebody who has been gagged and bound.

In a recent discussion with houseparents, we looked at situations where this had happened to us and found out how we

[6] An understanding of the other person's feelings so strong that one almost feels like him.

dealt with it. One of the houseparents said that when this happens to him, he leaves the house and goes for a long walk. Then when he "cools off" he can come back and begin to think whether there is anything he can do about it. Another housefather said that he starts smoking heavily and that that relaxes him a little. One of the housemothers says that she starts getting very mean with her husband even if he is not the cause of the frustration. (We had a wonderful laugh at that and realized how clearly we could see the mechanism of projection in what she described.) These solutions are not often available to children and especially to children in institutions who cannot go off freely, reach for a treat such as a jar of cookies, and who are not supposed to get mean towards anybody. In seeing how we adults deal with a strong feeling of frustration, we realize that it is not an easy task for a child to deal with it and we have to understand that the temper tantrum is sometimes the only way out.

Nevertheless, it is the houseparent who has to deal with this, and in a group situation rather than when he is alone with the youngster. In general, it will be helpful to let the child know that he is really not alone and abandoned and that we are deeply concerned with the reasons for his unhappiness. Since at the moment the tantrum occurs the child can hardly listen to all we would like to say, it seems best for the houseparent to touch the child gently and firmly and help him this way to calm down.

Jim, an eleven-year-old quite strong boy, felt that Don had cheated him in a game. Jim jumped up in a terrible rage, red in the face, swept the game on the floor, and shouted that he would kill him. He hammered on furniture and chased after the frightened Don. The other boys looked fearful and at the same time ready to join the fun. Don was hiding. The housemother tried to calm Jim by talking to him, but there was no response. She walked over to him, put her arms around him in a restraining as well as kind gesture, and spoke to him in a soothing voice. It was obvious that Jim did not hear what she was saying, but the calm voice seemed to have some effect. He strained hard against her and still shouted that she was an old witch and that she should let him go and that he had to kill this boy. The housemother was unprovoked but very firmly held on to him continuing the restraining movement but also talking in the same friendly voice. Slowly Jim grew almost limp in her hands. He was sweating profusely. When he had calmed down sufficiently, the housemother said simply and matter of factly that he might want to wash his face and he could go and get this done. This way she gave him the opportunity to leave the circle of boys before which he had put on a spectacle. While he was gone the housemother suggested to the others to make no mention of what had happened, explaining to them that this was quite hard on Jim. The boys having observed her calm handling of the situation and feeling quite safe because she had helped Jim as well as the boy whom he wanted to attack were perfectly willing to accept this.

It might be said that such situations don't always work out that well, and this is certainly true. Not every medicine works, even if it is the best one for the sickness that it is supposed to cure. But this cannot prevent us from trying this over and over again and from seeing whether it is not more helpful and more related to the basic cause of the temper tantrum than the other means we have used. Certainly at times when a child in a temper tantrum cannot be quieted down quickly enough and when the group situation is already a strained one, it will be wisest to remove the child from the group. Again I would suggest not leading him into a room by himself but giving the youngster the comfort of a kind human being while he is struggling with the strong emotion of hate.

The houseparent in a group situation must be aware of

what the tantrum can mean to the other children and, therefore, must handle this behavior not only in terms of the child
himself but in terms of the others. If he has a group of generally very frightened youngsters, he will have to remove the
child in a tantrum as soon as possible and he will also have
to use the opportunity to later discuss with the others what
they have seen. Children often can take these situations easier
when they understand them and when they are allowed to
express some of their fears about them. As much as the youngster in the state of tantrum needs the understanding help of
the houseparent at this moment, the group needs to feel the
protective role of the adult and know that they can rely on
somebody who is not just delivering them to a force that
attacks them and that is similar to their own frightened emotions.

One of the discipline problems occurring often in institutions is related to the *misuse of property.* I am using a situation given by Jack Simos.

On a nice summer afternoon, several eight-year-old boys take
some wool blankets to a remote spot on the institution grounds
where they build a tepee. They have not asked permission to do
this and the staff is not aware of the fact that the blankets are
out of the house.

The boys forget the bedding out of doors, and during the night
a heavy rainstorm occurs. The next morning, the tepee is discovered, with the blankets soggy and shrunken.

Let us see what this situation means to the institution and
what it means to the child. On the surface it means that valuable blankets have been destroyed and that the children have
used property without asking for permission of its use. It
means to the children that they were fulfilling a basic boy-
hood need for adventure and fun by pretending to play Indi-
ans, by being in a remote spot of the grounds where they could

feel very much on their own, and by heightening the sense of adventure in not telling anybody about it. They did not purposely leave the blankets out in the rainstorm, but they forgot them. Though they had great fun in playing the adventurous game, they now feel quite guilty and frightened because they too know that they have destroyed property.

Obviously they have not committed a criminal act. On the other hand, will it be helpful to them and their own feelings if the adults say nothing and just pretend that nothing happened? Actually, if the adults do nothing the children will feel (1) that the adults don't really care much about them, and (2) their guilt will increase and they will get quite confused about adult standards. It might be helpful to tell the boys that they apparently had lots of fun, that the houseparent in no way would like to spoil their fun, and that if they again want to play something like that they should ask for material and it will be given to them. At the same time it will be helpful to let them see that they too are responsible for community property and, though one does not want to spoil their fun, one expects them to participate in the responsibilities that go with it. The housemother, therefore, can discuss with them what they think they can do about it and work out some arrangement for paying something toward the replacement of the blankets with part of their allowance or some work.

It is often almost pathetic to see how children in institutions do not learn anything about the value of money because it seems to them that everything comes out of a big bin that is always full. The child will be helped considerably by learning where money comes from, just as in a healthy family a child should know something about the way money for the family is procured. In the above example, the children will learn that adults do not want to spoil their fun and do not begrudge them adventure, but, at the same time, feel that they can be responsible for the way it is carried out.

In discussing discipline as one of the major problems of group living, we have seen that it is not something that can be separated from the general living situation. It becomes part of the understanding of the child and the group situation and it must be handled by the houseparent himself in an understanding and helpful way. It should always be related to the causes of behavior and not only to its manifestations.

Limitations are related to the safety of the individual as well as of the group, and this safety is not only physical but also emotional. In using limitations the houseparent must be constantly aware of the need of each individual child and must learn something about his own reactions to certain forms of behavior.

We have certainly not exhausted all the problems that arise in the living situation. They are as many and varied as life itself. The few that were discussed were chosen mainly because of their frequent occurrence and because they might help to point out some basic considerations.

THE SELECTION AND TRAINING OF HOUSEPARENTS

Personality

We have in the preceding section seen the importance of the houseparent in the group living situation and discussed some of the problems confronting him. It became clear that the houseparent actually is not a parent and cannot pretend to be one but has to be a group worker with great understanding of individual and group dynamics and the ability to handle children intelligently and consistently in a day-to-day living situation. This is an exacting demand and raises the question of who the houseparents should be and what training we may demand of them.

According to the preceding material, it might seem as if a trained group worker should be the houseparent in an institution. There has been a great deal of discussion regarding the educational background of houseparents. It is my opinion that the houseparent in our children's institutions need not to come from the ranks of fully trained professional group workers. This requirement would be impossible to fulfill. It would be like demanding that all care in hospitals be carried out by the medical profession itself. We have seen that it is possible to give excellent lay service, if it is done under competent professional supervision and with certain requisites. In my opinion, the houseparent or group counselor can fulfill a helpful and professional role if he receives a certain form of training, works under professional supervision, and is willing to accept for himself the safeguard of professional discipline.

Since the houseparent is the hub of the wheel in the group living situation, I will go into detail about each of these qualifications. I do not think I have to say too much about the kind of a person the houseparent should be. This has been presented in numerous writings and it is almost self-evident. He certainly has to be a person with real love for children, a person who is willing to accept children who are not the easiest ones to handle, a person who is willing to learn on the job and to change attitudes if necessary. Very often one hears the comment that a person is especially suited to be a houseparent because he has raised his own children and has done a good job of it. We must realize that raising one's own children in no way guarantees that one is able to accept children of a very different kind and who have not come from a secure home. The housemother who will continually compare these children with her own or the housefather who will forward the argument that it never hurt his own son when he gave him a few slaps are not especially suited to understand that they are entering a completely different role than the one they filled with their own children. The few slaps probably did not damage the relationship between father and son, because the youngster had experienced a basic love and acceptance from his father. But to the boy in the institution the housefather is not previously known. The boy had no prior experience with him and, therefore, the slap will mean nothing but a repetition of a hated and unsafe home environment.

There have been many discussions about whether a houseparent should be an older or younger person. I do not think it matters as long as the younger person can show maturity and is able at times to accept a mother or father role and as long as the older person is young enough in his outlook on life that he understands the feelings and wishes of children. A little twelve-year-old once said to an over forty-year-old housemother, "Now I know why we love you so. You enjoy the same things we do." And a twelve-year-old boy one evening called his twenty-two-year-old counselor "Mom" and held on to her.

I do not think we need much discussion about whether the group counselors should be men or women. The only essential point is that in every children's institution both men and women should be available so that the children develop identification with their own sex and the ability to relate to both sexes.

The work of the houseparent certainly cannot and should not be separated from the daily living tasks such as eating, going to bed, waking up, etc. That means there has to be some skill in this role. I think that we have sometimes put too much stress on the housekeeping role of the houseparent. Certainly it will be useful if, when a housemother sits down in the evening with a bunch of adolescent girls, she can do a little mending or knitting, or if she can help them prepare a party, do some sewing, or help them with some cooking they want to do in their own cottage. It will be helpful if the housefather can do some simple repair work, so that the boys can see him do that around the house or can help him with some tinkering.

But all these are qualities that anybody dealing with children should have. The intensive housekeeping task, such as basic cleaning, cooking, and the like, should not be imposed on the houseparent if he is really supposed to carry responsibility for the group living situation in a growth-enhancing sense.

Supervision by Group Worker

The most important help which the houseparent should get on the job is *supervision*. I am comparing this again with the hospital and the medical staff. The houseparent must have an opportunity to discuss his problems related to the group living situation with somebody who is an expert in this, who has real appreciation of the difficulties of the situation, and who knows the problems of individualization in a group. The main role of the professional social group worker in an institution will be as supervisor of houseparents. (We will discuss later some other roles the group worker will carry in children's institutions.) Referring back to our discussion on the education of the social group worker, we see that he brings with him the knowledge required in using the group living situation as a therapeutic tool and he also is equipped with the capacity to transmit this knowledge to others. It will be important to discuss in detail what is meant by supervision and what are the methods by which it will be most helpful.

The social group worker who is supervisor of cottage parents has to be an integral part of the institution. He is the one who has to integrate the knowledge of the individual child with the group living situation. He is the transmission belt between the formulation of the treatment plan (derived from discussion by the clinical staff) and the practical application of this treatment plan in the group situation. When a child enters an institution a case record will be available and there will be some understanding of the child's difficulty. The first tentative treatment plan will usually be arrived at by a case conference between the caseworker, the psychiatrist and psychologist (if these services are available), the head of the institution, and the social group worker. It might be decided that this particular child needs additional individual interviews, frequent contacts with his caseworker, and a group situation that is not too aggressive and allows for a great deal of withdrawn and sullen behavior without to many pressures.

The role of the group worker and the head of the institution during this conference will be mainly related to considering the group where this child should be placed and what kind of houseparent personality might be most helpful. This does mean that the social group worker must have an intensive and intimate knowledge of all the houseparents and of the grouping in the different units, whether they are cottages or another form of division. The group worker must have diagnostic knowledge of each one of the units at any given time. He has to be aware of the fact that they are not static and may change, but he also has to see which of the factors are comparatively stable, such as, for instance, the personality of the houseparent in a particular unit. The group worker will achieve this kind of knowledge by (1) the individual contacts he has with the houseparent, and (2) systematic and continued "spot observations" of the units themselves. These observations are not "inspections," nor made to check on the houseparents, but they are the means of keeping a current diagnostic picture of those units. Quoting from a report of such a "spot observation" by a group worker:

In walking through unit X at any given time, except during work period, one gets the impression of a lazy Sunday afternoon. The atmosphere is relaxed, girls lounging around casually conversing with each other. The girls seem comfortable and happy. There seems to be no undue tension in the air.

The group itself seems well established. There are natural leaders such as Sonja and Anna. There are followers such as Ruth, Hannah, Anita. There are some antagonisms, to be sure, as between Stella and Gertrude. Also certain thorns in the group, such as Barbara, who serves as a provocateur. There are isolates such as Bonnie and Betty. As a whole, however, this can be considered a stable group which can serve as a helpful medium for the eventual adjustment of each individual in the group.

We see here how the "spot check" gives a diagnostic picture of the group as a whole and how helpful this can be if new intake is considered or if the houseparent wants to discuss problems relating to individuals or regarding program for this group.

From individual records the group worker must know the picture of every individual in the group so that he can help the housemother in determining her attitude towards specific individuals.

The group worker must be thoroughly informed about policies of the institution so that he can interpret them and help them to be carried out.

All these are means to give effective supervision. Supervision in relation to the houseparent means help given to a person who himself carries a highly responsible professional task and who will want continued learning in relation to this. I can see seven functions of supervision in relation to the houseparent: (1) Help the houseparent understand better the motivations of the individuals in the group. (2) Help the houseparent relate those to actual behavior in the group. (3) Help the houseparent to use himself best in relation to the needs of the individuals. (4) Help the houseparent recognize some of his own feelings in relation to the group and to individuals. (5) Give the houseparent direct help with programing in his unit. (6) Help the houseparent to see his work clearly as an important part of the whole treatment plan. (7) Give the houseparent support in an exceedingly difficult task.

It will be most helpful if supervisory conferences can be individual conferences between the social group worker and the houseparent. They can be supplemented by several forms of staff meetings. The individual conference will be one of the most important learning situations for the houseparent as well as helping him to feel that not all the responsibility is put on him alone. The supervisory conference will have to be based on the establishment of a positive relationship between the social group worker and the houseparent. This can be achieved only if there is a mutual respect for each other's competence, the houseparent does not fear a "snoopervisor" in the group worker, and the group worker recognizes the contributions the houseparent makes to the treatment process. Also, it will be positive only if the group worker is thoroughly familiar with the kind of problems the houseparent is up against. To achieve that, the group worker would best have had some experience as a houseparent himself or—if that is not possible—should at least at times take on the relief role for the houseparent. These suggestions come out of my basic conviction that nobody can teach what he has not done himself and that in the long run teaching will become stale if it isn't rubbed against reality. It will refresh the supervisor's outlook and it will also give the houseparent confidence that somebody is talking with him who knows his problems not only in an academic way.

Supervisory conferences should be regular and should not be done on the run or only occasionally when a special problem arises. I am aware of the fact that this involves time. If we want to consider our children's institutions as treatment homes, this time must be available and not be looked upon as luxury. There is no need to drag out these conferences, and they also must be held at the convenience of the houseparent so as not to disturb his work with his group. Frequency has to be related to the needs of the houseparent. Once a week should be the minimum.

The conference will be held around any problem the houseparent himself brings up, with the focus on helping him directly with this specific problem as well as bringing out some of the general principles so that he can transfer this learning to other situations. This capacity on the part of the group worker to start out with a specific problem and yet relate it each time to some basic principle and future use is an exceedingly important one. Conferences dealing exclusively with everyday problems but not helping towards some conceptualization and more general application would not be learning experiences. Conferences starting with theoretical concepts and not relating to the problem that the houseparent sees at this point would be stale and would not help in the particular therapeutic situation.

In the following excerpts of supervisory conferences we will see what the method was and whether they really helped the houseparent and in this way benefited the children.

Mrs. A discussed James' request to go off campus to buy pop and doughnuts. Boy is refused this permission. Mrs. A, however, felt remorseful about making such a refusal. She asked me whether she did the right thing. She pointed out that there is a rule about going off campus after supper, but it seemed to her that she was not sure about this rule and whether it had just come down to her through the grapevine.

We focused on the merits of judgment rather than the technical aspects of whether it is a rule or not. I pointed out that rules should not be screens to hide under. We decided to discuss why she seemed so upset because she had to deny a child. She said she did not like to say no but she feels she should not "give in all the time."

We see here how the houseparent actually is questioning her own method, but is confused about how to find out the right way to deal with a child. She is looking for something very definite to tell her what to do. She thinks first she has found it in a rule, but then when this does not seem sure enough she wants to ask the supervisor what to do. If the supervisor at this point would give her an answer solely as to what she should have done, he would not be helpful, since she would not know how to deal with this at another time with another child. If the supervisor would just say, "Use your own judgment," he would leave the houseparent alone with an unsolved problem.

The supervisor tries to help by first letting the houseparent see that the rules are really only an outgrowth of their own thinking and, therefore, the thinking has to continue. He then helps the houseparent find out why she is so concerned with this incident and what her own feelings are. This certainly is a beginning of the process of learning. The houseparent will begin to see that in all decisions we have to be aware of our own feelings, because it is the only way to arrive at a discipline of them and to be able to focus on the child. What we see here is a deep respect of the group worker for the professional role of the houseparent and the beginning of helping her to a disciplined use of herself.

The following excerpt concerns the very practical question of how to help youngsters to accept work chores. There had been some discussion about a housemother who had invented a form of game for sorting laundry.

In my conference with Mrs. B I expressed my feeling that this was just as beneficial to a child as playing games. We need to develop imagination in making constructive use of an evening chore. Mrs. B mentioned that she would like, if possible, to do something of this nature when children washed dishes. She feels, however, that it is part of a child's education to learn to wash dishes. We discussed at some length the question of whether a chore needs to be a drudgery. I pointed out that when house-parents can help children with chores they are showing the children by their action rather than by words that they are accepting these children and gradually the child will learn that the world can be a friendly place and that work is not a rejection or something to be despised.

Mrs. B pointed to another problem in this area, which is the effect on the relief cottage parent should she establish a precedent of helping children wash dishes, or even making a game out of washing dishes. I assured her that this can be worked through consultation on both their parts and the relief cottage parent. I put emphasis on the fact that she should feel free to act naturally without undue fears and apprehensions.

Here a basic question of attitude is discussed: should work be a drudgery or is it helpful to the child to see it as an enjoyable part of life. This is not an unimportant question in institutional life, where work frequently has been used as punishment, and where often the idea of making work enjoyable has met with great resistance. Mrs. B. feels actually guilty herself if she considers work a game and she is trying to hide her feeling of guilt by saying that this would have a bad effect on the relief cottage parent. The help given by the group worker lies in supporting her real wish to make work enjoyable and at the same time assuring her that the relief cottage parent will also be helped with this. The group worker-supervisor helps the houseparent to overcome some of her fears by making her feel comfortable and acting the way she would like to act.

In another conference the supervisor helps the houseparent with her feelings of insecurity in relation to other staff members and to her own status in the institution. These questions will seldom be brought up theoretically, but they will be expressed around day-to-day problems.

Mrs. A pointed out that once she makes a mistake she does not want to retract because she "wants to save her reputation." She gave an example of when the jitney was stolen. It had been pointed out to her that a mistake was made in keeping two boys punished who were actually not in their cottage at the time the stealing took place. However, because of her feeling she needed to save face she did not modify nor retract the punishment inflicted.

She led from this to a discussion of how boys play one cottage parent against another or cottage parent against the residence director, etc. Because of this she felt strongly that she needed to save face. We discussed this in relation to reality and she herself agreed that the residence director did not allow himself to be played against. When children came to him to overrule the cottage parent he did not fall into such a trap. She could see that in this respect there was no justification of her fears.

During this conference a few more points came out, for instance, her feeling that more maintenance help was needed for major cleaning and that there was some conflict in the cottage between the study and enjoyable activities, such as swimming. She felt that swimming at times other than evenings would be more beneficial to the children.

The record shows that the houseparent is using the supervisor to get rid of some of her feelings about her own status in regard to the residence director. The complaint about different kinds of punishment, maintenance help, and the conflict between work and recreation all show that her dissatisfaction lies largely at this point in the area of administrative relationships. The sensitive supervisor will pick this up and try to discover where the dissatisfaction is coming from. If there is a reality basis to the complaint it is his task as a member of the staff to work out more satisfactory relationships. This is one of the reasons that the social group worker in this position should be in a supervisory relationship instead of being merely a consultant with no line authority. It is important for him to be a full member of the staff with administrative responsibility. If the complaints are not based on reality but on an inner dissatisfaction of the houseparent, it will be important to help her with this, since she can help the children only if she herself feels satisfied and that her own contribution is recognized.

Individual conferences will help the houseparent with specific situations and again relate to some basic principles so that the learning can be carried over to other situations.

Ed reads a comic book. The cottage mother pleads with him to put the comic book away. Ed responds but only for a moment, then teases the cottage mother as he picks up the comic book again. His manner is somewhat taunting, as it challenges the cottage mother to make him put the comic book away. After this goes on, other boys particularly Danny become irritated with this "tug-of-war." They turn on Ed, expressing hopes that he will be removed from the cottage. They climb over him surrounding him. At the beginning Les plays a protective role. He keeps some of the boys off Ed but in a few moments he too shrugs his shoulders and walks off. Now Danny grabs Ed by the neck and shakes him while others gleefully look on and they add a cuff or a taunt. Ed grimaces with anguish. The cottage mother finally pulls Lee off Ed. Ed is furious. He first chases the boys and then with a martyr manner withdraws to his room. The boys make a great war game out of this situation, setting up barricades with table and chairs, and arming themselves with mops and brooms. The cottage mother admonishes the boys and tells them that they shouldn't do it because of Ed's brute strength and the danger of tangling with him.

The cottage mother describes this situation to the supervisor because she feels anxious and inadequate in this situation. It will be important that the supervisor first of all give her the reassurance that this is not an easy situation for anybody to take. It involves hostility and defiance of herself shown by Ed; it also involves a situation of group hostility against one member actively carried out. In the supervisory conference—after giving the housemother reassurance that she is not expected to feel happy about such a situation—the supervisor can go into the details of these two problems. The first one will go back to the help an adult needs in learning how to accept hostility. The supervisor will have to point out to her some of the reasons that Ed is acting the way he does so that she understands the causes of his behavior. He will then help her to understand her own needs in not wanting to be defied because it also shakes her own self-confidence. He then has to give recognition to the fact that the group situation requires action on the part of the housemother, since not she alone feels provoked but the other youngsters in the group feel this way too. There has to be some understanding why Ed has this position in the group. It is clear that some other boy might defy the housemother too and would only gain admiring approval from the rest of the boys. What are the relationships in this group and what is Ed's status that he can annoy the boys so much in acting the way he does? Maybe this group situation also gives a clue to his need to show off and be the defiant one.

The rest of the group also gains satisfaction out of the fulfillment of quite primitive hostile needs by bearing down on one member who is already in disfavor with the powerful person present, namely, the housemother. Actually the group at this moment is not the representative of high values or standards but is just as much gratifying its hostile impulses as Ed was gratifying his. When she understands this the housemother will see how she plays into the group's aggressive behavior by admonishing them not in terms of the brutal strength of the majority against one boy but in terms of the brutal strength of *one* boy, and so justifies their behavior. Through such a discussion the housemother gains some direct help by understanding better the hostile behavior of the group and the individual. She will also be able to recognize how helpful it is to her to understand her own feelings regarding Ed and why she needs to "save face." She will see that a "tug-of-war" is not helpful either to the boy or the group situation. She will learn that, according to Ed's emotional needs, she might let him read the comic book and not even start her objections to it. Or—if Ed is a boy who badly needs some firm limitations and actually is hungry for them—she will know that she has to take the comic book away from him and suggest to him other things he can do. This too might result in a great deal of hostility by Ed, but if this firm limitation is part of a therapeutic measure she can calmly insist on it.

The discussion of this one small incident can be an immense learning opportunity for the houseparent in terms of understanding individual dynamics, group dynamics, her own feelings, and methods of handling difficult situations.

Another example:

Mrs. D told me that her method of dealing with children if she wants a task done is to ask them to "please do her a favor." She looked for approval of this method which I did not give at this point but since it was towards the end of the conference I asked her to think over until the next time the question of why we want a child to carry out tasks, and should that request be in terms of doing the cottage parent a favor, or in terms of the child needing help to accept the realities of life.

It will be important for the supervisor to see whether this method is used constantly by the houseparent or only occasionally. If it is occasional it is justified, because people enjoy helping others whom they like and it is perfectly all right for children to see that they too can do a favor for somebody else. Yet, if this is a pattern of behavior on the part of the houseparent one will want to see whether she is personalizing everything the child does and not helping the children to internalize the demands of work placed upon everybody. I am using this example because we see here how much caution the supervisor himself must use in not jumping to conclusions and how he too must individualize each houseparent and his or her particular way of working with people. It shows how the supervisor has to be a person who himself has gone through a vigorous training of professional discipline which has taught him not to impose his own standards on others. It points up that supervision is not merely technical help, but as we are speaking of it here is one of the most powerful tools in education as well as in safeguarding the therapeutic integrity of the institution program.

There is no question that the supervisor will have to deal with resistance on the part of the houseparent, even if the houseparent wants to become a very effective member of the staff. All of us want learning and are afraid of it at the same time. Many houseparents come to their work as mature adults and therefore bring with them a wealth of life experience, but at the same time a great deal of resistance to additional learning. There is very often resistance to the concern with problems of individual children. It is not demanded of the houseparent to get involved in individual treatment process, but it must be demanded that they accept the necessity of knowing the causes of behavior and dealing with the child accordingly.

Mrs. J said that she felt that she knows all her boys very well; that she has control over her cottage and that this is enough for her. She does not feel that she should be a psychiatrist and delve too deeply into children's problems. She told me about Jim and how he first came to the cottage, what trouble they had, but that gradually she had talked to him and handled him and that now he was a good boy and was no trouble at all. I asked her what it was she meant by being a psychiatrist. She explained that the residence director had expected her to know not only that Jim had improved but why he had improved and what had led up to his having problems in the first place. I pointed to the example of turning on electric lights. For some people it is enough to know that when they pull the switch the light will turn out. But other people might want to know more. They would want to know what made the light be turned out when the switch is pulled. Perhaps right now she feels that it is enough that Jim has improved under her guidance. But one of these days there might be another Jim with whom she will deal in the same way but somehow or other he will not respond. At that point she will want to know why it is that with one boy a certain approach meets with success while with another it doesn't.

The supervisor accepts the hostility that the housemother expresses and understands her anxiety about not being able to fulfill a task that seems too hard for her. He does not answer with a categorical demand that she do certain things because they are required, but he gives recognition to her feelings that at this point she really is not especially interested in understanding the causes of behavior. At the same time he shows her how her own attitude in regard to this might change. He also skillfully uses a simple example that makes the understanding more easy, since it lacks the emotional connotations of working with human beings.

The supervisory conferences offer the houseparent release for their own feelings, give them a sense of security and direction in relation to their work, help them develop their individual ways of approaching children, make their work part of a concerted treatment effort, and help them develop competent professional attitudes.

Recording

In the preceding excerpts of supervisory conferences we see that they are largely based on the problems the houseparents bring verbally to the supervisor. Is this sufficient or should there be a greater amount of recording done by the houseparent? In the education of group workers and in research on group life we are using extensive process records. These are written by the worker conducting the group, who incorporates in them his observation of individuals in the group, the interaction among the group members, and his own role in the group work process. Such process records are cumbersome and very time-consuming. They are indispensable for the learning process of the professional group worker and for research purposes, but they are impractical and cannot be handled in day-by-day group living. Many institutions, therefore, have decided to use no form of recording. The result is that the houseparent does not see a picture of the development of his work and his reports are often not based on any kind of continued observation. That is also the reason why the houseparent often is not involved in treatment conferences or, if he is involved, participates little. While other clinical staff has documentary proof of the development of the child, the houseparent relies on his own memory, which generally can encompass only outstanding events or a very recent situation.

If group living is to become a conscious part of the treatment process, a way must be found to record the development of group life. Houseparents and administrators alike have often asked for some device by which this can be accomplished. I want to make some suggestions in this regard. They have been tried out only in a few places and to test their efficiency several institutions should experiment with them for some time. This way only will we know whether they are really helpful. It is presupposed, in these suggestions for recording, that the houseparents have supervision as described above, for any recording done otherwise could only be haphazard. Supervision by the professionally trained group worker is the heart and core of any effort toward integrated treatment in the living situation.

One of the devices of recording should be a daily log. It must become part of the houseparent's job to have half an hour per day to make entries in this log, just as a seaman must do this whether the weather has been favorable or not. The entry in the log will be meaningful only if the houseparent is sensitized towards what to include. It is unnecessary to record all the activities occurring during the day. The log must not be thought of as a check-up on the houseparent, but rather as his medical chart regarding his patient, namely, his living group. The entries can be classified under four headings:

1. Conflicts occurring within the group and how they have been solved.

2. Incidents of control exercised in the group and by whom. (The whole group? Individual members? The houseparent?)

3. Outstanding behavior of certain individuals. (Negative and positive. How did the houseparent handle it?)

4. Specific content of discussions. (Gripes, suggestions, positive comments.)

If these four major areas are given, it should be made clear to the houseparent that in general it will not take more than one to two pages of writing to comment on them. The main purpose of the log is for the houseparent himself to see progress in his group, to diagnose better the group situation and the individual members, to have a basis for his supervisory conferences, and to be able to participate intelligently in treatment conferences.

In addition to this daily log I would suggest a *written* summary on each individual of the living group to be made routinely at given intervals appropriate to the purpose of the institution. Then, before conferences about treatment or placement outside the institution, the houseparent should write a short report on the child under consideration. The individual summary should be related to five points:

1. The child's relationship to the adult.
2. The child's relationship to his contemporaries.
3. The child's acceptance of himself.
4. The child's attitude towards school and work.
5. The child's use of leisure time.

These five points will be helpful in determining progress in the treatment situation.

For general purposes these two forms of recording seem to be sufficient to demand of the houseparent. On the other hand, they are the minimum to be asked for, and an institution that does not supply at least these records cannot pretend to have made a real effort toward treatment. Recording is not a luxury that one can afford only if time is left over, but is the means of a systematic effort in behalf of a child. No medical treatment is given without recording. We should learn from the medical profession how to do this with consistency but with the least time involved. Perhaps by reducing recording to a few essential points we might make it easier in institutions where demands on those concerned with the living situation are especially heavy.

If the institution is established for the purpose of research, certainly more detailed records will be necessary. In such cases the traditional group work records, as I described them above, will be of special help. In addition to them other devices, such as, for instance, tape recording and the use of observer records, should be considered.

Additional Training Methods

We saw supervision as the crucial and indispensable form of education of houseparents. At a conference of the Delinquency Project of the Children's Bureau in Madison, Wisconsin, in 1953, some additional educational devices were agreed upon that are applicable to houseparents in children's institutions. Two forms of staff meetings were specified. One would be educational staff meetings in which specific problems of group living would be discussed as well as dynamics of individuals. They would be a direct supplement of individual supervisory conferences and often carry the same content. The clinical staff of an institution would be used heavily as resource in this kind of meeting. The second form of staff meeting would be the treatment conference. It should become practice for the houseparent to be included as a contributing member in treatment conferences. These staff meetings present an excellent learning device, mainly in relation to individual dynamics and to incorporate the team concept.

Another teaching device is *in-service training*. Without question there should be an orientation course for new houseparents. In small institutions it cannot be given for each individual houseparent, but perhaps an effort could be made to coordinate several institutions and run such introductory courses at certain times of the year. The content of the courses must clearly relate to the needs of houseparents and not be a general course in psychology or group dynamics. The following points should be covered in such an introductory course.

1. History, purpose, and description of the specific institution.

2. Understanding of the role of houseparent or counselor as part of the institutional team.

3. Discussion of some forms of individual dynamics and understanding of defense mechanism, such as, for instance, projection.

4. Some understanding of the dynamics of group life, such as the role of the newcomer, conflict, etc.

5. Some understanding of program activities related to individual and group needs.

All these subjects should not be treated theoretically in an introductory course, but should be presented with a great deal of record material through the discussion rather than the lecture method.

The Universities of Minnesota and St. Louis and the Pittsburgh Program in Child Development and Care stand as pioneers of lengthier houseparent courses, lasting three months to a year. Still, no standardized curriculum exists today.

Some Schools of Social Work have given extension courses for houseparents. At the University of Minnesota, in the 1950's, a course called "Working with Groups" was given for several semesters. There was no prerequisite for this course, so houseparents of varied academic backgrounds could participate. In addition to subjects covered in the introductory course there was intensive discussion of records brought to class by the houseparents. This made it possible to greatly individualize the content. The houseparents came to class once a week for a whole semester. They felt that this arrangement was especially helpful, since it ran concurrent with their work and influenced it immediately. This course included visits to different institutions and to community agencies working with children, allowing the houseparents to see practices in different places and to widen their own horizon. The course had an unusually positive value not only in terms of the specific content taught but also of giving satisfaction by attending the university and through the group bond that developed in class.

Another training device widely used in the country today is *two- and three-day institutes*. They cannot be completely related to the needs of each individual institution, but they have proved very stimulating.

The houseparent or counselor is under especially strenuous demands from his job because it involves a living situation and is not restricted to "office hours" with a specific limited purpose. Because of this, it is essential that the houseparent have satisfactions outside of his job. One of the most serious occupational diseases of the houseparent's work is his being completely absorbed by institutional life. Even among the most accepting and warmhearted persons this has led often to a disgruntled personality. Satisfaction finally could be found only by demanding the return of affection from the children. Yet they should not have to fulfill this personal need.

Often the source of imagination dries up completely because no new stimulation is added. This leads to a desperate monotony of institutional life. Satisfactions are found only in living vicariously the lives of other people, either the children or, through gossip, other houseparents. No therapeutic atmosphere is possible if the houseparent is not helped to have a healthy and stimulating life outside of his work. It is not the task of this book to go into the devices in personnel practice for avoiding such occurrences. But I want to point out that in institutions which lie somewhat outside of large cities or other centers of stimulating cultural life a special effort must be made on the part of institutional administration to give the houseparent stimulation, outside interests, and opportunity for learning and enjoyment.

We have talked a great deal about the importance of group life for the children. We must not forget also the great importance of privacy and the opportunity to be by oneself to children as well as the adults who work with them. It is absolutely necessary that there be opportunity for comparative solitude and not being exposed to the demands of the group all the time. In a rather crowded institution a boy once cried out, "No wonder I get mad so easily here. There is never a moment I can get off by myself." And one of the houseparents once said, "I feel like running away myself just to get away from everybody." As group workers, we have to be especially aware of the need of people to be alone at times, because we know that the need for companionship does not mean being with other people all the time. The understanding of group needs includes an understanding of the balancing need for privacy, and this applies to both the children and the adults who work with them.

ADDITIONAL ROLES OF THE GROUP WORKER

I have put great emphasis in the previous section on the role of houseparents in relation to the group life of the institution. The professionally trained social group worker has acted mainly in the role of supervisor of houseparents. There are four additional functions in the institutional treatment process which he may fulfill:

1. Direct work with special therapeutic groups or club groups or specific councils.

2. The supervision and coordination of program with a therapeutic purpose outside of school work or work assignments.

3. Supervision of volunteers, if any are used by the institution.

4. The exploration and making available of community recreational resources to the institution.

In a larger institution not all these functions can be carried by one worker alone. I would suggest the separation, if possible, of the function of working directly with therapeutic groups, councils, and clubs from the others. The group worker working with the children in direct treatment relationship has quite a parallel function to the one of the caseworker and it might often be better if he is not related to any of the administrative aspects of daily living. I do not think this essential, though, and can see all the functions combined in one person in a small treatment institution or perhaps divided in some other way among several group workers.

Special Treatment Groups

Many children in institutions are so badly disturbed that they have great difficulties in relating to other people at all. Any kind of relationship in the living situation hurts them and makes too great demands on them. Only the very small treatment home prepared to work exclusively with children of a certain kind of difficulty, as, for instance, the Orthogenic School in Chicago, can successfully handle these children directly in the daily living group. An institution directed toward treatment but dealing with a larger number of children with different forms of behavior disturbances will not always be able to handle the problem directly. In such institutions specific therapy groups will be indicated.

It is up to the group worker's skill to arrange the best type of grouping. We do not know fully about the impact of group associations, but basic guidelines exist. We have established some very rough grouping rules, such as not to place too aggressive children with too withdrawn ones, but on the other hand to maintain some balance between more outgoing and more retiring behavior. Child guidance clinics, such as the Pittsburgh Child Guidance Clinic or the Amherst H. Wilder Child Guidance Clinic in St. Paul, or the Jewish Board of Guardians in New York, have done a great deal of experimenting with grouping. Fritz Redl in his Detroit Group Project and in his writings about Pioneer House [7] has also done a great deal of thinking about grouping. In all experiments

[7] Fritz Redl and David Wineman, *Children Who Hate* and *Controls from Within* (Glencoe, Ill.: Free Press, 1952).

until now, the population of the agency or institution has never been large enough to do a scientific experiment on grouping. Because of the needs of the children available, the groups had to be organized as well as possible on the rough principles that I mentioned. It is important, though, that the few known criteria of grouping not be violated in the special therapy group. Besides having to avoid the placing together of too great extremes of behavior symptoms, we also know that a too wide age span is not helpful to children. We have learned that differences in intelligence do not seem to play an important role. This thinking is borne out in the therapy groups conducted by Slavson in the Jewish Board of Guardians.

These special therapeutic groups may be formed for different reasons. They may be formed for the purpose of allowing the child to experiment with relationships to other children in a more protective and freer environment than is possible in the living group. They may be formed to allow youngsters to discuss specific problems growing out of their difficulties. These discussion groups will appear more in institutions for adolescents and will include some interpretation of behavior.

These special groups may be either activity groups, using our knowledge of program and activities for therapy purposes, discussion groups, using verbal communication exclusively, or a combination of both, leading from activity into group discussion or from group discussion into activities, if the group feels the need to experiment with certain reality situations in a more protective environment. An activity group of eight-year-olds, for instance, used almost a whole period for discussion when the youngsters had worked with clay, modeled a great many people, and then had smashed them all to bits. Out of this rather violent activity had grown a discussion regarding their brothers and sisters, with a great deal of hostility shown in their relationships. For almost the whole session these children discussed with their worker their feelings about their brothers and sisters and gained some understanding of their relationships to them. This meeting was followed by a special session for which they had clamored because of the guilt that had been engendered by their strong show and open verbalization of hostility.

On the other hand, a group of adolescent girls who felt awkward and rejected by their own age group and who had discussed a great deal their feelings of inadequacy in relation to boys asked at one point whether they could arrange for a party with boys just for this particular group, because they felt comfortable with each other. The party in this case served as experimentation of some content of their discussion.

I have chosen the following record of a special group in a home for unmarried mothers because it is like any therapy group for adolescent girls except that it deals with the specific problem of pregnancy out of wedlock. The group worker records:

The girls said what they liked most about their group and about the group worker was that she was someone in whose presence they could say anything they wished. They said they just had to say nasty things about the housemother and they knew that the worker would not repeat them. I explained that I realized that sometimes when we were very disturbed we just had to get mad at somebody and say nasty things so for that reason I just listened to the things they said and had understood some of the reasons why they might want to say them.[8]

In such a group the group worker will easily be used as the person who is the all-accepting one while hostility is strongly expressed towards those who are in a therapeutic but also administrative relationship. It is important that the group

[8] Sally Story, *Group Work in a Shelter for Unmarried Mothers* (Master's Thesis, Columbia University, School of Social Work, 1951).

worker does not fall into the trap of thinking of herself as only "the good mother" but realizes that here is a need to displace hostility on somebody else. In the preceding excerpt the group worker recognized the negative feelings of the girls and very skillfully let them see that they were displacing them on somebody and that the housemother was not necessarily the "bad mother."

Finally, Eileen began to whisper and giggle in Martha's ear saying that she had a question which she would like to ask. I said that she could feel free to ask anything that she liked. She finally whispered it to Martha who laughed and said, "You might just as well ask it out loud now, because people will be thinking it anyway." Eileen's question was directed at me: If I were in love, would I have intercourse with a man before I married him? All faces in the room turned to me. I realized that they wanted to know how I felt about their situation and so I said to Eileen, "Aren't you trying to discover how I feel about what you have done?" She agreed that this was partly so. I said that they must have some idea about this from being with me or they would not have asked the question.[9]

In the beginning of the relationship the group worker is tested out and the girls want to be sure that they can discuss their problems freely. They do not ask this question directly, but ask it indirectly, and the group worker sensitively enough understands what they are really asking. She helps them also to see that just in asking the question they have proved to themselves that they can feel perfectly free with this person. From this moment on the girls feel that they can really discuss their problems:

We went back again to the problems that girls might have which would make them seek illegitimate pregnancy. We brought up first the problem of girls being so young that they did not know

[9] *Ibid.*

any better and that they were just experimenting. We included the fact that some people felt, since they'd never been loved, that the first physical touch from a man was real love. Libby, however, showed more insight. She said that she felt that a lot of girls were pregnant because they were rebellious. I asked Libby if she would not tell us more what she meant by this. She said that she felt that many of them hated their mothers and had been afraid to say so; that this was one of the ways they could get back. I said that I felt that Libby had a very good point. I also said that I realized that this was a very difficult thing for most girls to see. Most of us, even though we were not illegitimately pregnant, had a feeling that we should always love our mothers, that there was something wrong if we both loved and disliked our mothers. I said that mothers felt the same way sometimes toward their daughters. I asked the girls if there were other people in their families that they might be rebellious towards. They mentioned their fathers and the jealousy between themselves and their sisters.[10]

The excerpt of this record shows the anxiety of the girls and the way they grope toward understanding their difficulties. The interpretation of some part of the behavior comes from one of the girls herself. The group worker makes no attempt to generalize this, but helps relieve their guilt by accepting these feelings toward mothers. But this explanation is not wholly allowable. Such pregnancies occur for various reasons.

In recent years there has been great controversy about the question of whether dealing with emotional problems in a group is group therapy or not and who should do what to whom? I am afraid that if the history of our attempts to deal with emotional difficulties should be written by a later, more objective writer, the helping professions will come in for severe criticism because of their exaggerated jealousy concerning the use of therapy media. A large part of the literature deals mainly with the status of the therapist himself instead

[10] *Ibid.*

of with the helping tool. We still suffer from the lack of a clear consensus regarding some very basic problems related to the use of the group as a treatment tool. We do not know enough about the best way of grouping, we do not know enough about what specific program has what specific relationship to which specific emotional disturbance. We are in an area of controversy regarding limitations and have few objective studies regarding their effectiveness in therapy.

The reasons we are in this state is not that we have not had enough experimentation. There has been a great amount of it by the three major professions involved, psychiatry, psychology, and social group work, with both adults and children, and this experimentation is often well recorded. Progress is hampered by the fact that there seems to be comparatively little willingness to learn from one another, each person thinking that he has to start every experimentation all over again. There is also often dogmatic adherence to one or the other point of view with little open-mindedness toward what the other fellow has to offer. For this reason I do not intend here to enter the controversy as to who has the right to do group therapy and who has not. I will simply try to clarify in what area I think the group worker has a special competence for being helpful to specific institutional groups, and in this chapter particularly those in children's institutions.

The group worker is trained in the understanding of individual and group behavior, knowledge of the relatedness of program media, and the disciplined use of himself. His specific knowledge relates to his understanding of the emotional impact of interrelationships between people. He has some understanding of pathological behavior, but needs consultation and help from the psychiatrist in this area. We see, therefore, both the strength and the limitation of the group worker, and according to this knowledge we can give him a place in the treatment of disturbed children. The formed group is, therefore, one of the concerns of the group worker. He will be sensitive to the needs of the children in regard to making this group a helpful tool, sometimes in the form of a club group, sometimes in activity groups, and sometimes in discussion groups. No claim is made that the group worker has yet discovered the best media, and research on this is needed. He works with the knowledge that is presently available and he must be willing to cooperate with any other of the professions interested in human beings.

The social group work method, as described in a previous chapter, has developed considerably, and the social group worker in the institution will, therefore, use this method. In the special therapeutic group he will adapt it to the stage in which he finds his group, for one of the principles of the group work method is to start where the group is. If the group worker in an institution finds a group of twelve-year-olds who are not ready to take on the kind of activities and work that twelve-year-olds usually want but who are in a much more infantile stage, he will start there. He will, therefore, have groups in which originally very few decisions can be made, though this is something towards which he is striving. He will have groups in which the infantile need for a great deal of acting-out behavior has to be accepted to begin with.

The social work profession does not adhere to the theory that acting out alone is therapeutic. In the many years in which social workers have dealt with people of all ages, all walks of life, and in many difficult situations, they have found that relief comes in expressing one's fears and anxieties, but this alone is never the basic therapeutic medium. Real help comes only when the person can come to grips with his own problems and feel capable of handling them. At times this is achieved by the outside person giving him clear recognition of reality limitations so that he can struggle with them and conquer them. The same applies to the disturbed child in a group situation. At many points the group worker will let the child know that there are limits that cannot be overstepped and that he has to come to terms with them. This we consider helpful to the individual child as well as to the interrelationship of the children. To say it clearly: The group work method is based on the emotional needs of each individual in the group as well as on the understanding of what impact those needs have upon each other. The group work method allows and demands the use of limitations. The following excerpts of records will show different aspects of how a group worker might deal with such a formed group in an institution.

I am starting with an example in which we see the handling of hostility in terms of the difficulties of the youngster as well as in relation to the institutional situation in a formed group in a treatment institution for preadolescent children. This is a group of ten- and eleven-year-old boys who could not be placed in foster homes because of their aggressive acting-out behavior. The excerpt is from the record of one of the regular group meetings.

Michael and Ralph soon chased each other out of the room, still squirting water. The others ran out too, except Wayne. George came in at this point and I told him that his pop was saved and brought him his cookies. Meanwhile Wayne too began acting up. His anger suddenly flared and he began destroying things, obviously wanting me to chase after him. He threw half the ping-pong table on the floor and reached for the other half. I held it down and told him that the table was for his fun and I wouldn't let him hurt it. He squirted a mouthful of pop at me and seemed surprised when I did not flinch. However, he was still very angry and he heaved a chair up over his head and began to bring it down in my direction. He seemed very surprised when I kept coming toward him and he swung it around and crashed it on the floor. At this point I held his arms down and said that he was so angry that I felt he would hurt himself, me, or too many things, and I would hold him so he could not do this. While I stood with him I slipped in a puddle of water and we both landed hard. He lay there for a second and cried. I said I was very sorry, he knew I did not mean to hurt him, that this was an accident. He ran to the other side of the room and looked furiously at me. He crawled into a cabinet and said he was going to bend the pipe sticking out of the wall. I said I didn't know what it was but it might be dangerous to bend it. George, who had been quietly watching, agreed to this. Wayne began to bend it and I touched his hands and said again that I knew he was mad at me, but I could not let him do anything dangerous because of it. He came out of his closet and began to threaten me with the ping-pong table. He looked more relaxed and almost had a grin on his face. I said I could see he was not angry anymore and now he was just doing this to tease. We both gave big smiles at this point. I held the table for a moment and he found a way to save face. He said I just had to find his pictures (they had been painting previously) which I did.

It is obvious in this record that the worker uses limitations because of three reasons: (1) to protect property which might be dangerously destroyed, as for instance the pipe in the wall; (2) to help the youngster realize that he is dealing with a human being who can be hurt; and (3) to protect him from an outburst that he might not be able to handle when it goes beyond certain limits. All through this use of limitations, though, the worker lets the child feel that she understands his need for attention and acceptance. She is not dealing in a punishing way with him, as seen when she apologizes for hurt that has come to him by slipping while she held him and when she accepts his need to have something done for him by going and getting the picture for him. Nothing dramatic has happened up to this point to help Wayne overcome his infantile behavior. But we hope that the combination of acceptance with the introduction of some reality and safeguards against his too hostile impulses will be one link in the chain that will help toward recovery.

We can quote numerous examples where the worker has to deal with hostility directed either toward himself or toward other members of the staff. Acted-out hostility is very difficult to bear, even if it is intellectually accepted. Houseparents will have to accept it a great deal in the day-to-day living situation. Small formed groups may relieve them of some of the strain of this hostility that demands so much from the person against whom it is directed. The group worker working with the formed group is in the fortunate situation of the clinician who has to accept this behavior only for a limited period of time (groups usually run for one to two hours) and, therefore, he can accept more hostility. We see here how the group living situation and the formation of special therapeutic groups can supplement each other.

In the following excerpt the group worker heads off a dangerous outburst of hostility by working with the indigenous leader of the group. This is only possible after the group worker has established a positive relationship with the members of the group, including the natural leader. If such a relationship has not formed, this attempt would be futile or would perhaps increase hostility by the group's resenting the use of the indigenous leader or the latter's misusing his power. The use of this method stands or falls by the previously well-developed relationship.

I met Peter on the steps and he informed me that the kids were going to have a good time tonight. They were going down to Mr. X (the resident director), break all of his windows, slash his tires. I asked calmly why the kids wanted to do this. "Oh, none of the kids like him." When I inquired further I found out that Dick was the instigator for the following reasons: (1) Mr. X would not let him have musical instruments. (2) They could not run the movie projector the way a previous director had let them do it. (3) He just didn't like him. Peter and I discussed these rumors for a few minutes but I did not push the issue too much then. I was fairly sure that Dick was at this moment out exciting the kids about the possible plans for that evening. I knew also that many of the kids had said that they do like Mr. X and that they think he is a pretty good guy and most of them feel they can talk freely with him. I went upstairs to talk to Leo. Leo does influence the group a good deal. Sometimes he even takes the father role. I discussed the situation with him as his being one of the group and a person that they respected, looked up to, and who had a pretty good judgment about what to do and what not to do. He seemed very concerned about the situation and said that he really had felt that Dick was getting quite out of hand lately but that he, Leo, was able to hold him back at times. I said that if Dick really felt he did not like Mr. X a better way to work it out would be to go to him and talk it over with him. Leo said he understood this and that he would try and help the kids talk about whatever these rumors were.

After supper Leo invited Dick and two other boys to come into the library where he could talk to them. He started out by saying that several things had been taken from his room and he did not know who was responsible, but if he ever found them or if anything more was taken, or anything was damaged, that everything would have to be *paid off in full*. He was very emphatic about this. He then continued that if anything else were damaged around the center that that would have to be paid for in full. He assumed quite an authoritarian role at this time and yet the kids listened carefully to him and did not seem to fear him. They discussed some of their problems and seemed to consider their planned action especially since the limitation had come from one of them.

The worker herself comments, concerning this episode, that she wonders at times whether she is not expecting too much of Leo in asking him to assume more responsibility than usually a thirteen-year-old should carry. She realizes that at this moment she was taking a risk in having him assume such an adult role. Yet the immediate outburst of hostility could be handled best by a mature member of the group. It was important that the group worker always be present in this situation so that an eventual abuse could be prevented.

We know that the group situation very often relieves the feeling that one is alone with all the problems that bear down hard on everybody. Somehow problems seem easier when one knows that others have similar experiences. However, it would be very wrong to think that a group approach should be the only one. The relief that it gives can also sometimes prevent an intensive enough involvement of the individual for the purpose of working on his own problem. The group can be a help as well as an escape. This shows the importance of both casework and group work services in an institution.

In the small incident quoted in the following, these thoughts are expressed by the girls themselves.

Kate came forth with the idea that sometimes she found the casework situation very difficult for the simple reason that when a caseworker asked a girl a question, it seemed so awfully obvious that the girls became very hesitant and did not want to speak. Kate went on to explain that she found the group situation much easier because in a group, all the girls were in it together and nothing seemed directed toward one person alone. Kate said, "You sort of feel that there are other people with you."

The formation of groups will be suggested to the children or young people in the institution in different ways. In some instances it will be clear in the beginning that this will be a discussion group concerned with the problems that many of them have. In other instances, especially with younger children, it will be presented to them as an opportunity to have their own special club. The initial formation of such a group must always allow for expression of acceptance or refusal of such a plan. Medicine seldom can be crammed down the throat of a patient. In the psychological area this is even less possible. I remember a psychiatrist who explained to a group of adults who were very resistant to treatment that he knew that there was nothing a psychiatrist could do *to* people, that he only could do something with them if they wanted to be part of the treatment. In group association this means that attendance of specially designed groups must be as voluntary as possible. In allowing voluntary attendance, we also have an invaluable measurement for diagnosis in relation to the individual or the group situation.

The following record shows the way a group was started in an institutional setting. It was a therapeutic group conducted by the group worker in an institution for adolescent girls.

I told the older girls I would like to see them in my office in the evening. . . . When the entire group was present I said that lately different ones of them had come to me individually or in groups to talk about some situations involving all or most all the entire group of older girls. Perhaps they might wish to have a regular time to get together to discuss some of these things. I referred to a group discussion of two weeks ago and said that through getting ideas together on that problem I wondered whether they felt they were getting along better. There was general agreement that this had helped somewhat. I said there were still some things that they might want to discuss and we could examine them in a group discussion. I wondered whether they would like to plan regular group meetings once a week for this purpose—what did they think about it? Several of the girls immediately showed much enthusiasm for the idea. Susan and Hannah said they didn't know why they did not care for the idea—they just did not think it would work. They brought in some arguments about the limited time they had for such meetings. Other girls contradicted them. It was agreed that the majority opinion was that they wanted to have such group discussions and the time was set. I added the meeting would last an hour—we could plan on beginning next week.

.   .   .

Earlier in the day several of the girls referred to the fact that we had a meeting that night. At the set time all the older girls including Susan and Hannah came into my office. There was no question about their coming and I did not comment on it.

I briefly reviewed the purpose and focus of the group meetings as stated before—that the girls could bring up any situations or problems affecting the whole group. I added that they might also wish to bring up things about which they were individually concerned, and about which they wished to discuss the thoughts and ideas of the other girls.

The meeting was primarily a "blowing off steam" session.

The special group is started because of the need of the girls to discuss many of their problems. Those who do not want to come to the meetings are not forced to appear but are accepted without having to make explanations when they do appear.

We know that the group situation is quite frightening for some children, especially when they have not yet had a taste of it. The taste can only be acquired by trying it out. Knowing this we sometimes fall into the trap of forcing the child into the group "for his own good." In general that only leads to a great deal of resentment on the part of the youngster and, because of this, attendance in the group bears out all his fears. He does not involve himself in the activities or discussions, he shows hostility because he was forced into a situation he was afraid of, and this actually makes the use of the group as a treatment medium impossible. In an institutional setting this is accentuated because the child already lives in a group that he has not chosen himself. We can see how the skilled group worker helps children to start in a group without forcing them into it.

Billy said he didn't want to come to the club. Gene said "Why not, you are crazy." I said, "Maybe you think you have to play with the clay. You don't, you know. There are many other things to do." Billy was tossing a ball from hand to hand. "Ah, I don't like to be in here—but I guess I have to." I said, "You don't have to stay in the club. It's just if you want to." Bill said, "Don't I have to stay?" He started toward the door. I said, "You know what, Bill? Perhaps you could give it a try. Would you stay for a little while, and then if you don't want to stay you can go with the others and play." He said, "All right." . . .

At the end of the meeting Billy said, "Why can't we stay until it is time to go to bed?" I said, "Once we get to doing things, it's hard to stop working." I told them we would meet again next week.[11]

The group worker accepted the boy's resistance to being in the special group, but by making it clear to him that he would not have to stay, she gave him an opportunity to try out the situation. It is usually a new experience to the children that they are not forced into either the situation or the activity. They are almost set with their whole being to fight the demand that is imposed on them. If it is not forced upon them the way they are used to, they can relax and see reality without having it colored with their own feelings of hate and rejection.

Nancy just sat. She said, "This isn't going to be much fun." I urged Nancy to look through the cupboard. The first thing I

[11] Phyllis Dickinson Fairman, *An Application of Principles of Clinical Group Work to the Recreation Program in a Temporary Study Home for Children Referred for Foster Home Placement*, for Master's Thesis, School of Public Affairs and Social Work, Detroit, Michigan, p. 72.

brought out was the heavy crayolas. She said, "Well, I'm glad to see we have something new." Later she began to dig in the box of colored rope. She asked "What could you make of this?" I suggested belts, pot holders, rugs. Nancy pulled out several pieces that were braided and asked, "How do you make a rug?" [12]

Though these special groups are formed by an adult, they soon develop a bond and an "in-group feeling." When this occurs the members will want to determine group membership and will not want to have it imposed on them. This puts the group worker into a dilemma: On the one hand he respects the right of a group to make its own decisions regarding membership, but on the other hand, in an institution where we have a changing population new members will need to have the opportunity of attending such groups and new ones cannot be formed all the time. In general this problem is solved by asking the group members to permit the introduction of a new member, since the newcomer might feel especially in need of such association. Real difficulties arise, though, when the new member of the group is somebody who has shown behavior in the group living situation that is unacceptable to his contemporaries. The following excerpt is an example of such a situation. It is taken from a treatment home for preadolescent children, the group being a special club for some of the boys. Seven were present at the meeting.

Before we started the meeting Roy came into the room and asked very shyly if he could join the club or go sliding with us. There was strict opposition among all the boys present. I put my arm around Roy's shoulder to give him some support and in order to help him to accept the hostility that came from the others. I asked the boys why they didn't want to have him in the club. The answers were: "He swears too much; he makes so much noise in the morning. He has horrible table manners. We don't like

12 *Ibid., p. 72.*

him." Roy bowed his head and said that he knew that he was that way, yet he was very anxious to get into the club and make friends with the rest of the boys. . . . The club finally decided to give Roy a chance of behaving during the next week and they would consider his membership at the next meeting. Roy seemed satisfied with this answer and, feeling that he was accepted by me and had got some support, he left the room.

The group worker comments on this meeting by saying that Roy needed badly to be accepted in a group and he needed the experience of trying to join with them. At the same time it could have been too damaging if he had had to stand the onslaught of the accusations without any support by somebody who would show that he liked him. It has to be pointed out that sometimes in taking the part of the youngster we may alienate him from his contemporaries more than he was before. It is very important to consider the group situation and to be very aware of the attitude of the group to the adult in order to know whether one can handle the situation in this way.

Planning Groups

Some of the formed groups with which the group worker will deal in institutions are related to a specific planning purpose. Many children's institutions will have a council where the children themselves do some planning of leisure-time program or in which they bring out feelings regarding administrative situations. These councils can fulfill several basic purposes, namely, to give the youngster the feeling that he is participating in a common endeavor, and to give the institution the means of being informed on what the children think about the living situation. As an example I am using a record of a committee meeting concerned with writing a pamphlet describing the institution to new boys and girls. This committee consisted of children, the group worker, and some house-parents.

This was a staff-appointed committee asked to meet now to consider what ought to go into a pamphlet describing the Home to new boys and girls who might be coming to it, and to meet later to "hash over" a rough draft of such a pamphlet. They were picked for the various points of view they could represent, and for their ability to participate in a group on a joint project of this kind. . . .

We early directed the conversation to Buddy, feeling that he could make a real contribution since he had been here so short a time that he could easily remember the things he had wondered about before he came. From the beginning we had no further doubts about whether he would be willing and able to participate in the discussion. We sometimes had to wait for the words to come out, but Buddy seemed relatively unconcerned about his stuttering, and I had no feeling that self-consciousness about it kept him from saying things at any point in the discussion. The other youngsters, too, were very accepting of it, and neither broke in to speed it up nor ridiculed him.

Patrice participated least. It may have been partly her position in the group—having been here a relatively short time, yet not as short as Buddy. A couple times when asked a direct question she replied after some thought, but with comparatively insignificant points. Joyce's suggestions were often to the more or less objective facts about the Home, and she worded them rather pedantically. At one point she said very seriously that she would like to help write the pamphlet, and it was suggested that she try writing a little section, and that she and I could talk about this a little further, and I emphasized the point that one of our problems might be that we would have too much material, and, therefore, would have to cut. She understood that.

Buddy was the first to bring out some of the intangibles. He mentioned that one of the things that had surprised him was the way the other kids came in and talked to him right away when he came. By this time Clyde said, "Yeah, the kids here are real friendly." In discussing what the counselors are like, Ronnie contributed a gem: "The first time I saw a counselor he was playing with his yo-yo; I was sure surprised."

Both positives and negatives were brought out—there were hard duties and there were easy ones—and you had your choice! You could only go to the movies once a week (Clyde) but you got "treats" every afternoon, and got an allowance (also Clyde).

There seemed to be excellent examples of really democratic participation. Neither youngsters nor staff seemed to hold back, the staff attempting to help the youngsters see wider applications or contradictions in the things they suggested. The children accepted each other's contributions well, most times being willing to wait until someone else was through before speaking. They corrected each other—as when Clyde spoke about catching birds in the park, Joyce said we shouldn't do that, and Clyde agreed— and supplemented each other. Even Clyde, who started out asking "how long this would take" devoted complete attention to it for the longest time I have ever seen him in a committee meeting.

There is no question that in this meeting the children received a great deal of satisfaction from the fact that they were actively involved in an important activity. The staff gained insight into the different ways the children saw them and the situation in the institution, and finally a far more realistic pamphlet was written than would have been prepared by the staff only or by the children themselves.

We have discussed in the preceding the second function of the group worker in the institution, namely, the dealing with specifically formed groups, relating either to certain emotional problems or to planning and participation in institutional life.

Supervision of Recreational Program

The third function of the group worker is his responsibility towards the recreational program in the institution. Recreational life must be completely integrated into the living situation and must be carried mostly by the houseparents. Recreation outside of the living group situation is confined to that intended to create a bond between the different units in the institution through special events, and that which is carried on outside the institution in different community settings. Recreation cannot be separated either from the treatment aim of the institution nor from daily life, especially in children. Erik H. Erikson says of child's play that it is

not the equivalent of adult play, that it is not recreation. The playing adult steps sideward into another reality; the playing child advances forward to new stages of mastery.[13]

Play, therefore, cannot be neglected and must not be used as punishment or reward like candy which one can offer or take away at will. Albert Deutsch in his book, *Our Rejected Children*, points out that monotony is almost the worst aspect of our institutions. It is surprising to see that this applies not only to the institution for delinquents but also to institutions for dependent children. Often the concern of the institution extends no further than school education and work duties and, in the better institutions, clinical facilities, but the vital importance of play is disregarded. There is very often a great lack of imagination in the recreational program. In our culture sports certainly have a great importance to the youngster, and the ones who can excel in them gain real status and satisfaction from them. Frequently the sports program is the only form of recreation offered. Though it has a place for the youngster who is capable of fulfilling its demands, it leaves

[13] Erik H. Erikson, *Childhood and Society* (New York: W. W. Norton & Co., 1950), pp. 194-195.

the child who cannot participate successfully on the sidelines.

In some institutions the thinking prevails that every minute of the day must be occupied with busy work, with no allowance for the more relaxed or unorganized play of children, as, for instance, fishing in a brook or lying under a tree and staring into the sky or sitting together and just dreaming about all sorts of things one will do when one is grown up. On the other hand, some institutions think that children know best how to occupy themselves and do not give any stimulation in new games or activities. We must not forget that most of the children who come to our children's institutions have had a rather hectic life with little opportunity for relaxation and also very often a life poor in stimulation of their play instincts. I have seen children to whom childhood games that are familiar to almost all adults were quite new.

I have never forgotten when, as a young worker, I visited two children in the courtyard of a block of houses in the slum area of one of the large cities. I began to play a singing game with these two children and in a few minutes I was surrounded by a mob of children (I remember I counted up to almost fifty) who clamored to join in this game and who did not know a single one of the nursery songs. I stood in the light of a summer day surrounded by ashcans and the horrible smell of open toilets and I played singing games with children who seemed to think that this was fairyland emerging out of their drab life. Many of our children come from similar circumstances and there is a hunger and thirst for this stimulation, even if they often interrupt it with bitter swearing and spitting and angry withdrawal.

Recreation, therefore, cannot lie in the hands of an activity-centered worker. It must be based on understanding of individual and group dynamics and must take into account the therapeutic purpose. Imagination in recreational work must lie in the understanding of individual needs and specific cultural values. We cannot use games with thirteen-year-olds that are considered sissy in the environment from which they come. Dodge ball, for instance, would be considered a perfectly acceptable game in that age group, but the "tough guy" will think it far too highly organized and it will not have enough challenge for him. In their book, *Social Group Work Practice*, Gladys Ryland and Gertrude Wilson have an excellent chapter regarding the intelligent use of program in relation to needs. Fritz Redl has also enriched our knowledge about recreation in relation to the disturbed child.

The recreational diet and its implementation are of utmost importance in the treatment of the ego-disturbed child. In their various aspects, they offer the child a chance for expressional discharge within organizational, sublimational, and frustration-acceptance levels mainly circumscribed by the particular ego disabilities from which he suffers. The program tools of the outer world have been too challenging and frightening to the unstructured ego of this type of child. Just to mention a few, highly competitive games, arts and crafts, situations where achievement goals cramp impulse needs, toys and gadgets whose inner satisfaction potentials they have not been able to visualize, all have thrown these children into a recreational wasteland or, perhaps more appropriately, jungle, where their main adjustment has been to resort to random and destructive impulsivity. The clinician recognized that one of the most vital and ego-nutritive experiential areas is that of gratifying play. Normal children seem to have an inner guiding hand which helps them to find these outlets so necessary to their emotional health. With the ego-disturbed child, making up for this missing mental hygiene vitamin is one of the most important functions of the residential milieu. Our assumption is that a certain amount of ego repair and change can occur in this way alone.[14]

[14] Fritz Redl and David Wineman, *Children Who Hate*, loc. cit., pp. 36, 37.

Redl and Wineman also point out that the activities of play program in the living situation have to be modified from those used in individual play therapy. In the group situation we deal with reality and the interrelationship of people directly and not in a symbolic way, as in play therapy.

It is one thing to encourage a child to claw out the doll-sibling's eyes. They can easily be replaced. But none of us would advise this as clinical strategy where a live prop is involved, like another child in a therapy group.[15]

In quoting Erikson we said that play is the child's life, and we pointed out that it therefore, has to become largely part of the living situation, falling into the domain of the houseparent. It will be the role of the group work supervisor to help the houseparent understand this and use it skillfully.

Let us see what some of the children's needs are and how we can understand them better and fulfill them through play.

1. *In play the child gains satisfaction through the learning and mastery of skills.*

Dennis was a very frightened child unable to relate to either adults or children. He shrank away from any physical touch and usually sat somewhere alone in the corner of the room while other children played. There was no question that Dennis was yearning to join with them, but for many basic reasons he was filled with a feeling of complete inadequacy. When he was encouraged to participate in some activity with the group he got even more frightened and crawled further into his shell. One day the counselor was alone in the room with Dennis. She was putting away the ping-pong balls and paddles. Suddenly Dennis got up, came to the table, and rolled the ball along the table. The counselor asked Dennis whether he might not like to learn how to play ping-pong?

[15] *Ibid.*, pp. 70, 71.

Dennis looked frightened and shook his head. The counselor, sensing his fear of being found to be inadequate, suggested to him that she would draw the curtains and she would teach him how to play ping-pong without anybody being able to look in. Hesitantly Dennis reached for the paddle. For several days the counselor practiced with Dennis secretly and individually. The boy at times became quite excited about the possibility of his being able to master a skill. One evening when others were playing the counselor asked Dennis whether he wanted to play a match with her. In the safety of their relationships, but this time in the open and before the eyes of other children, Dennis was able to carry out the match. This was quite an important step in helping Dennis to overcome his fears and to join in more normal relationships with other children. The actual skill achieved through a warm relationship with the person who was responsible for the day-by-day living situation meant a great deal in the recovery process.

2. *Play fulfills a need to release aggressive feelings in an acceptable way.*

Jack Simos describes an incident in an institution:

Two girls, Phyllis and Thelma, aged ten and ten and a half years, while playing on the playground found some matches.

They sneaked candles out of the linen closet. At bed time they lit the candles in their room. Their housemother coming in to say good night smelt freshly lit matches.

This little incident shows how the child fulfills a need for adventure and for aggressive feeling by actually using a dangerous toy. The housemother, realizing their needs, will be able to turn this into constructive channels through other play activities. She can, for instance, suggest to the youngsters that they can have a cookout over the weekend and that they can be the ones to start the outdoor fire. She will make this a program full of adventure and give the satisfaction of playing with fire but with safety rules and with an understanding of what is involved. This way the children will get the fulfillment of some of their needs without damaging others and they will learn how this is possible.

3. *Children can learn the art of sublimation through play.*
Sublimation means our capacity to deal with our basic impulses in a way that is acceptable in our society.

Janice was a fourteen-year-old girl who had spent a large part of her life in institutions. She had moved from one place to another, seldom gaining any real affection. Janice's hunger for affection became so great that with the onset of early adolescence she got involved in many sex experiences. Janice, when she came to this particular institution, had no other way of coping with her instincts but to live them out. Janice's counselor was a young woman greatly interested in art who kept in her room many art books. While helping with the cleaning Janice saw some of the books and her curiosity arose because of the naked figures in some Michelangelo paintings. Her interest in art was at this moment purely related to what seemed to her a sex content. The counselor let Janice look through the pictures and showed her some of the beauty that arises out of color and design. Janice got so interested in the paintings that she asked to come back and see more of them. The counselor encouraged her and suggested that she might want to do some drawing herself. It was interesting to see that Janice started working first with charcoal on rough paper and that a surprising amount of artistic ability could be seen. Her subjects were almost exclusively adolescent nude figures in stages of despair, either kneeling, crying, or lying in each other's arms with agony in their faces. Janice got some help in understanding that she expressed her own fears, but she also got help in seeing that she had discovered in herself a great strength by being able to express some of those feelings in a way that meant a great deal to others. There was an unforgettable evening when Janice knocked at the counselor's door and said, "I have a picture for you this time, something very special." With eyes filled with joy she presented to the counselor the painting of a large flower in bloom in deep reds and beautiful glossy green leaves. The usually solemn and rather repressed-looking youngster said happily and full of excitement: "My first picture in color. It belongs to you. It is so beautiful. I will not use charcoal again." Out of play had grown a real liberation of feelings, an ability to put them in their place, and in addition a new purpose in life. Janice actually later went into art work.

4. *Play can help master relationship with others, with contemporaries, and with adults.*

Sue, a girl of fourteen, had very little status in her group and seemed to be quite removed from the other girls. The housemother recorded:

Sue (age fourteen) had three years of music before she came to us about ten months ago. She told the social worker on her way over that she refused to touch the piano while she was here and perhaps never again. A week or so ago she relented and asked her worker of her own accord if she could get her music for her. She made it a point to see me this noon to tell me that some one was bringing her music after school. She could hardly contain herself.

Later Sue was playing "The Bells of St. Mary." Several girls went over to watch her play. "Gee, I never knew Sue could play like that." Sue smiled a million dollar smile and went right on. Some of the girls started to sing and all those present joined in.

The same evening Sue said, "It's three whole weeks now, Sister." (Sue is eneuretic. She was trying to tell me that she hadn't wet the bed for three weeks. This was a real victory for Sue.)

We see how the youngster gained status with the others, how she began to join in with them, and at the same time how this made her free to talk to the housemother about her eneuresis. It helped her with relationship to children and with her relationship to the adult.

5. *Play and activities allow children to be in a giving situation.*
Human beings in general do not always like to be on the receiving end. The child in his family has many opportunities for give and take, emotionally as well as in relation to giving things. We know what satisfaction it brings to a child to give a gift to father or mother or relative. Children in institutions often miss this very gratifying opportunity. Emotionally they might often be quite incapable of giving, but even if they are, the opportunity to show their love through tangible gifts is sometimes denied them. There is an opportunity in handicrafts to let the children feel free to decide whether they want to make something for themselves or for others to whom they feel close. It is important that the child not be pushed into having to give away what he has made, because he must feel free to use something that grew out of his own creativeness the way he wants to use it. There is a wonderful therapeutic effect in being able to give out of one's own will:

Don asked if he could make a clay bowl for one of the "mothers" for Christmas. I said he could. He asked now if I would help him. I said that I would. At the next meeting Don arrived anxious to see the bowl. "Boy, I live for Monday to come," he said as he admired his product. He sanded it until it was smooth, and decided to decorate it with a Mexican design. As he worked he said he guessed he would have to make three vases, "It wouldn't be nice to give one mother one and not give the others any." I said, "Which of the mothers would you like to give this one to?" Don said, "I don't know. I like all the mothers about the same." The others admired the finished product. He did not give the bowl as a Christmas gift, however. Then a full month after he had finished the bowl, on a day when he was working on a second bowl, by chance he saw one of the matrons in the hall. He took the unfinished bowl to show her. When she admired this, he ran to get the first bowl and gave it to her as a gift.[16]

All these five values add up in the child to feelings of pure enjoyment as well as some resistance and unhappiness, of weakness and frustration as well as of real strength. We have to know that play and activities do not bring happiness exclusively, but being part of life they entail two-way feelings as we find in so many aspects of our struggle to become a part of human society.

The richer the program is, the more varied the opportunities for different individuals at different times, the more helpful it will be. It is perfectly clear that not every houseparent, not every group worker, can have skills in all different areas of programing. What they have to learn is to appreciate the many different aspects, to acquire as much skill as possible, and to use resources where they are available. It is especially important that they keep imagination alive in themselves and do not fall into the monotony of program planning that we see not only in institutions but too often also in our community centers. There is no reason why activities should always consist of certain handicrafts or sports. There is a multitude of possibilities in using, for instance, the environment of the institution, nature, art, nearby historical sites, etc. There are few children in families who do not hear at one time or another discussions about the daily events of public life. There is no reason why this cannot also be done in institutions. In some places the older children have divided reading the newspapers into separate assignments and they report at the dinner table and discuss some of the issues with the house-

[16] Phyllis Dickinson Fairman, *op. cit.*

parents. It brings to the children life outside of the institution and helps them see themselves as an active part in a democracy.

I remember once when I had a conference with a director of a small treatment home and one of the boys burst in, telling quite excitedly about the way he had argued in school for his favorite candidate in the coming presidential election. The director listened to him, discussed with the boy some of the issues involved in this campaign, told him that he himself was for the other candidate, and gave some of his arguments. All this was done in a friendly relaxed way, letting the boy see that one can have different opinions and that this is perfectly all right. The boy also got the feeling that so shortly before a presidential election the director too realized how important this was and did not cut him off. I am sure that besides learning about how to discuss political issues this boy learned that he is part of a citizenry responsible for public life and that his director has a respect for his ideas even if he does not share them.

The same day I visited another institution and saw a club group conducted in which there was a great deal of voting. Yet all through this meeting the presidential elections were not mentioned. When the meeting was over one of the boys jumped on another and said, "Listen, you dope, I heard you are for X," naming one of the candidates for presidency. The group worker conducting this meeting had completely missed a vital opportunity for program planning.

In a home for adolescent girls I saw how dramatics were made an excellent tool for therapy. The counselor who handled these sessions was fortunately undogmatic about them and allowed over a period of time change from creative dramatics to the presentation of a written play, and back, sometimes allowing for the girls' needs to express a great deal of feelings in creative dramatics, another time accepting their need to be somebody else and to hide their own feelings behind assumed roles.

In the informal play situation the houseparent has an invaluable opportunity to observe while the children feel more unhampered from restraints than at any other times, and also has an opportunity to establish a warm and more informal relationship. A new housemother once came into an institution where a great deal of rigidity was usual and where there was a cold distance between the houseparent and the youngsters. The first evening the children played hop-scotch in front of the cottage. The young housemother watched for a moment and then suggested that she would play along with them. Nothing she could have done could have helped as much towards the feeling of warmth and actual affection that the children felt towards her from this moment on.

The group worker's function in relation to recreation, besides helping the houseparent, will be in three additional areas:

1. *The group worker must keep contact with other community agencies that can provide recreational outlets for the children in the institution.*

In places where the institution is close enough to large cities, it will be very helpful for the youngsters to participate in agencies which serve all children as, for instance, the Scouts, the Y's, or some settlement houses or community centers. The group worker's role will be to know these community resources well and to be able to interpret them to the children if the child should be referred to them, as well as to interpret the needs of the children to the agency. His role must not be just a technical one, as, for instance, giving the children the location of the place or driving them to it. This kind of contact too must be related to the general aim of helping the child to become more adequate in his relationships to other people and, therefore, the referral must be a thoughtful, well-prepared one and related to the needs of the individual child. It is important, for instance, to know whether the particular agency deals mainly with natural groups and the child from the institution will be looked upon as an outsider; it is important to find out whether group leadership is oriented towards understanding the child or is mainly activity oriented. After the child is participating in an agency, the group worker will have to keep in contact with it in order to gain additional understanding of the child.

The knowledge of community resources in the recreational and informal educational area will also be a help to the houseparents. The group worker can help to make the life of houseparents more enjoyable and meaningful by letting them know about agencies that will serve *their* needs.

2. *Coordination of recreational staff, as, for instance, the swimming instructor, art instructor, or occupational therapist.*

The coordination of all those services is indispensable if all of them are to serve the therapeutic purpose. The supervision given by the group worker is certainly not in the area of specific competence of the specialist. The group worker cannot and should not supervise the art instructor in art, the swimming instructor in the best way of teaching swimming, or the sports director in training a team. The supervision and coordination will be in relation to understanding the individual needs of particular children as well as to the group situation at a given time.

3. *Coordination and supervision of volunteers.*

Not all institutional settings use *volunteers*. In some settings this will be impossible because of the specific disturbances of the children. In most children's institutions, though, the volunteer will be an exceptionally valuable person. I have very often heard administrators in institutions resisting the use of volunteers because they felt that they were not reliable and, therefore, too damaging to the children, who felt very disappointed if a promise for an outing or a certain activity was not fulfilled. I think that this relates mainly to the poor use made of the volunteer rather than being inherent in volunteer participation. If the volunteer is used to substitute for staff, we will see conflicts. If the volunteer is used because of a specific contribution that only he can make, then he will become really valuable in the program.

The volunteer brings to the institution the interest of the community. He also brings to the child the feeling that there is somebody in the outside world who is concerned with him, though it is not his job. Both those attributes are inherent in volunteer service and invaluable in dealing with people. They apply as much to work in adult institutions as in children's institutions and we have seen in recent years that this specific attribute of volunteer service has helped towards great progress in our mental hospitals. If the volunteer recognizes himself as somebody who can make a specific contribution to the institution, his feeling of responsibility will increase. The volunteer also must be treated by the staff as somebody highly welcome, neither superior because of his possible position in society nor inferior because he does not have the professional education, but as an important member of the staff.

The volunteer needs an introduction to the institution almost as intensive as that of a new staff member. He cannot give his best if he does not know what the purpose of this institution is and with what kind of children he will have to deal. If this is made clear to him it will again increase his own feeling of responsibility. It is not surprising that a volunteer who teaches clay work in a children's institution may not appear on schedule if his introduction to this institution has been only that the kids should learn something about handling clay and if in several of the meetings he has seen youngsters wasting material, throwing clay around, and making his task rather difficult. If he does not understand what this activity means to the child and why they act the way they do, he simply cannot consider his job an important one. The volunteer who understands that these are children with many aggressive needs, that his helping hand may mean that they will regain some confidence in the adult world, that his always being there when he has promised will mean that they can learn to believe that promises are kept—this volunteer will not easily drop a meeting.

We see, therefore, that introduction is an important part of working with the volunteer. But it is not enough. The social group worker must also give individual supervision to the volunteer to be sure that the activity he conducts is really helpful to the individual child and also to give the volunteer himself constant help and real interpretation of what the institution tries to do. Volunteers will want to write short observations of their work if they know that these will be used. The group worker notes about a conference with a volunteer in a small children's home:

Erick opened the conference by telling me of a conversation he had with a girl who was doing volunteer work in another institution. With apparent pride he told her of how he has conferences and writes reports. He had shown the girl the report form. She said that she wished she had such a set-up because she is thrown on her own. Nobody gives her any help with what to do. She asked for a copy of the report form, which he had given her.

We are wrong in assuming that we can make few demands of volunteers. We must stay within the limits of the time that the volunteer can give. Yet he will have much higher respect for us if we make our demands strong enough that he feels his work has meaning and is not just an afterthought.

The volunteer also will want to learn. He has chosen this activity because he enjoys it and because he wants to gain from it. I am quoting from another supervisory record.

I asked about the activity of the other boys in the shop. Merrill (the volunteer) mentioned that Don had started a chest. Merrill felt this was really too difficult a project for Don, but Don was so anxious to make it and Merrill had let him go ahead. Merrill had helped him a great deal and he thought this chest would turn out all right. I said that in deciding whether to let children go ahead when they wanted to do things beyond their ability, we have to ask ourselves certain questions and balance up certain factors. One thing we have to ask, will the desire for doing this particular project be overbalanced by a possible feeling of failure in not being able to complete the project? We must also ask, if in order to get the project completed, the worker does most of the work himself, and we have to find out whether the fact of having a completed project has more value to the child than if he has a simpler project which he has completed himself. We have to ask ourselves these questions and then decide according to the individual needs of the child.

Learning this way the volunteer will gain a great deal of insight into people and will feel related to the aim of the institution.

I am quoting one more record, this time written by the volunteer himself, to show how elated he can be when he sees that his understanding has helped improve the meeting.

To my mind a very successful—though unorthodox—meeting. When I got there, Gene came rushing downstairs with a tale of woe. It went like this: he had been sick when his craft club met, and could he come to the club tonight to finish his horn? Well, I told him this was all right—if the club members approved. They did. Gene brought along a beautifully prepared horn (a wall "vase" with an ingenious hanger); it was well done and I told him so. As soon as the club began, he put his work aside and volunteered to help the others. Feeling experimental, I said yes—and retired somewhat to the background. Gene was amazing to behold! He helped carve, saw, select horns, and gave advice. The regular boys soon turned to him naturally. Gene had a "huge" time! At the end he insisted on cleaning up. And then said, "I was a pretty good boy tonight, wasn't I?" Then he impulsively hugged me— and ran upstairs. What are the implications of all this? I think Gene deserves a lot of help!

This volunteer will want to discuss in his supervisory conference the implications of Gene's behavior. The supervisor probably will pick up on the last sentence, "I think Gene deserves a lot of help." The supervisor will want to help the volunteer to see that *every* child deserves help and not only the one who gratifies us with acceptable behavior.

Summary

The same principles and functions as described for the social group worker in the preceding section will apply to the small treatment and study home for disturbed children. Some of these centers will be used also for research and, therefore, more intensive recording will be needed. Some centers have used clinical staff as houseparents. In my observations I have seen that intelligent, flexible houseparents can fulfill their task just as well as this clinically trained staff *if they receive the kind of supervision which the social group worker can give.* The clinical staff, which is trained exclusively in one-to-one relationship, has not always been the best for fulfilling the houseparent role in the living situation. Their understanding of individual dynamics is great but often they have little understanding of the impact of group living and they are not used to handling group situations. There is no question, certainly, that some people trained in clinical one-to-one relationships are also gifted in working with group relations. They all will profit greatly from additional knowledge of the dynamics of group behavior. In general, the role of the group worker, even in small research-oriented treatment homes, will be the same as the one described for other institutions, with the exception that in some of those centers the group worker will actually take on the role of the houseparent or counselor.

There is not yet an official survey of the way group workers are used in institutions for children. In the listing of Residential Treatment Centers for Emotionally Disturbed Children published in 1952 by the Children's Bureau, twenty-two out of thirty-six institutions mention social group workers either full-time or part-time on their staff. This does show that the importance of group work in institutions has been recognized. The listing does not allow us yet to know which function they fulfill in the different institutions.

I would like to summarize *the function of the social group worker* as I see it in *children's institutions*.

1. Supervising houseparents, giving individual supervision as well as in-service training in staff meetings and short introductory courses.

2. Doing direct leading of therapeutic groups, specially formed clubs, and councils.

3. Being responsible for and helping with the recreational program as part of group living.

4. Supervising other staff concerned with the recreational aspects of institutional life.

5. Being responsible for contacts with community group work agencies and for referral of children to them.

6. Supervising volunteers.

In addition to this the group worker is responsible for all

those tasks that every member of the professional staff is responsible for, such as participation in treatment conferences and research.

The *houseparents* or *counselors* must accept a professional role, since they carry out a responsibility which is vital to the institution. This professional responsibility includes the acceptance of supervision as well as learning to use this learning intelligently and on their own. The relationship of the houseparent to the social group worker should be like the modern concept of the relationship between nurse and supervising doctor in the hospital. Houseparents are not unthinking servants but they are professional people coordinated and helped by the person in charge of their specific program.[17]

Children's institutions are no longer used mainly for custodial purposes. All of them have become treatment centers for more or less disturbed children. Our aim is not to adjust the child to the institution, but to help the child to become a capable and independent member of a democratic society.

Robert Havighurst said, "We must have an education which makes the individual able to participate as a free man in a world society." This general aim of education is the same in our institutions and it applies to the most unhappy, most difficult, most hateful, and most lonely child. We will never achieve it through buildings or gadgets. We will achieve it only through people working with such children with deepest love and greatest understanding.

[17] See also Child Welfare League of America, *Standards for Services of Child Welfare Institutions,* New York: Child Welfare League, Inc., 1964 and U.S. Children's Bureau, *Institutions Serving Delinquent Children: Guides and Goals,* No. 360, 1962.

4. SOCIAL GROUP WORK IN INSTITUTIONS FOR UNMARRIED MOTHERS

Function always relates to the competence of the profession and the setting in which it is practiced. According to his competence the group worker's function in an institutional setting will always be the same, but he must adapt this competence to different settings. There are many institutions where group living encompasses only a short period of time. In all institutional settings we are dealing with people who have gone through a strong emotional upset and the quality of the group living situation is extremely important regardless of the length of stay.

The stay in an institution for unmarried mothers is usually only a few months, and yet those few months can be and will be of crucial importance. Homes for unmarried mothers were originally thought of mostly as shelters for the girls, who felt the heavy impact of society's disapproval of their behavior. They were mainly conducted by religious orders, who added to the offer of shelter their belief that the human being in distress also needed help towards change. They were focused on changing the sex behavior of the girl, since there was yet no knowledge about the causes of such behavior. We see again as we have seen previously how increase in knowledge has helped towards our more helpful treatment of human beings.

Unmarried motherhood has many causes. It depends a great deal on earlier experiences of the girl, on her age, and on the attitudes of society around her. In cultures where unmarried motherhood is the accepted pattern we will have none of the conflicts we find in our society, and even in our culture we might find the proud, more mature woman who consciously has accepted unmarried motherhood because of her deep love for a person she cannot marry for some reason. We often find in our culture the young woman or adolescent who has entered such a relationship because of many feelings of dissatisfaction, revolt, and unhappiness. Yet, this does not apply to every girl, especially not in times of changing mores. Again, as in all behavior, we will have to find the causes related.

NEED FOR CASEWORK SERVICES

In institutions for unmarried mothers, we find a variety of individuals, but they have in common the removal from their usual environment with all its implications. This fact itself establishes some bond. Most of the unmarried mothers in institutions are young adolescents and carry with them adolescent drives of dependence and independence, of wanting to be adults and still being children, of hating adults and looking to them for shelter, of struggling with establishing their own values. They usually have undergone an experience of poor relationship with adults and their sex behavior has very often been a protest against negligence or too strict supervision. They are going through an adult experience while not being ready for it. They are frightened, resentful, and feeling guilty.

The few months in the institution take on a much greater meaning than any other period in their lives. The way society meets them at this point is crucial. The adults in the institution represent at this moment society, very largely because contact with the rest of the adult world is comparatively cut off. Because of the great anxiety caused by the unknown advent of childbirth as well as her guilt feelings and the need for making adult decisions regarding, for instance, acceptance or placement of the child, the young woman is in desperate need both of acceptance and of understanding herself. The latter applies to almost all age groups found in a home for unmarried mothers. These institutions, therefore, have recognized comparatively early the need for casework services. The caseworker has the important task of helping the young mother to understand some of her feelings, to bring them out into the open, to relate to a person who does not sit in judgment over her, and also to help her plan for her child and for her own future life.

MEANING AND VALUE OF GROUP LIVING

What does *group living* mean to the unmarried mother? The atmosphere in such a home is an intensely emotional one. Every single person is filled with anxiety, expectancy, and hostility. They are "on edge" and easily provoked. They feel separated from the stream of normal life because they actually are rejected by it and their own bodies become strange to them. In a group situation this means an easy flaring of tempers, a tendency to tears and to quarrels, a feeling of desperate loneliness amidst others, a sense of suspicion towards oneself and everybody else. If the situation in the home is accentuated by no stimulation, just waiting, the atmosphere becomes still more charged with hostility or with despair. This is the time when group work services are not only desirable but essential. What they can offer is the relief of this tension, a change of the whole atmosphere in the institution as well as an opportunity for the girls to gain some confidence in other people, which often is badly lacking. This is not an easy task to achieve.

I quote from a record in which the girls themselves describe well their own group situation.

I explained that, generally, girls of their age were interested in having their own groups with their own officers, and planning their own programs. They were very vocal about this subject. They explained that they didn't think this would have worked. It would have left too many girls out. I asked what they meant by this. Evelyn said that now that she is gone, we can mention her name. She said that Nancy would never have been asked in any group because no one liked her. The girls seemed to agree on their dislike for Nancy. They said that she felt that she was better than anyone else. She was always telling stories which they knew were not true. They said there were other girls who would not have been chosen for groups too. They also said that in a group as large as theirs, they really did not trust each other. They were very envious when one girl was in a position of leadership or when one girl bossed them. They were also quick to see that girls really didn't have very much in common. They said they came from different backgrounds and different cultures. They also said we come and we go so much it would be very difficult to form into any group. They mentioned the fact that they felt there was always a spirit of mistrust in the house. They weren't quite able to put their finger on it, but there was an undercurrent which they could not quite touch. They said that the way I had worked had given these girls confidence that they could work together as long as I was planning things. They explained, when I asked them about programs, that they liked a variety of things. Sometimes, they got very tired and restless and did not want to sew . . . that they liked change. The feeling that something was going to happen which would break the routine that they were not quite sure about. They explained, again, that it was very boring not to have anyone coming in.[1]

[1] Sally Story, *Group Work in a Shelter for Unmarried Mothers* (Master's Thesis, Columbia University, School of Social Work, 1951).

The girls realized how difficult it was for them to form into a group. They felt the "mistrust" that prevailed in the house. They had not yet reached a stage where they could do something about this by themselves, but somehow they felt that this was improved when the group worker was with them. They expressed their feelings of restlessness and of boredom and they also realized that they expressed hostility and their need to express it. It is obvious that a great deal of work had to be done to help them to relate to others in a more positive way. It is surprising how this can be learned in a comparatively short time, mainly because of the urgency of the situation. It cannot come by itself. It needs the help of the group worker, who can focus on those interrelationships and can help the girls see how their own feelings relate to the difficulties they have with each other.

Handling Interpersonal Hostilities

In the following quotations an informal committee meeting conducted by the group worker turned into the discussion of relationships towards a girl with whom most in the group had special difficulties.

Quite out of context, Joan turned to me and said, "Have you heard that Louise is coming back to the home?" I indicated that I had not. Joan said, "Well she is and, boy, will that mess up things." I asked what she meant and Joan said that the girls did not like Louise very much and that she couldn't even get along in a work home. She told of some staff comment she had overheard on Louise's return. I asked how she felt about having Louise return. This provoked immediate response from those who were sitting near us. It ranged from "Ish" to "She is a pain in the neck." I asked what Louise had done to make them feel this way about her. Joan said, "Oh, it is her airs. She thinks she is so hot and can do almost anything. She has *education*." Ina broke in and said "Well, golly, Irma has as much education as she has and she doesn't act that way." Irma said, "Well now, I guess an educated person really doesn't act that way. They would know better." I wondered why Louise used her education to express her unhappiness.

We have seen how a committee meeting did not start on its business because the girls were much too upset about somebody whom they disliked re-entering the group situation. It was important that the group worker be sensitive to this and not call them back to "business." When the girls expressed their feelings, the group worker simply asked for facts and let them express themselves further. At this point in the discussion we can see how the girls resented somebody who felt superior to the rest of the group. They wanted to feel that they were "all in the same boat." This was the one safety they were gaining in a situation where they felt quite rejected by the rest of the world. They realized differences in background, but they did not want this to be used in a superior way. The group worker's role would be to understand the feelings of the girls but also to help them accept the one who is returning. This was very essential, since hostility that has been built up before a person even enters a group can take on large dimensions and make work with the group as well as with the newcomer impossible.

The discussion continued:

"Did she feel that a person with education should not have a baby out of wedlock?" Irma remarked, "Well, that's what I cannot understand; she acts like she is proud of this experience, and by golly, some of us . . . most of us do not feel that way about it." I wondered if sometimes we do not act one way when we really feel another. Irma responded with "Sure, but why does she have to talk, talk, talk all the time? You ask a simple question and you get a life history." I asked if she understood why some people do talk about an experience a good deal. Joan injected with a good deal of insight, "Well, I suppose she has to talk about something . . . she even reads her letters aloud to us."

The group worker did not defend Louise. This would have been unrealistic, both because her behavior obviously was very disturbing to the group and because the worker taking her part might alienate her more from the group. She simply asked questions regarding the way people express their feelings and let the girls find the answers for them. In the beginning the girls found general answers for the causes of such behavior, but we see Joan in the last sentence relate some of her understanding of causes for behavior directly to the rejected girl.

I said that I understood that Louise lived some distance from the home and wondered if that might have some bearing on her need to talk with and about something. Geri said, "Washington is far away but, gee, we all get lonesome, but we do not dwell on it."

The girls realized their own feelings but they wanted to maintain their proud independence and in their expression of hostility towards Louise they exaggerated their own strength.

I asked if they had ever talked with Louise about how she felt in the home or whether they had attempted to accept some of what she said on the basis that she really was very unhappy.

The group worker tried to be very direct at this point and in her question lay a suggestion of what the girls should do. The following response shows that this was premature and that it was not accepted by the girls:

Joan said, "Gee, I'm afraid to try. You never know what you are getting into. Anyway, she picks up and drops people. As soon as a new girl comes, she gives her the rush, then when she has exhausted them she turns to someone else." Irma, with her slow drawl, pondered awhile and then said, "She sure is looking for somebody to be her friend." I indicated that I thought it would be rather hard for Louise to come back to the home and wondered whether there was anything the girls could do to help the situation. Irma again took the initiative and said, "I just guess we should try to be friendly to her." Ruby, who rather worships Irma said, "Well, if you can, I guess I can too." Some of the others agreed to this. I indicated that it probably would not be easy at first, but if Louise began to feel that she had some friends in the house, she probably would not be so tense.

The change in attitude towards the disliked girl came through some understanding that especially one of the girls, Irma, had gained in that discussion. Irma apparently was one of the very well accepted girls and, therefore, her understanding that this difficult girl needed friends and that she would try to give her this friendship carried enough weight that the others were willing to join in with her. The group worker sounded the warning so that this did not become too unrealistic and made it clear to them that difficulties might still arise in spite of their trying to accept Louise. Hand in hand with such a group discussion would have to go individual contact with Louise so that she too could learn her part in the group situation. This kind of discussion is helpful not only for the moment but it improves the whole climate of the institution and also helps the girls to understand what makes for human relationships.

Receiving the Newcomer

The fears of the newcomer are especially great in such an institution. Because of the feeling of guilt, the institution very often is pictured in her imagination as punishment for wrongdoing. Nowadays, usually casework services help the girl to know something about the place she is about to enter, but this does not prevent her from continued feelings of anxiety as long as she has not actually arrived. The person responsible for the living group situation will have to play an essential part in receiving the girl. In the following excerpt, which describes the arrival of a newcomer, we see the importance of the first contact.

Mrs. G, the caseworker, brought Ruby, a new girl, to the kitchen and introduced her to the girls. Ruby then sat in the dining room eating alone, so the housemother went in to sit with her. Ruby said she did not like to eat alone. Housemother assured her that she would not have to feel alone at the home, that there was companionship if one desired it. Ruby readily told her whole story. While she was talking she toyed with her food and said she was not hungry. Housemother indicated that she did not have to eat unless she wanted to.

We see how important it was that the housemother did not let the girl eat alone. At this point she needed the feeling that somebody was interested in her and she needed badly to tell her story. The housemother with great sensitivity did not go into the details of the story, knowing that the girl could work this out in other contacts, but she gave her what she needed at this moment: her warm attention, the reassurance that there would be companionship if she needed it, and the indication that nobody would force things on her, symbolized in letting her refuse food if she did not want it. Some weeks later Ruby commented, "You know I was scared when I first came here, but when I found that everyone here was in the same boat and that everyone was so helpful, I didn't feel nearly so bad." "Being in the same boat" would not have been enough. It was important that the common experience was consciously directed so that it became a helpful one instead of one that would intensify fear and guilt.

Utilizing Group Discussions

Elsie was one of the youngest residents that I have known. She had just turned thirteen and her pregnancy had occurred without her understanding much of its import. Elsie was an intelligent girl with artistic ability, but had been sheltered so closely that she had been easily misused by an older man. Elsie was very unhappy and very frightened when she came to the institution. Most of the girls were considerably older than she was. They were kind to her, but they certainly had many different interests from hers. To Elsie the regular club meetings that the group worker held meant the difference between months of deep despair and a healthy experience of which she today talks as one that gave her not only a great deal of knowledge about herself but in which she learned to get along with people very different from herself and learned that time does not have to hang heavily on one's hands if one continues working on certain skills.

For instance, Elsie was yearning for school, but she could not continue her school work while expecting her child. The group worker helped her to get a typewriter and Elsie acquired a skill in typing which would have taken much longer at school. In the club meetings the girls did some singing and the group worker accompanied them on the piano. Elsie said that she had started piano lessons and asked whether it would be all right if she could practice some. She soon became a vital part of the group, in spite of her youth, because of her ability to play the piano, and she again increased a skill, making her feel that the time was not just wasted in waiting. She was asked to be part of a planning committee that worked out programs for special events, and her young and enthusiastic mind helped her make good suggestions that gave her status even in the eyes of the older girls.

She was frightened by the many discussions regarding childbirth that the girls had among themselves and she asked the group worker whether they could not have such discussions in group sessions. The group worker and the nurse of the home conducted the meetings, giving pertinent information as well as allowing for discussion periods, which brought out much anxiety and many of the girls were relieved. Elsie contributed to these discussions by expressing most frankly her fears but also by openly expressing relief. At one time in the discussions she said, "I understand much better now. I just will have to relax. I do remember when the cow had a calf. She just lay down calmly and I guess that's what I will have to do." Elsie also needed a great deal of reassurance regarding her status after leaving the institution. Casework interviews were a source of great help because realistic planning was introduced. At the same time she asked anxiously about group discussions on the same subject, wanting to know whether others believed that it was possible for her to become a normal little girl again.

PROGRAM COMBINING THERAPEUTIC MEDIA

For a long time it was thought that the burden of distress was best relieved by intensive work. We all realize that there is therapeutic value in work, but only if it does not take the degrading aspect of punishment. We then learned that distress is relieved by talking it out, but we know now that this is not enough if it is not accompanied by a positive solution for dealing with the expressed feelings. We then suggested that recreation and creative enjoyment would be a helpful medium, and we found that this was true, but only if it was not used as a flight from reality. It is clear that all these media, *work*, *catharsis* and *insight* into one's feelings, and *creative enjoyment*, create a really therapeutic environment only if they are used in conjunction.

The relief of monotony of institutional life will come best through an intelligently thought-out program that combines these three media. A small excerpt of a record shows how this is recognized by the girls themselves.

Kitty remarked that she was going to enjoy sitting down while she still had an opportunity. This led to a discussion regarding delivery. Kitty shuddered and said, "Boy, I hope they gas me up and let go." Mary, who had just shortly had her child, answered, "It wasn't really so bad, but I shut my eyes when they put my little girl on my stomach after delivery," and she added, "I guess I wasn't sure whether it was all real and whether she was all right." The group worker said that many people feel that way. Joyce, who is the next girl scheduled for delivery, twisted in her chair and said, "I wish this business were over and I knew a little more about it." Kitty asked when the group could start some real discussion on childbirth and have the movies that had been suggested.

We see in this informal discussion the anxiety that the girls have about the birth process itself, and how the group worker lets them express this in her presence. The record continues:

Suddenly Kitty asked the worker, "Are you a social worker?" Worker said yes and explained that she was one kind of social worker, a worker that helped groups . . . a social group worker. A social group worker enjoys working with groups, helping them plan activities that they might enjoy and discussing things they would like to know more about or might be puzzled about. Kitty remarked, "Boy, can we use you."

The group worker's interpretation of her function includes the provision of enjoyable activities and of helping the group plan for them as well as the opportunity to discuss their feelings. This coming after an expression of great anxiety gives the girls the needed reassurance that their needs are considered and can be fulfilled.

Program in such an institution can be as varied as program in any other place. It will relate to the situation of being pregnant, but not exclusively. In many of these institutions it was found especially helpful to the young women to have some of the perfectly normal activity that would be offered to their age group at any other time. Picnics and parties represent so much enjoyment in life that they were especially highly considered. They also fulfilled the craving for some special food. Most pregnant women nowadays live according to some form of a diet. In a good institution the diet too will be individualized, according to the different needs of the girls. Nevertheless, diet always means some deprivation. In people who are emotionally deprived this has additional disturbing meaning. Parties are usually one way of relieving the monotony of diet and the gratification of "breaking the rules." It is important in such an institution that the group worker and the dietician work as a team on this question. If they work separately the situation may lead to additional tension and additional guilt feelings. The girls might use the group worker against the dietician. If dietician and group worker work closely together, meals can be planned so that the party allows for special food without harming the girls.

An excerpt of a record shows how much meaning food has to the person who feels rejected and hostile.

The girls said that everything was fine for the picnic supper except the nurse had decided that canned wieners should be used. Barbara was particularly disturbed and was quite expressive in dislike for the canned wieners. "Whoever heard of a picnic with canned wieners?" Geri asked worker if she thought they could all chip in and buy some others at the store.

The discussion continued with a great deal of anger and hostility expressed. The girls were ready to use the group worker against the nurse who had made the decision.

Worker suggested that perhaps the girls should try one over the fire to see whether they would work. Mrs. J (the nurse) accepted this and so did the girls. Edith roasted one and broke it into pieces for the other three. There was a silence and then Barbara said, "Well it isn't too bad if you plaster it with mustard." Edith commented, "I think we can use these—after all, they let us have cocoa."

The worker did not let herself be used in the argument. She helped the girls to make their decision according to the reality of the taste of the wieners. She allowed them to save face without arguing with them. These small incidents sound trivial, but they are the ones that make the stuff of life and help us to learn to get along with others and with limits imposed upon us.

The short time available might help the girls to learn skills in homemaking or to widen their horizon about other possibilities they have never discovered in themselves. Often our thinking is that they especially want to do something related to babies, but some girls cannot take this because they actually reject the idea of motherhood. To some it might be much more important to have activities that have no relation to their state of pregnancy but relate to everyday community life. A good library and some discussion of books might be just what they need. Painting has often proven especially valuable because it is an outlet for feelings and a creative experience for which few people have opportunities. With the younger girls everyday kinds of games are something they actually need, because their need to be children is just as great as the need to understand their adult role. After a grab-bag session Tena, a fifteen-year-old, said, "You would start all this interesting stuff just when I'm going to the hospital." And when they talked about campfire singing and perhaps having a campfire outside the home, Julie commented, "Gee, it would be fun to have an old-fashioned marshmallow roast."

USE OF VOLUNTEERS

As in every home, the *use of volunteers* can be very valuable. I repeat again as I have said before that the use of volunteers is one of the best ways to interpret a program. The citizen who is directly informed about a program and who has participated in it will be best able to support it in an intelligent way. In a home for unmarried mothers, the use of the volunteer has to be handled with special caution because of the need for confidentiality. The girls have to be sure that confidentiality is respected, and the volunteer can only be a person who understands this and is willing to adhere strictly to it.

The following quotations are from a group worker's record of her introduction of the volunteer to her job, and it gives us information about what the volunteer is expecting in her work and what has to be done to make work for her comfortable while also making it profitable for the girls in the institution.

I met Mrs. B in the reception room. She appeared to be a warm, vital, rather motherly individual with a pleasant smile. I asked her if she had ever been at the home. Mrs. B indicated that she had not seen the home so I showed her the place and arranged to have the conference in the room where the sewing activity she was to conduct would be held.

This is the first meeting between the volunteer and the group worker. The group worker wants first to be sure what kind of a personality the volunteer presents. Her description indicates that she is the kind of person who seems to be suited to work in the home. The group worker realizes that it is important to know the surroundings into which one comes and she therefore first shows the house to the volunteer and also arranges the conference in the room in which the volunteer will work with the girls.

After some preliminary chatter Mrs. B told of her other experiences at community centers, etc. She said she had thought about the work here a great deal and had a million questions to ask. I remarked that that was wonderful and I would help her as much as possible.

It is important that the worker start with something that is familiar to the volunteer, because every new situation fills people with some doubt about their competence. By giving her an opportunity to talk about the places where she has worked she helps her to be on more secure ground. This also establishes a friendly relationship between the worker and the volunteer and the volunteer feels free to ask the questions she has in her mind.

She asked first about ages and backgrounds of the girls. I explained that there was variety in both ages and backgrounds and sketched briefly the current picture of the home. She asked about economic background. Again I mentioned that this varied a great deal depending upon the residents at the time, but no girl would be handicapped in choice of project simply by the lack of funds. The agency is willing to arrange for any reasonable expenditures.

The volunteer starts out wanting to know something about the girls she is working with. The worker relates some of the questions directly back to the project they have in mind, namely, the sewing. This leads into some of the specific discussions regarding this project.

She seemed to be eager to know as much about them as possible. Did they like fashions? What were the sewing backgrounds, etc.? I indicated that we did not have that information but that it might be an excellent way to begin the activity . . . that is, general discussion of what they wanted perhaps stimulated by samples and ideas that Mrs. B would bring.

Here the worker uses the question of the volunteer to help her directly with some program suggestion.

"Well, how will they react to me?" she asked. I indicated it was not possible to foretell the reaction. The girls are interested in making something and they want to start as soon as possible. They also know that the instructor is skilled and has taught other classes of girls. I wondered how Mrs. B expected them to react to her. She laughed and said, "Well, I suppose they will react just like my other classes . . . a little shy at first and then when they get started in a project they will warm up." I indicated that it seemed to be a normal reaction. The girls had been responsive to all other activities. Most of them are unhappy about their present circumstances, and it was one of the functions of the home to help them adjust in as many areas as possible. I also explained that probably if the girl is seriously disturbed, she might not participate in the group immediately. If Mrs. B felt she needed help with a particular girl or found some girl who was having difficulty adjusting in the group, then I would discuss it with her.

The volunteer expresses some anxiety in meeting the group, the way everybody feels fear before a new endeavor. The group worker reacts to this in three ways: (1) She reassures the volunteer by giving her some indication of how the girls have reacted to previous activities. (2) She allows the volunteer to express her own feelings regarding what she expects. (3) She promises continued help if the situation should become too difficult.

"It's nice to know that I'm not alone in this project," Mrs. B remarked. "Now that I have that straightened out in my mind, my other questions are about method and equipment." Mrs. B asked whether she should set up units or have projects. I said that the girls could help her decide on what type of things would be most satisfying . . . the interests expressed by the girls would give her the most clues.

Without naming it, the worker is interpreting one of the basic group work principles, namely, the right of the individual to participate in the choice of program.

"There is only one other thing that I have been wondering about, what if I recognize a girl?" asked Mrs. B. I indicated that this might be possible and asked her what she thought she might do. Mrs. B indicated that she supposed she would wait to see if the girl recognized her first and if not she would proceed as though they had never met. I said that this probably was a good way to handle it. I explained that confidentiality was a factor and that the girls used first names only. I explained the importance of keeping this confidentiality.

The question of confidentiality is not introduced first by the worker but arises naturally out of the questions brought out by the volunteer. This makes it much more practical for the volunteer than if it had been presented in a routine fashion. If it had not come up, the worker certainly would have had to broach the subject herself. Yet in general we can be quite sure that this question will arise in the course of the discussion and we can wait for interpretation until it becomes more meaningful.

There was discussion on the best time for the class. Mrs. B also asked that I come to the first part of the first session to help with "breaking the ice." I said that I would be happy to help with introductions, and that I was certain that once the group assembled and they began to discuss a mutual interest things would progress very nicely.

We see that the anxiety of the volunteer is not completely allayed by the discussion and that she still needs tangible evidence that the group worker will be there when she needs help. It is very important that this help not be refused. The group worker is accepting her anxiety and at the same time gives her the feeling that she respects Mrs. B's competence and is sure that she will be able to carry on.

I quote next from the first meeting conducted by the volunteer and in part observed by the group worker to show how much this introduction has helped.

Mrs. B met me and asked if I would sit in on this meeting because she was not certain what the response would be. I again assured her that the girls wanted to sew and would warm up as soon as they felt secure with her. I also indicated that I would sit in on the meeting and help her if she felt she wanted help.

The girls came in in pairs and picked up their chairs as they entered. I introduced them to Mrs. B informally and after several had come they began to respond by introducing themselves. Mrs. B in a pleasant manner asked how much experience the girls had had in sewing.

The worker repeats to the volunteer the importance of the project to the girls and also stands by as long as the volunteer thinks that she needs this help. During the following part of the meeting, the worker stays in the room and observes that Mrs. B is establishing a friendly and easy relationship with the girls. At one point she observes that the girls were so absorbed in their activity that they didn't seem to notice visitors passing by the room. The group worker realizes that Mrs. B is now quite obviously capable of continuing the meeting by herself. At an opportune moment she leaves.

After the meeting I complimented Mrs. B on her excellent beginning and the ability to give the girls warmth. She was pleased and said she felt she would enjoy working with the girls. I said that we might want to arrange a time periodically to discuss the progress of the group and talk about any individual problems that might appear.

It is important that the volunteer not be left after the first meeting without having heard any comment regarding the way she has handled the meeting. The comments of the group worker give her an additional feeling of self-confidence and open up the possibility for positive supervisory relationships. How much the volunteer gained through this work and the accompanying supervision is seen in the excerpt of a supervision record written after several months.

Mrs. B told of Anna's flat statement that she had never made anything, her shy manner, etc. I asked her what she had done about it. She smiled and said that she had not thought of that consciously before, but she helped her choose a simple project and encouraged her whenever she could. "You know, I can see those kids loosen up. When they come in at first they are shy and maybe afraid. After they have been in the home a while they loosen up considerably." . . . Mrs. B commented that she was learning so much about people.

Mrs. B began to individualize the girls and relate the activity to their specific needs, this way making her contribution a really helpful one. At the same time she herself gained satisfaction from a job well done and from the enjoyment of learning.

I chose the Home for Unmarried Mothers as an example of the vital importance of the quality of group experience in institutions with short-term placement. This kind of institution—and also detention homes—plays an especially important role because of the intensity of emotions involved at the moment of entrance into the institution. The social group worker's task is to create a climate that allows for free expression of feelings as well as to open up ways of dealing with them in a manner that makes them less painful to the individual involved and allows him to live with others.

The example chosen should point out again the interlocking of *all* therapeutic measures, individual interviews, physical care, group discussions, activity programs, and interest shown by the lay community. With the increase of unmarried mothers of school age, cooperation with the schools becomes very important. No unmarried mother should be deprived of education just because of pregnancy.

Larger homes for unmarried mothers will use the professionally trained group worker in pretty much the same role as described in relation to children's institutions. Smaller homes might use the services of a group worker who comes in from the "outside," taking on these functions in a more limited time span.

5. SOCIAL GROUP WORK IN INSTITU-TIONS FOR HANDICAPPED CHILDREN

We talk a great deal about fighting prejudice, thinking of prejudice in terms of race, color, and creed. We forget that in our society some of the people who suffer most from prejudice are the ones with physical or mental handicaps. While medical knowledge marches forward in great strides and provides hope for many, a large part of our population is not aware of this progress and adheres to preconceived notions regarding certain handicaps.

Because in Biblical times leprosy could not be healed and was one of the most dreaded diseases, we are still segregating people with leprosy in the twentieth century, in spite of the fact that modern science can arrest it more easily than other sicknesses which sound much less frightening to the modern world.

Epilepsy is another such unfortunate disease. Many epileptics still have difficulties in obtaining jobs and in being admitted to social affairs. And yet modern medicine is able to control epilepsy to a large degree and we know that seizures would occur less frequently if the person with this sickness would not have to stand up against so many pressures. Because in ancient times people were frightened by the writhing of the human body in a seizure and marked it as the work of the devil, the intelligent well-qualified epileptic of the twentieth century is still looked upon with suspicion. In a group of young adults who suffered from *grand mal* seizures, not a single seizure occurred in over twenty meetings. Nevertheless, an otherwise progressive community agency raised serious questions regarding the attendance of some of the members of this group at their social affairs because they were afraid of an "attack." It needed a great deal of interpretation to let them see that their judgment was based on prejudice against a sickness they knew very little about.

A college student told me that because of her speech handicap her parents had always kept her in the house and never allowed her to play with other children until past the age of adolescence. It was the parents' own fear of having "a damaged child" that made them increase the handicap under which their child was suffering.

Besides the misconceptions and prejudices that directly reflect on the personality of the patient, there are prejudices related to their capacity to fulfill certain tasks. It is not so long ago that we expected a blind person to be able only to make brooms or sell pencils in the streets, while we note today that they can fill practically every job that a sighted person can fill. The person with cerebral palsy who has difficult muscle coordination is really very handicapped, but we have seen them fulfilling professional responsibilities.

Aside from the prejudice of society around him, the handicapped person has to deal with the overprotection that comes frequently from his closer environment, with his own feelings of inadequacy and frustration, and with the reality of the limitation of his handicap. Work with handicapped people will lie in the area of training them to stretch the limits imposed on them, of relating them to their own disability as something that must be accepted without being thwarted by it, and in relating them to an environment that will react to them differently than it will towards persons without handicaps. One of the young seizure patients who had gained a great deal in the therapeutic group work discussions said at the end of the treatment situation, "What amazes me most and helps me most is that I'm not afraid of people anymore and that I like myself better." The pride in oneself and one's own capacity that we hope to achieve in all education is also the goal in working with the handicapped, and this also includes the mentally handicapped. Often far greater effort is needed to achieve this.

GROUP WORKER'S ROLE

In institutional work with handicapped children we have to consider the same questions as in other institutional work with children. One housemother in an institution for the blind said to me, "I soon learned that they are children like all others, with their difficulties and with their lovability." The role of the group worker, therefore, in such institutions will not be different from the one in any other institution; the difference will lie in his own better understanding of the specific handicap he is working with and his capacity to help others on the staff to relate to it. It is important that he help the houseparents to individualize the children and realize that they are working with Susan, who is blind, or Joe, who has seizures, but never with *the* blind or *the* epileptic child, and that the handicap means different things to different people. He will have to adapt his approach to the specific handicap of the child. A blind child, for instance, will especially need human touch and the sound of a pleasant voice, while the deaf child will recognize human affection mainly through touch and sight.

In working with children who have cardiac diseases, the group worker will have to deal with the need of all children to be active and yet offer these children restricted forms of activity. He will have to use his imagination in finding activities that will give the youngsters outlet for their energies. At the same time he must be able to interpret to them why they cannot do certain things and allow them again to express their negative feelings about being different from others.

Helping Parents Accept Handicapped Children

Group work with parents will be especially important in such institutions. The parents of the handicapped child very often feel extremely guilty about this situation. I have seen otherwise well-informed parents who continually search in an almost irrational way for the causes of their child's affliction. The parents of three children, two of them perfectly healthy and one a severely spastic child, were continually searching for the answer as to how this happened. They were intelligent people and realized that it could not be their fault, and yet one day the young mother said almost desperately, "Maybe I should not have had her that summer; I was just too tired out and too occupied with the other two." It was perfectly clear that rationally she knew that this had nothing to do with her child's sickness, but unconsciously she was still punishing herself for what had happened. It is a frightening experience to any healthy adult to be confronted with a child born different from other children. Youngsters handicapped at a later age usually do not constitute quite such a serious problem as regards the feelings of the parents.

Mentally handicapped children are even harder for parents to take, because our society puts a high premium on intellectual achievement and mental retardation usually presents a kind of final failure. Group work with parents of mentally handicapped children has proved of immense value. When they were alone, they considered their situation as such a shameful one that they did not want to talk about it. In group meetings they began to see themselves as part of a larger fraternity and they helped each other to overcome those feelings of frustration, unhappiness, and futility. They achieved better understanding of themselves as well as of the children and their possibilities and limitations, and, therefore, they could help the children get along better when they were out of the institution or could accept their being institutionalized.

Special Problems of Houseparents

In working with houseparents in institutions for handicapped children, it was seen that special emphasis had to be placed on their understanding and accepting the parents. The houseparents very often felt that they were the ones who did all the work and, therefore, they felt jealous and resentful when parents visited and received in that short time so much affection from the youngsters. The houseparents have to be helped with their feelings of resentment towards the actual parents and be made to see how hard some of these parents have to struggle to accept institutionalization of their children. They have to be helped to see that the parents have only a short time with their children and need to feel accepted by them, because otherwise their guilt increases even more.

In general, the group worker's role will be mostly working with the staff. Institutions dealing with the handicapped usually represent long-term placement and, therefore, there will be greater need to help with the daily group living situations. The houseparents need somebody with whom they can discuss the problems of the changing group, of how to relate individual children to group life, of how to handle discipline, which will be handled somewhat differently in an institution for mentally retarded children than in an institution where children can easily follow verbal explanations.

The group worker especially will have to take on the responsibility of making the group life of the houseparents themselves a stimulating and enjoyable one. Because of the long-term situation in these institutions, life can become very monotonous for the staff and this may reflect in the work they are doing with the children. A person who is only half alive cannot give stimulation to others. Houseparents need stimulating group life in the institution as well as interests outside of their place of work. It is extremely important to make a real effort in this direction. In many institutions the houseparents' group is an extremely ingrown one. They talk only to each other, discussing continually the problems of the children under their care or the problems directly related to their own living situation on the campus, as, for instance, the food, etc. Very often this results in a great deal of gossip and an almost morbid interest in everybody else's business. This can be avoided only if there are events that take the staff out of the "rut." Healthy family life among houseparents certainly is one of the most helpful factors, because this resembles closest the regular community situation. Hopefully, institutions no longer will be located in isolated areas. Community resources then will be readily available to both staff and clients.

Relationship to Teaching Personnel

A third special role the group worker will carry in these institutions is the relationship to the teaching personnel. Most institutions for the handicapped have strong educational purposes as the heart of the institutional effort. Very often the school is on the institution grounds. The group worker with his knowledge of individual as well as group dynamics can be the mental health consultant to the teachers in such institutions. Their focus must be on educational rehabilitation, and the worker can help them with the emotional implications of their work and be a resource for grouping and special attention in the classroom. At the same time, he will be the link between the teacher and the houseparent. In one of the larger institutions for deaf children, I heard special complaints about the fact that teachers and houseparents worked at cross-purposes, each expecting the other to take on responsibility for a child's behavior.

When Marge, for instance, threw a temper tantrum in the morning, the housemother did not force her to put on a certain dress but thought it more helpful for her to keep on what she had and discuss this calmly with her after return from school. The teacher, unaware of this, immediately commented on Marge's inappropriate dress and sent her back to the cottage, telling her that she was not to return until she had changed. The housemother had a more upset Marge on her hands.

In keeping a regular tab on the pulse of the whole group living in the institution and seeing it as a task to coordinate such services, the group worker will help to establish a system in which quick communication and cooperation between the different staff groupings is possible. This is partially an administrative responsibility and might be carried by the superintendent, but for educational purposes this task can be taken over by the group worker. In establishing a friendly cooperative spirit between houseparents and teachers through special events and common staff meetings and courses, they will spontaneously accept the responsibility of communicating with each other. If they once in awhile fail to do so, it will not lead to bitter accusation but to a realization that a mistake was made and can be avoided the next time.

Large custodial institutions of the mentally retarded have often given up hope of any individualization of the residents. Case work contacts are often impossible because of the inability of the patients to verbalize, and the institution has seen no way to give them any other individualized attention. The group work method aims at and can accomplish individualization in such a group and is using as its tool a great deal of nonverbal material. In a large institution of low-grade mentally retarded children, two volunteers with group work training started working with groups of ten or twelve members picked at random out of the mass of patients. In a few months they saw an amazing increase in the capacity of these patients to do certain things for themselves. The difference actually was so great that there was a feeling on the part of some of the staff that the project should not be continued, because it gave such advantages to some patients while the others had nothing. What it really proved was that such services are indispensable if we realize that even in these institutions custodial care alone is not sufficient.

We can help many patients to become more satisfied and use their limited capacities better than if such attention is not given. One of these groups, for instance, was a group of adolescent girls, and the worker indicated how much it meant to them to have some of the adolescent need of adventure fulfilled. Of course, she had to adapt her methods to the low mentality of the youngsters. Limitations, for instance, had to be given quite definitely and very completely, and planning could be done only on a very short-term and simple basis, but it was important that it was done at all, even if it consisted only in preparing some simple paper strips for a party. There was a feeling of accomplishment in such small ways.

In institutions for the handicapped main emphasis of the group worker's function will lie on work with the houseparents, on coordination between the teaching staff and the houseparent, and on direct group work with parents of the institutionalized children.

The group worker should help establish small activity groups among patients which can give them opportunity for planning and enjoyment.

As with everyone else on the staff, he will need to be an interpreter to the community for helping overcome the many prejudices that exist in regard to our handicapped population.

6. SOCIAL GROUP WORK IN INSTITUTIONS FOR JUVENILE DELINQUENTS

But when you get hunted—that's different. Something happens to you. You ain't strong; maybe you are fierce, but you ain't strong. . . .[1]

The being hunted, not always by the law, but *feeling* hunted, is part of being a delinquent, and, with the intuitive understanding of the great writer, Steinbeck has seen that this does not put new strength in the person, but that it only produces a pretended strength—fierceness—a sullen defiance of the world. As a contrast to this, let us look at what Karl Menninger once said about mental health

. . . as the adjustment of human beings to the world and to each other with a maximum of effectiveness and happiness. . . . It is the ability to maintain an even temper, an alert intelligence, socially considerate behavior and a happy disposition.

It is a long road from hunted fierceness to "maximum of effectiveness and happiness."

[1] John Steinbeck, *The Grapes of Wrath* (New York: Viking, 1939).

WHO ARE DELINQUENTS?

Who are delinquents? There is Jerry, who together with a bunch of four or five boys opened a car, jumped into it and drove it with wild speed through the night. By morning they had run the car into the ditch and soon were picked up by the police. It was Jerry's first offense, but he had been known in school for stealing, boasting, and bad language. Jerry's home is crowded, one room for four children. Both parents work hard, but it is difficult to make ends meet.

There is Joyce, solemn and disheveled, found with obvious marks of the use of drugs. Joyce lives with her family in one of the comfortable suburbs of a large city in a nice home. The parents have cared about their children and are completely bewildered.

There is thin-faced Donald, with big hungry eyes, who has a long history of homosexual experiences and who is a chain smoker at the age of twelve.

There is laughing and kind young Celia, who has been found dancing naked in a night club and who doesn't quite understand the fuss that is made about all this.

There is eleven-year-old Hans, who was brought into an institution for delinquents in Germany just when I visited it. When asked what he had stolen, he said in a tearful voice, "old iron from the ruins." The stern reply was, "You know that that is not allowed, don't you?" The boy nodded tearfully. "With whom were you when you stole?" "With my mother," was the unhappy answer.

When we look at these pictures, we see clearly that the word "delinquent" does not give us any indication of the child himself, of who he is, what his problem is, what the causes are, why he is doing something that society cannot approve of. We find everybody among the delinquent: the highly intelligent, the dull, the one from high economic stratum and the one from the slums, the one whose disturbance has already gone so far that it will take years of treatment, the one who will need only a short time for recovery, and perhaps the one for whom we today do not know any remedy. "Delinquent" is a term that gives no definition of personality, background, or sickness. It only says that the child has been before the juvenile court or before some judge and has been declared delinquent.

Treatment or Punishment?

Because of this generalization, the treatment of the juvenile delinquent is very difficult. The problems that institutions for juvenile delinquents are facing are of such a variety that their task is most difficult. Foremost is the question of punishment or treatment for the delinquent, depending on different theories of human behavior. The confusion about this issue is clearly seen in a general information bulletin given to staff members of a Boys' State Training School. One of the paragraphs reads:

Our school has been created for the purpose of affording training and treatment for delinquent boys. We must remember that most of them have become socially maladjusted through no fault of their own . . . they are in need of special examinations and diagnosis, they are in need of specialized treatment and training. They are confused in their thinking; "all mixed up," as some boys will put it. They have not understood what society demands of them. They come to us frustrated and disturbed individuals; therefore, our purpose shall be to prepare these boys so that they may be restored to society to function as normal and adequate individuals according to their capacities and abilities.

We see here the expression of treatment goals and of individualization in diagnosis and the goal as the youngster's being able to function in society. Yet we see at another part in the same bulletin:

Boys may earn an earlier release provided they maintain the good record in their shop placements or their work assignments. A total of three days good time may be earned for each month of good conduct, and satisfactory achievement in school or shop placement. . . .

Misconduct reports and poor achievement will add to a boy's length of stay. A boy is permitted 30 demerits without penalty. Beyond that he is penalized one month for every 30 demerits that he accumulates. . . .

A boy is usually penalized an additional period of three months for an escape. However, the disciplinary committee may modify or extend the extra lengths of stay depending on the circumstances.

While the goal is treatment, the method is related to punishment, and the language used is the one that we find in adult correctional institutions, as, for instance, "earning good time."

Without discussing at this point the merits or faults of this system, all I want to point out is the confusion regarding treatment and punishment. We will be able to clarify and to come to an agreement regarding this only (1) if we learn more about the way people develop and their motivations for behavior, and (2) if we have long-time research on treatment methods. We do have long-time experience with repressive methods, and it is proved that those have not helped in the fight against juvenile delinquency. Only if we use our best scientific knowledge about people combined with our knowledge of methods that have worked in many other circumstances and then test those over a longer period of time will we be able to decide which ones are really helpful. What I am presenting here is the use of one method among many others. I am aware of the fact that the group work method is but one among many others. The group work method has increasingly been used in delinquency institutions since the first publication of this book. Yet more and better use of it is needed.

Inheritance, Intelligence, and Environment

For a long time we thought that all behavior and all qualities in the human being are inherited. The program with juvenile delinquents, therefore, could only be to train them like one trains animals, because it was thought that basically the inherited qualities could not be changed. We seldom find this concept in pure form in the United States, but it is sometimes still found in the way an attendant will express himself, for instance, by saying, "what can you expect of him; his parents are not any better." In 1950 I found in Germany in many institutions the theory of inherited behavior. (It had been greatly supported during the Nazi period.) I remember that I once asked a director of a training school why most of the boys were committed to the institution, and the surprising answer was, *"Schlechte Erbmasse"* (bad heritage). Out of this idea can grow only a rigid handling of the youngster, since, as I mentioned before, there is actually no hope for basic improvement but only a possibility of preventing him through fear from repeating behavior.

This school of thought was closely related to the concept that all delinquency was caused by low intelligence. Again, we will find remnants of this even in our present time. I recall in an institution for delinquents asking whether it might not be helpful to the girls to participate in deciding how their rooms should be painted. The answer was, "They can't do this, they are too dumb." When I asked whether they were all of low intelligence, the answer—given with great assurance—was, "There are no intelligent girls here—if they were intelligent, they would not be here." The theory of low intelligence being responsible for delinquency and crime seemed to be proved scientifically by psychological tests forty or fifty years ago. Up to 70 or 80 per cent of criminals and delinquents showed a very low intelligence level on the Binet test.

It was only during World War I that newly designed tests given to draftees showed that previous scores had indicated literacy and education rather than basic intelligence. Psychologists found

. . . later in civilian life that several reformatory populations were closely like draftees, and the people generally in respect to intelligence—age for age. . . .[2]

There were many other discoveries which disproved the idea that low intelligence was the cause for delinquency. For us today it is important to see that we do not still maintain this kind of thinking.

Our next theory regarding the cause of delinquency made environmental factors solely responsible for delinquency. There is no question that there is a great deal of truth in this. Crowded housing, the constant contact with adults in their most intimate relations, the frustration that occurs in slum living, has a great deal to do with driving a child away from home and into committing delinquent acts. Yet we saw that again this was not *the* cause of delinquency, but only one of them, since we have seen delinquency occurring in children from good social environment.

The next step in our understanding of delinquency came through the findings of psychiatry and, especially, psychoanalysis. We learned how much early environment can mean to a child, how important the relationships to father and mother are in the development of feelings. The new knowledge that grew out of this gave us some understanding of why children from homes that were socially well situated also showed difficulties. We learned what a cold and loveless en-

[2] Robert H. Gault, "Highlights of 40 Years in the Correctional Field and Looking Ahead," *Federal Probation*, March, 1953, p. 3.

vironment could do to a child, even if all worldly goods were available.

But this interpretation has also been misused and exaggerated, and when considered the sole factor in delinquency has even done harm. The wave of punishment inflicted on parents rests a great deal on an exaggerated application of this thinking. In simplifying the psychoanalytic findings, it was decided that the guilty ones are always the parents, because they have not given enough love and attention to their children. In recent years there has been a movement from punishing behavior towards children to just as punishing an attitude towards parents. The anxiety created in parents by this might prevent them from raising their children freely and happily. In fact, such thinking has often led to an almost tragic and irrational feeling of guilt on the part of parents when their children failed to fulfill the hopes placed in them, and especially when those children showed asocial behavior.

I remember the desperate cry of an intelligent warmhearted mother whose son had gotten himself into some difficulties: "I'm asking myself over and over again what I have done to produce this?" It was difficult for her to accept the fact that each human being is different and unique and something is created in them that is not exclusively related to direct heritage or to their wider environment or to the way their parents have treated them. It is strange that all of us accept the fact that some people are born with a tendency to gain weight easily when they eat, even if their parents have not this body structure, but we will not accept this kind of individualization in the emotional area.

Scientific findings have taught us that human beings are greatly influenced by their early relationships, by the social and physical environment in which they grow up, and by some factors that they inherit, though often not directly from their parents. We have not yet discovered what produces the factor which makes every human being so completely unique. It is our task to do further research on this. At this point in history we do not know the answer. It is very important that we acknowledge this limitation.

To summarize: Our belief in inheritance has made us give disciplinary training instead of education and treatment and has encouraged punishment.

Our belief in environment as a sole factor has made us neglect the emotional and psychological conflicts inside the human being.

Our belief that the emotional and psychological factors are the only important ones has made us stereotype our diagnosis and, in spite of the effort to individualize, we have used too many generalizations in trying to understand the individual.

If we combine what we know and in all humbleness accept the fact that we do not know everything, we will gain a much more therapeutic attitude and also recognize the need for more research.

Needs of Adolescents

Hyman S. Lippman once defined delinquency in the following way:

Delinquency is an outlet for hostility engendered in a people that is either subjugated or has been deprived of gratifications which are vitally needed.[3]

We can accept this definition here in relation to all delinquents, realizing that "gratifications which are vitally needed" might be different ones in different people or at least their degree might be different. For instance, everybody needs love and affection. Some people will be able to have a happy and constructive life receiving a minimum of this; others have to

[3] Hyman S. Lippman, "Preventing Delinquency," *Federal Probation*, March, 1953.

gain a great deal. If they do not receive this affection in large quantities, their hostility rises. There is also different capacity among people of gaining gratification of such vital needs, even if it is not directly offered to them by their closest environment. It is amazing to see, for instance, that there are children from cold and rejecting parents who somehow are able to find gratification of their needs for affection in a neighbor woman or a teacher or even in relationships with their contemporaries and so can provide themselves with the emotional food they are not receiving at home.

Who are our delinquent children?

In 1967 approximately 811,000 children were brought to the attention of the juvenile courts. There are four times as many boys as girls represented in this figure.

The majority of the boys are brought in for stealing or malicious mischief. Most of the girls are brought in for running away, sexual offenses, or being difficult to handle.

The majority of delinquents are between fifteen and seventeen years old. Approximately 35 per cent of them have been before the courts on one or more previous occasions. The age of first apprehension is mostly during early adolescence.[4] Boys show a much higher degree of delinquency than girls. We are not very sure, though, that this gives us a true picture. It might very well be that girls are not as easily brought before the courts as boys because of society's more protective attitude towards them. Our society allows the boy a greater amount of acting out. The boy's hostility is mainly expressed in stealing (and in most cases it is stealing of cars, which gives him the means of quick movement and a saturation of adventure spirit), while the girl expresses her hostility and her insecurity in sex delinquency and running away. We can easily see that this has a great deal to do with our cultural pattern. Sex de-

[4] See also "Juvenile Court Statistics 1967," Children's Bureau Statistical Series No. 93, 1969.

linquency may also satisfy the adolescent sense of adventure. A fifteen-year-old girl once told me in an interview that she wished she could go out and fight, as the boys were doing (this was during World War II). She expressed her great resentment about learning how to cook and sew. She would like to fly an airplane. And then she added, "Sure, I go out in the evening and let the boys kiss me. I really don't care much about them, but at least it is *something* exciting." Interest in sex was actually quite low in this girl, but the sex activity meant adventure and excitement.

Few delinquent acts are committed by a boy or a girl alone. Most of them are committed in a group or "gang." The group is extremely important to all teen-agers, but especially important to the one who feels insecure and who needs support to bolster his own feelings of inadequacy. We mentioned in a previous chapter that the group is for the adolescent the main source of security when he begins to reject the adult. The delinquent filled with feelings of angry hostility needs the protection of the group even more. Also, only the group makes possible for him the fulfillment of his adventurous desires and gives him, for the time being, the feeling that he is somebody important in a community that he himself respects and accepts.

How important the group is I realized again recently when a sixteen-year-old girl, who had a short time before left the institution, said to me, "Oh, I have not had a car ride for such a long time!" I reminded her that we had had a ride the previous day, and the reply was, "I don't mean *that* kind of a ride. I mean with the gang!"

Harry W. Lindeman, Judge of the Juvenile and Domestic Relations Court of Essex County, wrote in his report on the shooting of an Essex County resident by three young boys:

These boys were seeking status which they were unable to attain as individuals. They sought status within the group, approved by the group, in the performance of overt acts which, as individuals probably none of them would have committed. In each instance of delinquency, it was a common act performed by two or more boys. Singularly, no single act of delinquency was traced to any one boy, but rather to the group whose combined thinking, acting, participation, was motivated by this strong subconscious desire for status. Somehow this status was not created in them by their adjustments at home, in school, or through their religious programs.

I cannot stress too strongly how important status actually is to children. All children, yes all adults, crave status. It is a prime factor in developing well-balanced, well-integrated personalities. It is at the same time the one factor which is most likely to be overlooked by the average person and by otherwise well-informed parents. Many children have status within the home. It is equally important to the child to have a real status outside of the home, that is, in the community, in his club, in his recreation, and with his associates.[5]

This observation by the judge is a basic one. In our treatment of delinquents we have often underestimated the importance of their group associations. Status among their contemporaries means far more than status in the adult world, especially if this adult world does not seem to be very understanding of their needs. In considering prevention of juvenile delinquency there has been a great deal of discussion regarding the role of recreation. If this stays in the superficial area of merely occupying the youngster's time, it will be of little value. In work with delinquent gangs the knowledge of emotional drives and of the dynamics of group behavior is indispensable. The youngster in danger of becoming a delinquent needs not only playgrounds and equipment but needs even more an

[5] "Insecurity Causes Waywardness," *The Welfare Reporter* (Official Publication of the New Jersey Department of Institutions and Agencies), July, 1948, p. 12.

understanding adult who is able to help him and his gang gain the status they are craving and have exciting activities as well as to let them bring out the feelings that are in their way. In a discussion of the Glueck Study of Juvenile Delinquency, Marshall B. Clinard writes about their presentation of a preventive program which should relate to the youngster himself, family life, school, and leisure time:

The evidence would seem to support the reversed order. Since the majority of the boys stole autos or committed other thefts and burglaries in association with others, it is unfortunate that the role of groups and companions other than the family was not explored in more detail. . . .[6]

Group workers have done a great deal of this preventive work, with neighborhood gangs, in youth serving agencies, and in settlement houses. Since the 1950's, they have moved into work with delinquents on probation, parole and in institutions. Such community service lies within their competence. competence.

The need in youngsters for group association is combined with a more hidden craving for understanding by adults. Though delinquents pretend to be quite self-sufficient in their gangs, every contact with them has proved that they accept an understanding adult with a sense of relief. They usually meet adults first with great distrust, but when an adult has been proved trustworthy the acceptance is so complete that it shows the depth of the need.

How much understanding by an adult can mean in a crucial moment I myself remember well from an experience in my adolescence (and it is told here with belated thanks to Doctor Bernfeld). We were a bunch of sixteen-year-old boys and girls in a large urban center in Germany. In a culture that places a great deal of authority in the adult, youth is doubly

[6] *Federal Probation*, March, 1953, p. 51.

rebellious, and so we were. We felt that no adult would ever understand us, but we felt happy and well related to our own age group. We were reading a great deal and at the time of the fight between the Freudian and Adlerian schools of psychoanalysis, we were strongly partisan one way or another. At this time, young Doctor Bernfeld announced six lectures on psychoanalysis. We were burning to go, feeling that we were just as well informed as anyone else, but also knowing that our parents would only laugh at us, and, besides, we had no money to pay for those lectures. We thought, therefore, that it was our right to sneak into those lectures without paying and without telling anybody about it. Each of us alone would have been afraid to do this, but as a group we felt justified and secure.

Before the first lecture we were posted at the entrance where the lecturer would enter, since this was not the public entrance, and we tried to go in right behind him. Suddenly Doctor Bernfeld turned. He had seen us and he confronted us directly. I have never forgotten my own feeling. I was absolutely sure that we would now be thrown out in disgrace and that the man of whom we thought very highly would probably laugh at us and call us "children," about the worst insult we could think of. Doctor Bernfeld's first calm words were, "Did you want to hear the lecture?" There was no rush of explanation on our part, but only a suspicious and resistant nodding of our heads. We were sure that if he did not throw us out at this point, he would start with a lot of questions. Instead of that he gave us a long intensive glance, reached into his pocket, and said, "I have a few extra tickets. If you sneak in today, you are not sure you can make it a next time. If you want to hear the lectures, it is only valuable if you hear all six of them, so here they are." We could hardly thank him before he had left.

I doubt that Doctor Bernfeld ever had more intense and—I would almost say—more understanding listeners in his lectures than he had during the next six evenings. We did not miss a single one; we took notes. His incredible trusting and understanding gesture had even made it unnecessary for us to show off with this. We met after each lecture and discussed the content. I cannot remember the details of it. But I do remember the amazing feeling of peace that pervaded us, peace with ourselves and peace with "those adults." He had not only prevented the "delinquent act" of entering a lecture without paying for it, but he had restored a great deal of basic faith in an adult environment that seemed hostile to a group of adolescents.

TRAINING SCHOOLS

Not all delinquent youngsters are referred to institutions, but a great many of them enter them. In a group of university professors recently there was a discussion about delinquency around the lunch table. Suddenly each one was reminiscing about some delinquency he committed as a youngster and the almost always repeated thought was expressed, "How lucky I did not end up in an institution. If I had, I never would be what I am today." I think no flaming pamphlet could have been a more serious indictment of our institutional efforts than this kind of discussion. Actually, what was being said was, "I did the same things that hundreds of other children are doing who had to go to training schools. They are condemned to failure, not because of what they did, but because of the institution." Even if this is not the true picture (and I can see how many superintendents of training schools who work very hard to make their schools a treatment unit will feel hurt by these remarks), it certainly shows how the public feels about our institutions for delinquents, and we must admit that this is not all fiction.

Albert Deutsch in his book, *Our Rejected Children,*[7] has shown us the many horrible punishing ways in which we still treat children in institutions for delinquents. He has shown us practices that are of such inhumanity that they sound like the reports of Nazi concentration camps. We all know that such practices still exist, though we also know that there are many institutions that work very differently. The task of the institution for juvenile delinquents to become a place for treatment and education is an exceedingly difficult one and the road towards this is much longer and harder than for children's institutions. The factors that make this road so difficult are many:

1. Institutions for delinquents usually are state institutions and, therefore, very large, because the taxpayers do not want to spend money on those who have hurt their communities. The larger the groups, the more difficult it is to give individualized attention.

2. Because of the vagueness of our interpretation of delinquency, the child and the young person with whom these institutions are confronted show extremely different characteristics. The wider the margin of behavior difficulties, the harder it is to group the youngsters effectively.

3. The training schools deal with children whose symptoms consist in acting-out behavior. This kind of behavior is extremely difficult to take in a day-by-day living situation where people constantly rub against one another.

4. Community attitudes towards delinquents are still punishing ones and the institution which sincerely tries therapeutic methods will be easily accused of "coddling" youngsters who have made life difficult in the community.

5. With a better system of probation, institutions for delinquents have to deal with those youngsters who show the

[7] Boston: Little, Brown & Co., 1950.

greatest problems. In many of these cases our knowledge of behavior, its motives, and of treatment methods is not far enough advanced. We really do not know how we can best be helpful. Meanwhile, this kind of youngster is dangerous to himself and to his environment.

There are practical difficulties with which training schools are especially confronted, one of the major ones being the lack of personnel having a genuine respect and interest in the kind of youngsters with whom they work. Too often institutions for delinquents will have employees who have chosen this work mainly because they could not get other employment or because they were unconsciously seeking an outlet for their punishing attitude towards people. These are the difficulties and the realities with which training schools have to deal today. On the other hand, they have an amazing opportunity of trying on a large scale to work with young people so that they will not swell the ranks of our criminals. They also work with many young people who mainly need a trusting and understanding environment to regain the capacity for becoming a satisfied and satisfying member of society. Basically they are working with *children and adolescents* with the capacity of all children and adolescents to learn and to trust if an opportunity is given to them.

The group worker's role in this endeavor is one of the most important ones, not only because of the group living situation, but because we deal mostly with adolescents to whom this group situation is crucial even in life outside of the institution. Some of the group work method's basic principles, such *as participation in decision-making, the use of program in relation to needs, and the use of limitations combined with basic understanding,* play a vital role in the institutional life of the delinquent.

The functions of the social group worker in the institution

for delinquents will be approximately the same as those established in the children's institutions.

1. Supervision of houseparents.

2. Direct group leading of therapeutic groups, especially formed clubs and councils.

3. Being responsible and helping with the recreational program as part of group living.

4. Supervising other staff concerned with the recreational aspects of institutional life.

5. Being responsible for community contacts.

6. Supervision of volunteers.

Some of these functions will take on different aspects in the institution for delinquents, and there are some added functions, as, for instance, the important team work relationship with probation officers and police and *group discussion with parents of youngsters in the institution.*

I will enlarge on these parts that show some specific function or a specific form of function in the institution for juvenile delinquents.

Every child is fearful when entering an institution. This fear is intensified in the case of the delinquent. He feels that society is making him responsible for his acts and he is afraid of retaliation and revenge. He is set for punishment; he is set for loss of his identity and even in some way for loss of self-respect. All these feelings are not necessarily conscious, but they are rolled together into a ball of fear, hatred, and defiance. There are very few delinquents who come to an institution thinking that it will help them. Maybe this will happen in later times, but it certainly is not the case today.

Without question, the attitude of the houseparent and of the group that receives them will be essential. I observed the arrival of a sixteen-year-old in an institution which had poor physical facilities but a thoroughly able director who had known how to pick his staff. The boy arrived dirty and hand-cuffed to a policeman. The director immediately asked that the handcuffs be taken off. He talked to the boy a few min-utes, reassuring him that he could talk to him whenever he wanted to and that there was also a caseworker available with whom he would have individual interviews. He then introduced him to the housefather in whose group he would be. The housefather asked the boy whether he were not very tired and wanted to wash up before he even saw anything of the rest of the crowd. This unexpected concern for his comfort was the first impression which the boy received. After he had taken a bath and was refreshed, I saw how some boys from his cottage took him around, explained the different rooms and their use, told him about the work they were doing and about the rules that had to be observed. Though the cot-tage father did little directly with the boy, the climate that pervaded his cottage and the freedom he had given the other boys to introduce a newcomer created the helpful relationship.

PRINCIPLES OF GROUP DISCUSSION

Because of the nature of the delinquent behavior and its underlying hostility, therapeutic groups must be available for all the youngsters in the care of the institution. These groups will be important all during treatment, but they are indispensable and should become a regular part of the insti-tutional setting at the time of entrance and at some time before leaving. Just as we expect a good institution for delin-quents to have a caseworker available for the boy, to make sure that he can keep contact with his home environment, to help him to express feelings individually, and so that he will have a person all to himself with whom he can share some of his greatest worries and fears, it should become prac-tice to have introductory group sessions for everyone entering the institution. The same feelings that will be expressed in individual case interviews will appear in those group discussions, and it will be important to the youngsters to feel that they are not alone and that these problems can be worked with not only in secret gripe sessions in the dormitory or on the playground but can be discussed in the open in the presence of an adult who is willing to listen to them and who can also interpret the point of view of society and of the institution.[8]

These group discussions which are an integral part of the whole treatment process fall into three groups: (1) those that are introduction for the newcomer to the institution; (2) those conducted during his stay in the institution, as long as the youngster needs this kind of special attention; and (3) those that prepare him for release. They will relate to reality around the children and to their feelings, and will help them to understand some of the reasons for their feelings as well as to handle them. The group worker will not go into too much interpretation of unconscious material. The group worker is a social worker and—as his brother, the caseworker—he should be able to handle feelings in relationship to reality situations. If he sees the need for interpreting serious unconscious material, he will consult with the psychiatrist, or will ask the psychiatrist to take over if the situation is such that his own competence is limited. It is a basic principle of professional integrity to know one's own limitations and to ask for help or to refer the patient when the limits of one's competence are reached.

The principles for group discussions presented on the following pages have come from a wide experience with many different groups of this kind. There is no question that also

[8] For records of such group discussions, see Gisela Konopka, *Therapeutic Group Work with Children* (Minneapolis: University of Minnesota Press, 1949).

in this area we need more experimentation. Yet we must not eternally start every new therapeutic group project as if nobody else has tried this before. There is knowledge collected and we can use the experience of others. It is impossible to simply translate individual contacts into group discussion. In the research project done by Florence B. Powdermaker and Jerome D. Frank on group psychotherapy, they say:

For most doctors group therapy was more taxing and complicated than individual treatment because of the greater complexity of the group situation and their lack of experience in dealing with several patients simultaneously.[9]

1. Voluntary participation.

In discussing children's institutions we referred to the fact that help with emotions can only be given if the individual is willing to involve himself in this process. Voluntary participation, therefore, is essential. In an institution for delinquents this demand is even more vital because of the many other instances in which the individual, by necessity, must be forced to participate in certain activities. It is important that the youngster feel that there are islands in this setting where he can have his choice of participation. The question certainly arises whether this principle can be upheld completely if we consider that some of these groups are held at the point of entrance into the institution and, therefore, at the point of deepest emotional resistance of the individual to anything that is presented to him. August Aichorn understood this very well when he said:

To the dissocial child we are a menace because we represent society with which he is in conflict . . . they do not tell the truth.[10]

[9] Florence B. Powdermaker and Jerome D. Frank, *Group Psychotherapy* (Cambridge, Mass.: Harvard University, 1953).

[10] August Aichorn, *Wayward Youth* (New York: Viking, 1935), p. 125.

This principle of voluntary participation, therefore, should be modified in the sense that the youngster is asked first to participate in the group and it is made clear to him that he can drop out after a certain number of meetings if he wants to. This provides an opportunity for him to get to know what is offered. If the meetings are conducted well, they usually will have so much meaning that he will not drop out anyhow. If he nevertheless does withdraw, this in itself is an important symptom and we will have to see what the causes are. It can be that open discussion of feelings is still too painful for him and he will need more intensive individual attention before he can make use of the group. It can also mean that the youngster has too great difficulty with verbalization and discussion groups, and even individual discussions are beyond his capacity. In such a case, much more help might come from well-directed activities. We can see that the principle of voluntary attendance gives a helpful diagnostic tool into our hands. We would not want to deprive ourselves of it.

As an illustration I am quoting from such a discussion meeting in an institution for delinquent girls. Because of the distrust and resistance of the girls, the worker needs to explain carefully the purpose of the meeting:

I began by explaining that, as they knew, I was their social worker, only instead of seeing them on an individual basis, I was seeing them in a group. They could feel free to talk about any kind of problems they wish—what was bothering them at the institution and also any problems they might wish to bring up in regard to their own situation. They could feel free to say anything they wished; these discussions would be confidential and they need not fear being punished or losing privileges for anything they might bring up for discussion. I also explained that though they might have gripes or complaints at times, they could express them, but there probably would not be anything that I could do to change things. What we would be doing would be to discuss how they felt about them, why, and what they might do about them themselves.

It is not only the worker who begins to understand the girls better, for the girls also gained some comprehension of their problems. After the first discussion meeting in this group, Lisa asked the worker for an individual interview.

When Lisa was settled in the chair, I asked her what the trouble was. Lisa said she wanted to know how she could get along with the girls. At first I interpreted this as meaning that she was usually getting into fights with the other girls, but I soon found out that she meant that she did not know how to be a part of the group. She felt unwanted and did not know how to enter into conversation with them. When they joked around, she tried to, also, but somehow she couldn't say witty things. They weren't mean or anything, but she just didn't feel that the girls liked her especially.

Lisa recognized here her position in the group and her own feelings of being unhappy about this. She was not accusing the others and she began to see her own part. It was the task of the worker to help her understand the reasons for this and to change the behavior that brought this upon her. It is clear that this sometimes can be done in group discussion and sometimes is better done by referring it to individual interviews. These discussions show that the girls freely used the group worker for individual contacts outside the group. The group worker's role is to accept such interviews as part of her function because of the relationship established with the girls. Sometimes she may help them to get additional assistance from the caseworker. Increasingly, social workers acquire skills in both casework and group work. In the future, division of functions between the two will no longer exist.

2. *Intelligent grouping.*

The grouping will be around different aspects. It may be around a specific problem, such as, for instance, the arrival in the institution, or dismissal and adjustment to the world outside the institution.

It may be around natural groupings which have been observed in the course of institutional life. In larger institutions we often see in the living situation the development of subgroups which play an important part in the life of the individual youngster and this gives the keen observer another diagnostic tool. Who attracts whom and why? What are those subgroups doing when they congregate informally? It is possible that they have a very helpful influence on each other, and it is also possible that they are quite disturbing. Whatever their influence is, it will help us in dealing with the youngster to know about it and to turn this relationship into one that is helpful to him. Some of these groups, therefore, may be based on this natural friendship bond.

Grouping may be around specific forms of behavior which the youngsters have in common and which can be the starting point for discussions. It is not a recommendation that this should always be done, but in one of the institutions a group of eneuretics was formed and proved very helpful because the boys who were very ashamed of this condition could discuss this with others who suffered from the same difficulty. It will be important, while having the group discussions, to be aware of the interrelationships of members and to change the grouping if it does not prove helpful.

3. *Informal discussion.*

There is a difference between classroom teaching and therapy discussions. In recent years, because of our strange desire to call everything therapy we have created a disastrous con-

fusion in this respect. I remember once sitting in an evalua-
tion of a summer session at a small university and one of the
teachers saying, "Oh, we are doing fine. We are in the middle
of a terrible confusion and I think that's part of group therapy." One of the other teachers simply asked, "For what have
the students come here? For therapy or for learning?" This
question hit the nail on the head. They had come for learning and not for treatment, and the confusion, therefore, was
not helpful in the learning process. On the other hand, therapy sessions are sometimes treated like classroom lectures. I
remember a therapy series with delinquent youngsters which
consisted almost exclusively of lectures given by the person
conducting them. The boys hardly said a word.

The conducting of an informal discussion involves a great
deal of self-discipline, because a discussion leader must allow
others to say what he himself is thinking or even to say
things he does not approve of. He has the difficult task of
allowing freedom in the discussion as well as keeping a certain discipline in it so that the group members themselves
do not feel as if they are only floundering without knowing
where they are going. The informal atmosphere must be kept
alive all the time. There are some techniques that will be helpful in this, such as, for instance, comfortable sitting arrange-
ments, a friendly room or an outdoor setting, an opportunity
to eat while one is discussing something. These are helpful
props, but they are not sufficient if the group worker himself
has not the capacity to make the youngsters feel that this is
their meeting and that freedom of expression is genuinely
accepted.[11]

4. *Focus of discussion.*

The focus of the discussion must be on the feelings of the
youngster and not on a preconceived subject. This does not

[11] For detailed recordings of such group discussions, see Konopka, *op. cit.*

mean that sessions are conducted without any direction. They have their specific purpose, but the group worker must continually be aware of the youngsters' feelings and of what is meant by what they are saying. A discussion with delinquent girls in Germany started out by their asking whether there were also institutions for delinquents in the United States. It sounded on the surface like the questions of any high-school girl asking for information about another country. Yet behind those questions was really an expression of their hostility towards being in an institution and their secret wish to hear that in a free country such as America nothing like this existed. It was important, therefore, to allow the discussion soon to be concerned with themselves and their situation, instead of launching into a long description of the United States.

In one of the discussion meetings in a girls' institution the girls were discussing the reasons why they had come to the training school. Dottie had been quite agitated during this discussion and finally burst out with what was really troubling her.

It was being here [in the institution] that was so hard. She resented it and hated it and with this Dottie put her elbow on the table, put her hand up to her eyes and burst into tears. Between tears she told it was hard having every moment worked out for you so that you had no time for yourself. Rules and regulations she could more or less accept; but what was hard was losing your freedom. Here she broke into tears again. Not to be able to walk down the street whenever you felt like it; to be locked up like a criminal—that was what was hardest.

With this the others in the group moved into talking about what it meant to be in the institution.

It was important that the group worker not turn this discussion into a gripe session about the institution, but realize behind these complaints the feelings of rejection and hostility and begin working with them.

5. *Avoiding the quiz session.*

One of the most painful group discussions that I witnessed in an institution for delinquents was one that ran under the name of group therapy but actually was torturous inquisition. Though well-meaning, the person who was conducting the group session was used to interrogating mental patients and used this method in the group session. In rapid fire the boys were questioned about what they had done, why they had done it, what they thought about it now, what kind of friends they had before, etc. The questions were directed towards one person after another, pointing them out without giving them an opportunity to volunteer an answer. The boys looked terribly frightened and the answers were stereotyped ones, obviously aimed at pleasing the interrogator. The session was wasted from the point of view of diagnostic value as well as of therapy.

6. *Establishment of relations.*

The group worker must allow time to establish a relationship between himself and the members of the group. The inexperienced worker will expect in the first sessions an outpouring of feelings and will be disappointed if it does not come. But we share our feelings only with those we trust. The difficult beginning is well recorded as follows:

I asked if there was any particular spot where they wished to start—was there any question someone wished to raise. There was a long silence as I scanned the various members. They criss-crossed glances and grinned at each other. Perhaps there was something they wished to bring up about their cottages? Continued silence with a few exchanges of murmurs and grins. What about school?

There was still no overt response, so I ventured surely everything wasn't perfect. This brought forth a few teeters. Then I asked if someone would volunteer to say where she was finding trouble.

It would have been helpful to have preceded these discussions by having had a more informal contact with the youngsters. After a hilarious game in which the group worker participated actively, discussion started much more freely. Yet the most warm and giving approach will not achieve complete trust in one or two sessions with those youngsters who see in us only the enemies.

In a group the establishment of relationships will vary from individual to individual, will be stronger with one and less intensive with another one, and the time to achieve it will also be different with different members of the group. All this has to be taken with a great deal of patience and the knowledge that it is unavoidable. If, in the third meeting, for instance, one or the other begins to speak freely, the group worker can be satisfied with progress. It is important that he does not push youngsters too fast into opening up. On the other hand, he has to also be sensitive toward the unspoken wish of an individual to express himself. In about the seventh meeting I once asked a sixteen-year-old whether he wouldn't want to talk about his mother too (one of the others had just expressed a great deal of unhappiness about his relationship to his mother). I had seen him stirring and I had observed him during all those meetings listening intently but not saying anything. He again shook his head. I felt behind his denial that he really wanted to say what he was thinking, but that it was extremely hard for him. I reassured him that whatever he said would not be repeated anywhere, but that I thought it would help him if he let the others know what he was feeling, just the way he had seen it had helped them when they talked. He suddenly spoke up and received a great deal of attention from his friends. Two weeks later he came to me and said, "You know, it was the best thing that happened to me when you made me talk that day."

It is important also that the group worker realize that in those discussions his task is not only to relate the group members to him but also to each other. They sometimes will accept criticism far better from each other than from any adult and a positive relationship with another youngster in this kind of situation is a help towards productive friendships.

7. *Participation of worker.*

The group discussion leader must be willing to be active in the discussion if necessary and not be just an observer. We have stressed in the third principle the importance of not becoming too domineering in the group discussion and of letting the members express themselves freely. The dogmatic use of this principle has led sometimes to the group discussion leader being nothing but an observer and not giving direct help when it is needed. The youngster has to feel all during these discussions that the group leader is a human being made of flesh and blood and not an immobile machine watching him. At times it will be important for him to enter the discussion directly.

The boys discussed with great anger the way they were apprehended. They felt that they had no respect for some of the people who caught them and they expressed a great deal of dislike of the way all adults cheated and did bad things but they only wanted the children to do everything right. The worker interjected only with a question "*All* adults?" Very quickly the boys wanted to reassure him that he certainly was excepted. The worker thought it important at this point to help them see that he too was not perfect and that he might have made mistakes in demanding something from others, he was not completely ready to fulfill himself.

By giving them a personal example he made it possible for them to transfer their love of him to a wider understanding of adults and to realize that most adults, though not perfect, were trying to live up to some of the demands of society.

8. *Using different techniques.*

We have developed many techniques that can be used in a therapeutic way in group discussions, such as, for instance, guided group interaction, socio-drama, psychodrama, the use of visual material and discussion of it, and the use of resource people brought in for the discussion. Sometimes a dogma has been made out of a particular technique. The social group worker must be familiar with all of them and not insist that only the one or the other is therapeutic. He must be able to use each one whenever it seems most helpful.

In preparing a child for release from the institution, dramatic play often proved very helpful because it brought reality closer than just theoretical discussion. On the other hand, it very often seemed artificial when the youngsters were full of a desire to tell about past experiences. Resource persons were especially helpful during the time of introduction to the institution or of later ongoing therapy. It was, for instance, very desirable to introduce the superintendent of the institution into the group very early. By having him participate in one of these more formal discussions and by letting the youngsters see him in a group setting smaller than that in which they would usually meet him, the institution lost some of its fearful aspects. The superintendent symbolizes the authority of the training school and a positive relationship to him increases a positive attitude towards the whole institutional experience.

In the course of treatment the introduction of police officers was another very helpful device. Most of the youngsters consider police as their worst enemies. The presence at such discussions of an understanding police officer who encourages the youngsters to talk freely to him about anything they wish can mean the opening up of a completely new understanding of the role of the police in society.

9. *Constructive use of limitations.*

The use of limitations in the discussion meeting is very important because it is around limitations that many problems of the delinquent arise. Limitations are imposed by the interplay between members and one of the healthy aspects of the group discussion approach is the give and take that occurs between them.

We see in the following excerpt the frank and realistic way in which the girls limit each other's "showing off" and help in this way towards a more realistic self-understanding.

In regard to running away Anna said that it wasn't always a case of running away; she liked to travel and get around to different roller-skating rinks and meet different people, and her mother would let her go because she knew she could be trusted not to get into trouble. At this, most of the other girls snorted their protest, and Ginny challenged her by pointing out that she got up here to the institution, so she must have gotten into some kind of trouble. . . . Anna stuck to her point that she just wanted to get around to different skating rinks. Again the girls expressed disagreement and challenged her. Ginny and Susan were of the opinion that she could meet just as many people in skating rinks in her home town as going so far away as into another State. They agreed that she might like it for adventure but they did not agree that it was necessary from the point of meeting new people. They also expressed the opinion that in order to become skilled in the art of roller-skating, a person usually prefers frequenting a certain rink because one tends to become more accustomed to the floor.

It is not an outside adult who imposes on Anna the need to think further about her running away. Her own contemporaries take away from her glib rationalization and force her into doing some thinking about herself. It is interesting to see that in the same group discussion Anna begins to admit that there were times when she and her mother did not agree on her going away. Only after she admitted this did she begin to see why she left home.

Anna is a good example of a girl who had put a shell around herself and would not admit to herself or anyone else her reasons for her behavior. It was important that this shell crumble before anyone could work with her. It needed the intensive work of the caseworker as well as the kind of experience Anna had in this discussion group to help her work through her difficulties. In a summary about her we see the different stages through which she had to go.

When Anna came into the institution she was very quiet and conforming, but one sensed that this calm exterior was covering an otherwise hostile and rebellious attitude. . . . After a few months this proved to be the case. She became defiant, stubbornly refusing to take certain courses in school. She rebelled against responsibility in her cottage, many times refusing to cooperate and being very belligerent. . . . She seemed to get great satisfaction out of the fact that she was in constant trouble claiming that she was happiest when in difficulty.

She rarely projected the blame for her difficulties on other people, openly admitting that it was always she herself who made it necessary for punishment to be inflicted. She took great pride in her stubbornness, stoutly proclaiming she was not going to change her attitude no matter how long she would have to remain. . . . After a few months, Anna began showing a change of attitude. She no longer seemed to find satisfaction in participating in rebellious enterprises and made an honest effort to abide by rules and regulations. She became more cheerful and relaxed in manner, more friendly with girls and staff and seemed less hostile than formerly.

We see here how this girl had to go through a period of acting out her hostility before she could feel freer and more satisfied in herself. It was important that she be allowed to express feelings verbally instead of only acting them out.

The group worker's role in relation to limitations in discussion meetings will be to protect the youngster who is imposed upon too harshly by his contemporaries, to limit the one who is using his status situation to prevent others from gaining enough from the sessions, and also to limit content of the discussion to what is essential for the youngsters. He has to be flexible enough to accept some straying from the subject in the discussion, but he must be able to come back to it to make it satisfactory to the participants. In one meeting the girls had involved themselves in a discussion regarding their social needs and had begun to gain some insight into their rebellion against family and general society mores. One of the girls mentioned a picnic and this led into general griping about the food in the institution. The group worker let the girls express themselves on this subject, but limited it to a comparatively short time and then suggested that they refer this question to the council. She then helped them to see some of the connection between the need for food and their need for affection, this way leading them back to their original subject.

It is a difficult skill to be flexible and to be still capable of using limitations. The less mature worker will easily fall into the trap of being either completely permissive and nothing but an observer or of being too restricting for fear of losing his group. It needs security, self-discipline, and a great deal of experience to find the balance between flexibility and use of limitations.

10. *Relating reality situations to feelings.*

It is obviously not enough to help work out a program for placement of a girl in a community, but is also important to discuss her feeling about this. This is mainly the function of the probation officer. It will be helpful to have these discussions in a group too, so that the girls can see that there are individual differences in the way they react to certain situations. It will help them to be more realistic and may increase the extent to which they will stick to a certain plan while on probation. The discussions may be conducted by the group worker in the institution or by an outside worker connected with the probation department. The following is from a record of such a discussion.

The girls got on the subject of parole, and Gen, who will be going before the Commission next month, stated that she hoped she would get her parole but in the same breath said no fooling, she was afraid to go home; she didn't want to. When asked to explain why, she revealed that her main concern was that she would not be able to make a go of it in her own neighborhood. Having gone around with a certain crowd of girls, Gen admitted that she had procured quite a reputation and she was afraid that the right kind of girls would not be interested in making friends with her. If that happened, there would be nothing to do but go with the wild crowd, 'cause otherwise she would be rather lonely. And if she went with the wild crowd, she knew she would just slip right back into the same old pattern. She was scared to think of going home and wished her family would move.

We see here how Gen is more afraid of the reaction of her contemporaries than of the ones in her own family. She also realizes her own difficulty of not being able to stand up against this and, therefore, she would join in with the same old crowd. She quite realistically, therefore, prefers not to return to the same neighborhood.

Eve disagreed with Gen on the point of not being accepted by the community. She told of a recent home visit in which the kids had seen her, talked with her and had been very accepting. The kids were swell and decent; it was the big shots who would make it hard, the important people in town. . . . She wanted to go to an entirely new location where she could begin over again with a clean slate, where no one would know her.

Eve too sees some difficulty for returning to the same place, but for different reasons than Gen. Her difficulty lies more in relation to adults and her fear of their scorn makes her feel that she wants to start somewhere else. In discussing this with others the girls begin to see more clearly their own motivations.

Emily said she wanted to go home and prove to herself that she could make a go of it in her own home town. If she couldn't prove it to herself, then how could she ever prove it to the Commission or anyone else. Mary and Gert had the same point of view. Gert repeated that she wanted to go back to her home town and prove to everyone that she could make a go of it.

The group discussion helps to see and to discuss reality in the light of each individual's feelings and experience.

11. *Intensive recording*

As a last principle of group discussions, I name again *recording*. Such discussions as these should be recorded intensively. They need to be used for diagnostic purposes to understand not only where the youngster is at a given point but also the way he has developed in the course of time. We cannot be dogmatic about the kind of recording that must be done. The institute of group dynamics has developed a method of recording through the presence of an observer. This will be very helpful if the youngsters feel free to accept this observer. We cannot expect that this will always be the case, because some of them might be very suspicious toward anybody who writes down something they are saying. It will depend, again, on the relationship developed with them whether one can use this method.

Another recording method is the one developed in social group work in which the group worker himself reports group process and individual observations after the meeting. This recording will be helpful for diagnostic purposes but is not sufficient for research studies. Tape recording can be used only if the youngsters have developed enough trust in the proceedings so that they do not think that the recording may be used against them. Tape recording also has the drawback that it cannot record nonverbal material such as gestures and facial expressions. It is used primarily in conjunction with recording done either by the group worker or by an observer.

PLANNING GROUPS

It is a misconception to think that delinquents have not learned to do any planning for themselves or in relation to others. Some of them actually have highly developed skills in planning, as seen in the way they worked out a burglary or went about taking a car. Most of this planning is done in groups and there is interaction and awareness of the need to ascertain facts and to come to conclusions. It is the skills themselves that many delinquents have to learn in planning groups, but the use of those skills for constructive purposes and acceptance of planning on a more democratic basis than it is usually done in the gang situation. In most gangs the final decision is made by the leader or the few powerful members of a subgroup. It is a different form of planning when one has to listen to everybody, when the minority must be heard and considered, and when final decisions are arrived at either by vote or as a result of integration through discussion.

In many of our institutions group planning is neglected. The only demand is for the youngster to conform to rules and follow orders. This is exactly the pattern he has followed earlier, only that the boss was the gang leader. He will never learn to be part of a democratic society or to internalize society's demand on him if he does not gain some experience in group decision-making. The planning groups are, therefore, an essential part of education and rehabilitation for juvenile delinquents. They also fulfill a purpose by improving the climate of the institution. Human beings have different and more positive feelings if they participate in a common endeavor. The youngster who feels that he has some say about some aspect of institutional living will be much more willing to accept decisions that have to be made without his consent.

Some institutions for delinquents have experimented with so-called self-government. If the self-government was used to decide administrative matters and, especially, punishment or rewards for the individual, it was doomed to failure and was actually dangerous. We discussed in a preceding chapter the fact that children are often far more cruel than adults because they cannot weigh all aspects of another child's behavior and have not the experience and knowledge of different emotional responses. In an institution for delinquents, where we deal with children who are filled with especially strong hostile impulses, we must expect that this hostility will be used wherever the opportunity is given. If they are allowed to take over the punishing role in relation to contemporaries who are in a weak and unprotected position, they can very easily misuse this power. I was told by a twelve-year-old who had run away from an institution that he would never go back there, not because he was afraid of the attendants but because he was afraid of the other boys who had the power to punish him.

For what, then, should the planning groups be used?

The representative student council, for example, can concern itself with almost all aspects of institutional life if it is realized that the members are not asked to take on the role of administration but are asked to comment on what is happening. They are encouraged to make suggestions and their suggestions will be considered by the administration, accepted if they are helpful, and the superintendent will discuss it with them if they are not considered practical. The council, therefore, must not be just a pretense at decision-making, but must have real influence. At the same time it must be clear to the council from the beginning that the administration of the institution has the final decision. Only in this way can the educational and therapeutic aspects of the institution be guaranteed.

Ideally this council will meet with the superintendent, since he represents the highest administrative power in the institution and it will be helpful for the youngsters to know that they have direct access to him. It will be important that the superintendent be familiar with group work principles and able to use the group work method in relation to this specific task, just as he uses casework methods in initial interviews with youngsters entering the institution. If for some reason in the larger institution the superintendent cannot take on working with the council group, the social group worker will fulfill this function, but will bring the superintendent to the group at certain points in the discussion so that the youngsters may be aware of the interest of the administration in their thinking.

The council meetings must not be turned into therapy sessions regarding the inner conflicts of youngsters, but must be kept the tool for representation of the young people in administration and the channel for expressing their thinking.

In looking over the content of discussions in council meetings over a period of three years in a school for delinquent girls, I discovered three subjects which had received outstanding attention. They related to (1) complaints and questions regarding fair treatment, (2) demands for a more permissive attitude in regard to beauty aids such as cosmetics, clothing, etc., and (3) demands for increased recreational outlets. There is an interesting trend appearing in the course of the three years. The less punitive and restrictive the institution, and the fewer demands, we find, the more concern on the part of the girls with responsibility for their own behavior.

In the beginning the discussions were concerned with:

Why can some girls have white shoe polish in their rooms while others do not have it?

Why can't we exchange music records between different cottages?

Why can't we have communications with different cottages?

Why do we get a bad mark if we once forget to clean up a bathtub?

Why bad marks for talking in the laundry?

Why bad marks for calling to the housemother and talking to her in a loud voice?

Why should we have loss of recreation if we forget some mending?

Why can't we at least have lipstick when visitors come?

Why are we told that we must go swimming or get into a discipline cottage?

In the third year and with the change of climate in the institution we still find demands for better recreation; the girls, for instance, ask whether they can have a *long* hike or can do some overnight camping, but we find also some of the following discussions:

We have been allowed to go outside the institution for church services on Sunday. Some of the girls do not behave very well and giggle or show off. We think we should do something about this since it reflects on the whole institution.

This is an amazing change from projecting responsibility on everyone else to taking it on by themselves and being concerned with the reputation of the whole place. They feel now like representatives of an institution they want to be proud of instead of continually wanting to tear down.

The council also is used to do some planning for special events and again the girls feel that they too have responsibilities in carrying those out. When I visited this institution and talked informally with some of the girls, one of them mentioned with a real sparkle in her eyes, "From next week on I will be representative on the council. I am looking forward to this. You know the girls who were on the council did a lot of planning for our Fourth of July week end."

The superintendent also felt that the council became a real tool in improving the climate in the institution.

SPECIAL ACTIVITY GROUPS

From the very beginning we felt . . . that above all we must see that the boys and girls from 14 to 18 had a good time. . . . They were human beings who had found life too hard.[12]

This quote from Aichorn will frighten many working in institutions for delinquents, mainly because of his words, "above all." Why should these youngsters have a good time if they have harmed many people and really brought a great deal of misery to many? Aichorn's thinking cannot be understood if we do not recognize this as being part of a way of changing the underlying hostility. In all our dealing with human beings we have found that meeting hostility with its kind only increases it. By responding the same way the youngster has responded to us and to the world around him, we are starting a vicious circle. By allowing the young person times

[12] Aichorn, *op. cit.*, p. 150.

of relaxation and direct enjoyment, we give the wounded ego moments of rest, and help in this way with the healing process.

In times and in cultures where joy was regarded as sin, this kind of thinking certainly could not be accepted. Joy and idleness were looked upon as disastrous. In our increasing knowledge about people we have seen that enforced idleness is really dangerous. In some institutions we still find solitary confinement with nothing to do as a form of punishment. It is really one of the worst forms of punishment we can invent and it does everything else but rehabilitate the youngster. The loneliness combined with no outlet for body or soul increases the feeling of desperate frustration, and results in hatred stronger than before.

Out of this realization grew the thought of using work as a therapeutic tool. This really was progress. However, as so often in human endeavor, the healthy thought was twisted and misused in practice. Instead of letting work become an enjoyable and educational medium, it too was often used as vicious punishment and lost all its therapeutic value. Examples of this are almost too numerous to mention. I visited a girls' institution where the girls started working at six o'clock in the morning, either doing housework or sewing. This was kept up all day under the silence rule, which means that all this work was done without the girls being allowed to speak a word to each other. This same silence rule was kept during meals. The girls had "free time" after 7:00 P.M., and they were expected during this time to sit in the yard and do something, either shelling peas or knitting, but they were allowed to speak. Work was considered a tool of rehabilitation for these girls, but actually it became a bitter-tasting, ugly medicine that they would throw off the moment they left the institution. I saw in a more progressive institution for boys the demand on them to stand for hours around long tables shelling peas. There is nothing wrong with shelling peas, but it becomes torture to active teen-agers when it is done for many hours and under the watchful eyes of an adult who doesn't allow hands to rest idly for a minute. The healthy thought of "work therapy" was turned into one of the most fiendish torture tools.

When I talk here about the use of recreation, I in no way want to diminish the importance of constructive work and also the importance of formal education. Both must play a major role in institutions for delinquents. The best use of leisure time will be of no avail when the youngster has not been equipped with the tools of earning a living. I pay my homage and respect to the teachers and workshop instructors in our institutions for delinquents. I thoroughly agree with the increasing movement to improve the quality of teaching and vocational training. The special activity group program will strengthen the whole effort to help the youngsters with their inner conflicts and their adjustment to their environment. It will only fulfill this purpose, however, if it strives toward individualization, active participation, and is purely on a voluntary basis. It will also be a valuable diagnostic tool.

The activity group program of the institution for delinquents will lie less in the hands of the houseparents than in the children's institution. The reason for this is that we are dealing here mainly with adolescents, and they will need some recreational outlet outside of the relationship they have with the person who is responsible for daily living and who must help them to get to school and to work assignments. It also should not have the aspects of a classroom. Adolescents need independent groups and the recreational period should give outlet for this. Many of these groups will resemble community clubs or actually be in the community. The program must be carried out with much imagination as well as real understanding of needs. Let us look at some of the needs it should fulfill.

Relief in Enjoyment

The youngsters with whom we work in institutions for delinquents are *children*, and they need to forget at times their own conflicts and their conflicts with society. There is no need to keep this constantly before them. It is important, in fact, that they become children again like other normal children. In regaining this capacity, they might regain some of their more positive feelings toward themselves and toward others. This applies even to the older adolescent. In an institution where the younger boys received the services of a social group worker who had special clubs with them, an eighteen-year-old came to the social group worker one day and said wistfully, "Couldn't you just play with some of us older boys too? It would make us feel as if we are not so bad after all." With an uncanny intuition he had realized that those play activities allowed the boys to throw off for a while the deep feelings of guilt.

Feelings of guilt are important to every human being and without them we would not have conscience and the ability to improve behavior. Yet guilt feelings which are too persistent and find no constructive way to be alleviated turn only into blind hostility, starting new guilt feelings and, therefore, establishing another vicious circle. It is important for people to handle their guilt feelings by doing something about them. The "doing something about them" consists either in atonement by acting differently, in learning to understand why they arose, in avoiding behavior that will lead to them again, and in involving oneself in activities which are acceptable and enjoyable. We have to find ways of helping delinquents handle their guilt feelings through these many approaches, including the one of the small relaxed informal group and its creative activities.

In an institution for delinquent girls I saw a young and

enthusiastic nun introducing paintings of the great masters to the girls. I never saw a more happy and stimulated group. The girls arranged for an exhibit of old and modern paintings. With visible pride they pointed out to the visitor their knowledge of the characteristics of different painters and their enjoyment of colors and forms. It was very obvious that this was not a boring class in art appreciation, but a purely enjoyable activity that gave them an enormous amount of satisfaction through learning as well as through the almost adventurous moving into an area that had been unknown to them. One of the girls showed me with real delight the flaming colors of Van Gogh. I pointed out to her the strange relationship of El Greco's coloring to modern painting, and she immediately began to search through the available books to find more about this. In describing this it is difficult to reproduce the glowing excitement that was in all the girls and the pure enjoyment and release they seemed to feel through this adventure into art.

Outlet for Feelings on a Nonverbal Basis

Many youngsters do not easily participate in individual or group therapy discussions because they do not have a capacity for verbalization. This might relate to many different factors, such as age, social environment, intelligence level, emotional blocking, etc. Whatever it is, it must be recognized that the youngster cannot relieve his feelings through expressing them in words. As adults we very easily forget this and ask for this capacity far too much. I learned this best through an eleven-year-old boy with whom I was working in a Child Guidance Clinic. He was drawing and I tried to involve him in a discussion about himself and some of his difficulties. He finally looked up and said calmly, "Look, I am not much of a talker." After this I learned to see more what he was doing and what he was expressing in his drawings and in his movements rather than expecting him to involve himself in a great deal of discussion. Because of the considerable amount of hostile feelings which we find in institutions for delinquents, we have to give the youngsters material that allows them to express these feelings in an acceptable form. Hammering, woodworking, and work around machinery are activities that allow for a great deal of energy outlet and are very helpful to boys and girls. The younger adolescents will enjoy working on materials with vivid colors. I have found that some very anxious youngsters need a period of rather solitary and withdrawn activities, such as, for instance, weaving or sewing or leather work. (Boys like sewing too, mainly with felt material.) Most handicraft projects have to be the kind that can be finished comparatively quickly. Besides the regular sports, games also are especially helpful if they allow for expression of feeling. Creative dramatics are liked by the younger boys. The older ones, because they are more inhibited, prefer the presentation of a given play, but use these greatly to present their own wishes and needs.

In general we find better recreational outlets in boys' institutions than in those for girls. Very often I have heard the cry of institutional personnel that girls never show as much interest in activities as boys do. I think that this is mainly because of the kind of program we are offering to girls and the kind of attitude towards them that is still prevalent. The form of delinquency in boys is usually one not too frightening to people. You will often hear the expression, "Oh, well, boys are boys and I myself have sometimes run away or even taken something." The delinquency of girls, which is usually sex activity, hits against taboos of our society and arouses fear and guilt feelings in the adults who work with them. It is, therefore, often much more difficult for them to accept the girls and to offer them what they need.

Most of our girls' institutions assume that the interest of

the girls must lie in housework and activities related to their feminine and later maternal role. We forget that very often the girls have become delinquent because of rejection of this role and it is no help to them to force it upon them. It can be wanted and acquired only if they see it as something really desirable. It is often much more important to allow the girl outlets for her feelings in a manner for which she is ready at this time. I saw, for instance, girls' institutions which offered weaving as the main activity in leisure-time hours. This was very beautiful work, but completely unsuited to the needs of girls who could not calmly watch the movement of threads but who were filled with great inner tensions. The weaving did not calm them, as it was expected, but, on the contrary, increased their tensions. What those girls needed were sports and active handicrafts.

I have seen many girls who thoroughly enjoyed woodcraft just as much as the boys. They often like painting with big sweeping strokes and bright colors. The colors mean a great deal to a girl whose emotions are strong and whose life has consisted in trying to please men. Besides, they are young adolescents and it is as important for them as for any adolescent girl to be beautiful. How cruel is the attitude that takes this away from the girl. I saw an institution where all the girls, tall, short, heavy, and thin, had to wear the same unbecoming hairdo. In this same institution a girl had chosen red buttons for her gray Sunday dress which she was sewing. The superintendent passing by, ripped off the red buttons, and replaced them with black ones, because the red ones were too frivolous.

Girls enjoy dramatics and especially creative dramatics, even in later adolescence. The dressing-up for dramatics means a great deal to them, and the emotional outpouring that is possible in this activity is also important. A skillful group worker can help these dramatics to become an outlet for feelings, an enjoyable experience in creativity, and a valuable tool for diagnostic and therapeutic purposes.

As all youngsters do, children and adolescents in institutions for delinquents greatly enjoy special festive occasions. They will have far more meaning if the youngsters prepare them in their own groups, establish special committees, and go through the planning process for them.

The group worker will have to evaluate here how far his group has developed. Because planning has been seen as an important democratic function and because it is so vital to the normal community group, group workers have sometimes become too rigid about it. They have made a fetish of this process and forced youngsters into it when they were not ready for planning. Diagnostic skill must also be used in relation to this. In a group of thirteen-year-old aggressive delinquent boys, the group worker started out planning for a picnic. Very quickly he realized that attention was not sustained, yet he also knew that this picnic meant much to them. He relaxed the planning procedure, simply asked what they wanted to eat, and later let them participate in the actual carrying out of the picnic (serving, roasting wieners, etc.). He himself had "provided" for the picnic. While this might be wrong for many groups, for *this* group it proved that he really loved them, that he gratified their infantile needs for "father giving to them," but that he involved them where they were able to participate. The group worker would work on increasing their capacity to plan, but he was not dogmatic and punishing in working toward this goal.

We see in this small example how much skill, flexibility, and sound judgment are necessary, if we take seriously the idea of group activities as part of treatment, and not as just another recreational program.

Learning About Limitations

Learning about limitations is something which comes in everyone's life at a very early age. We learn not to touch fire because it will burn us or not to go near deep water because we might drown or not to touch father's books because he wants to have them in good order. The delinquent often has rejected the idea of limitation and is acting like an infant. He has to learn about them in many different ways. In the group living situation he rubs against the interests of others and they are not always in accord with his own. In the activity groups we find a great many opportunities for this learning without needing to enforce it, as has been sometimes done, in a more punishing way. The material that the youngster uses itself offers an opportunity to realize limitations. He will learn that wood splits if it is not treated right, that the smearing of several bright colors one over the other only leads to an ugly gray mess, and that clay, if not properly treated, will blow up in the kiln. Games also will offer opportunity of learning how to get along with the other fellow, especially if those games are the kinds where one is dependent on somebody else and, therefore, must accept the limitation that comes with dependency.

Outlet for the Spirit of Adventure

The youngsters in institutions for delinquents are *adolescents*, as we have repeated so often. One of the most outstanding needs of adolescence is adventure. If this need is not fulfilled, frustration accumulates and the youngster blows up, either by becoming more delinquent or by running away. Institutional life tends to increase the need for blowing off steam and doing things which the individual would not do in normal life. This is almost unavoidable because of the congregation of so many people who did not choose to live together and the necessity of more rules (times for eating, for instance). We must be aware of this and accept some exaggerated behavior in institutional living not necessarily as a sign of disturbance or rebellion in the individual but as directly created by this specific situation. Girls suddenly yelling at a certain time in the evening, boys pulling pranks on a hot evening, these are often simply signs of too much institutional living. (They appear—as we all know—also in student dormitories, where there is little or no restriction of freedom.)

These outbursts give us warning that group life has become too monotonous. To give outlet for the adventure spirit in an institution for delinquents is certainly not easy. Many events which mean adventure to other children are far too tame for these youngsters, and some of the outlets for this need are far too dangerous to be used. To fulfill this need, therefore, we need very special application of imagination.

Adventure means to find out something one has not known before and something that gratifies curiosity. Traveling and seeing new parts of the world fulfill this need very well. This may be difficult but not impossible to offer in an institution. Again, such trips undertaken by smaller groups under the supervision of adults who have established a positive relationship to the youngsters are not impossible. It is perfectly clear that not too many staff members can be taken out of an institution to do this, as most institutions are short-staffed. Yet, over a period of time, it should be possible to arrange for a few such trips. The help of volunteers can be used to have enough personnel available for such a trip. Even if it takes only two or three days, it will fulfill some of the hunger for new sights, for staying up at night and talking, and for the feeling of independence that comes with it.

Adventure spirit can also be gratified through such new and exciting activities as the journey into art that I described before. New knowledge of scientific discoveries also can have a great deal of meaning, especially when it is accompanied by a presentation of experiments. For younger children, imaginary trips with the help of visual aid programs will be very interesting. Almost any activity that interrupts the usual routine of everyday life will give some satisfaction of the adventure spirit. If one usually eats indoors, it is helpful to plan an outdoor picnic. If group meetings are mostly held in a certain building, it will be fun to conduct them somewhere else. If it is routine to have visitors on a Sunday, it will be a special gratification if visitors are allowed and invited for another day of the week. Nothing is more deadly than to know each day exactly what will happen the next hour and the next.

Acquiring Social Skills

By this I mean far more than the acquisition of social manners. I mean the ability to get along with other people and to feel comfortable and at peace with them. It is the most basic skill that we would wish youngsters to achieve. And it is exactly this that the delinquents are lacking. It will be important to find out in each youngster what the specific reasons are for his having difficulties in this area, and individual help will be needed. But the group situation can offer them an opportunity to try out their capacity for social relations in a reality situation. It is very important, for instance, to help adolescents to work out their feelings about the other sex and to help them establish healthy heterosexual relations.

Most of our institutions for delinquents are one-sex institutions and can easily and often do breed abnormal attitudes; they have often been called schools for the education of homosexuals. The youngster who is already in a state of conflict is thrown into an unnatural environment which does not give him any opportunity to work out the problems of relationship to the other sex through which every adolescent lives. It is important that the group worker be ready and capable of discussing questions of sex, openly and without embarrassment. It is usually not sufficient to give physical sex information (though very often a youngster who sounds very sophisticated has really very little knowledge), but it is also important to help him to establish some code of behavior that will make it easier for him to get along.

Besides those discussions it is very helpful if the institution offers contact with the other sex. Institutions for delinquents should always have both men and women on the staff, both in educational and therapeutic capacities. Girls' institutions especially suffer too often from staff limited to women. It usually becomes an unhealthily suppressive and monotonous atmosphere, deadly for the staff as well as for the girls. It is also important that the young people learn to get along with each other in a positive way. There should be at least weekly parties or picnics or other common activities where both boys and girls participate.

I remember an institution for delinquents which was a co-educational one. During the week the boys and the girls usually had their own activities in their own cottages, but every Saturday they got together in a large recreation hall, and there was a big dance in which all the staff members and their wives and husbands participated. It was an evening to which they all looked forward and in which the boys and girls learned to play and dance together in an acceptable atmosphere. I still remember how the director of the institution pointed out to me an especially attractive couple of two seventeen-year-olds who danced beautifully. When the boy brought the girl back to her seat he bowed graciously and the girl smiled. The director told me that John had been committed to the institution for burglary and Ann had been found as a prostitute in one of the worst establishments. John was learning a trade and Ann had shown such a high degree of skill in office work and so much reliability in her whole behavior that she was working in the office of this institution. Both youngsters were attracted to each other and began to talk about a future together in serious terms. This was far more helpful than if each had spent a long time separated from any contact with the other sex.

I am aware of the fact that these relationships will not always work out so happily. Yet we cannot expect youngsters to have healthy feelings about the other sex if we keep them segregated from each other. Our safeguard will lie in competent personnel.

Social relations are helped also because the institutions offer an opportunity to live together with all kinds of people, all races and religions. If this opportunity is not used consciously by the institution to help youngsters to understand each other, we might have tensions or only a transitory acceptance of the necessity to get along together while one has to, but no carry-over to better intergroup relationships in community life. It is not enough for a Negro youngster who has experienced rejection and humiliation to be thrown into groups with other youngsters. It is important that he begin to see that the community that has confined him to an institution is one that really accepts him as an equal with all other children, and will try to help him and the others to understand each other. This will be best achieved in the daily living situation by the housefather's or housemother's genuine acceptance of all youngsters, but it can be intensified in the special group program where anyone may be elected as a club officer and where questions regarding feelings about race can be discussed directly and openly. Special effort must be made to raise the self-concept of youngsters belonging to minority groups. Race relations do not improve by just throwing people together. There has to be a conscious effort to help them with mutual acceptance.

LIST OF ACTIVITIES

In summarizing this part I would like to give a list of activities which the adolescents in an institution for delinquent girls had made up and which they said they had considered fun when they had been at home. They gave this list in a discussion with the group worker with whom they had established a good relationship. It is important to know this, because I am sure we would not have gotten this same list with somebody with whom they had not felt completely free. The list is an interesting mixture of everyday activities as we would find them among other adolescents and of those showing enjoyment of delinquent activities.

Movies
Ice skating
Roller skating
Bowling
Spotting cars—racing (Marge)
Midnight swimming
Wiener roasts
Splash parties
House parties
Snake dancing (Marge)
Street dancing
Dancing
Community Center activities
Breaking into people's houses (Alice)
Hunting (Marge)
Winter swimming
Horseback riding
Parking (Kathy)
Overnight camping (Alice)

Drinking
Horse swimming (Marge)
Ringing doorbells (Kathy)
Mischief
Fights
Stealing flowers, apples (Kathy)
Fishing
Boating
Picnics
Boat racing
Motorcycle racing
Driving (Marge)
Spending money (Kathy)
Playing "Chicken" in cars (Marge)
Blackout (Freda)
Sports—soft ball, etc.
Drinking under the table
"Chivereeing"—weddings
Flirting
Truanting to stay home and listen to radio programs
Dressing up like boys (Marge)
Shop lifting
Stealing.

It is interesting to see that the kind of fun of which certain girls speak gives us a picture of their needs. For instance, if we put together the activities which Marge considers fun— spotting cars, racing, snake dancing, hunting, horse swimming, driving, playing "chicken" in cars, dressing up like boys—we gain the picture of a girl with strong masculine drives who gets satisfaction of her adventure spirit only in excessively dangerous kinds of activities. When we look at those named by Kathy—parking, ringing doorbells, stealing flowers and apples, spending money—we see a much more feminine pattern with less overt expression of aggression. We see her turning to activities which are more self-centered and more related to her sex drive.

We see how an open expression in an informal group can be an invaluable diagnostic tool.

Activity reveals unconscious material that case histories do not contain.[13]

The use of activity groups involves understanding of individual needs and of the use of program related to those needs. It fulfills diagnostic, educational, socializing, and therapeutic purposes. It is obvious that it must be carried on under the supervision of a social group worker well trained for this tremendous task.

USE OF COMMUNITY RESOURCES

Oftentimes have I heard you speak of one who commits a wrong as though he were not one of you, but a stranger unto you and an intruder upon your world.[14]

The relation to community resources is often hindered by fear of a sensational approach to the delinquent. We will overcome these attitudes only if we make our institutions accessible to the public, but not for visits to just satisfy curiosity. We must help people understand what the institutions are trying to do and let them see that the young people in them are not so different from other children. One of the superintendents of a large training school told me what a plague it was to have young college students or sometimes high school pupils arriving in masses at the institution to look at the youngsters as if they were animals in a zoo. It was disturbing

---

[13] S. R. Slavson, *Introduction to Group Therapy* (New York: Commonwealth Fund, 1943), pp. 106-108.
[14] Kahlil Gibran, *The Prophet* (New York: Knopf, 1923).

not only to the routine of the institution, but offended the dignity of the individuals served by it.

Interpretation of institutional life to the community will be best given by volunteers who are active in the institution. As in the children's institutions they will bring with them a spirit of outside acceptance and they will leave with a better understanding of institutional life. Regularly there have been complaints about the difficulty in finding volunteers for correctional services. One of the reasons is that we have not made these services vital and interesting enough. I am sure that we will find many young people's groups who will be interested in giving service to institutions for juvenile delinquents as a special project. It will be the task of the professional personnel in the institution to help them gain a healthy and helpful attitude in relation to this work. They might come with a great deal of missionary spirit and they will have to learn that young people in these institutions will not accept condescending or preaching attitudes. They will respond only if the volunteer meets them as an equal.

Volunteers can be used successfully to teach special skills or activities or as visitors for youngsters whom nobody comes to see. Sundays are very often the most monotonous and unhappy days in an institution. A larger part of the staff is off duty and the rest, therefore, cannot give much attention to the youngsters. On days like that visits from volunteers or special activities introduced by them will mean the difference between idle hours filled with increased feelings of abandonment, frustration, and hostility and a happy free day to which one looks forward all week and which provides a satisfactory experience. The same kind of supervision that was described in the chapter on the institution for unmarried mothers should be available to volunteers in institutions for delinquents.

Another community contact which means a great deal to

the youngsters is the relationship to national youth serving organizations. To many of them organizations such as the Boy Scouts, Girl Scouts, Camp Fire Girls, YMCA, YWCA, and Catholic Youth Organization seemed sissy and they did not join them. While they are in the institution, an intelligent program related to their specific needs and under the auspices of such organizations can give them a more happy taste than they expected and can at the same time make them feel that they are part of a wider community. It will be important again that these kinds of groups are not completely segregated in the institutional setting but that the youngsters join for special events with community groups of the same organization. It is essential that at such occasions they are not treated either with condescension or with curiosity, but are accepted as just another club or group. This will mean more than just taking them to a certain meeting. It will mean preparation of the youngsters in the community club groups and preparation of young people who come from the institution to meet each other on an equal footing.

Too often such contacts are exclusively arranged on a competitive basis, such as, for instance, the boys of the training school debating against boys in other groups or in competitive sports. This is not the best way to achieve the feeling of belonging to a community outside the institution. It might increase the bond with the institution but it prevents identification with a larger community. Common activities with others on a noncompetitive basis will make for mutual learning. One YMCA group which had visited regularly with some groups in an institution discussed once their experiences with their group leader. The leader later related that the boys had learned to their surprise that there wasn't much difference between them and those in the institution. They wanted to make sure that the youngsters after release from the training school would be accepted into their groups without any difficulty.

GROUP WORK WITH PARENTS

It is Sunday and visitors' day in one of the large training schools. Everywhere parents sit with their youngsters on the grounds, some in friendly and intimate discussion, some staring at each other without being able to say very much, some almost immediately starting a quarrel, and some talking intensely to the youngster who is dissolved in tears. Almost continually parents are knocking at the doors of the houseparents or the superintendent wanting to discuss some question relating to their children, such as discharge, what kind of clothes they should send them, whether they could receive packages, whether somebody had taken care of their teeth, why nothing happened, etc. After the departure of the parents the houseparents usually have a difficult job calming some of the youngsters. The superintendent is exhausted and many parents feel dissatisfied because not enough time could be given to them and because they still do not know the answers to all their questions.

This kind of unsatisfactory situation is repeated in training schools all over the country. Some of them have improved the situation considerably by the use of caseworkers who are available to the parents. But usually the caseworkers also are overworked and cannot give the attention that would be needed to be really helpful. Many institutions have sent out letters at the time of the arrival of the youngster in the institution trying to anticipate the many questions parents are asking. These letters have been helpful but have seldom diminished the need of the parents to discuss these questions all over again in relation to *their* particular boy or girl. Anxiety, guilt, and fear are not relieved enough through written communication.

Child Guidance Clinics in many years of experience have proved that, to be of real help to the youngster, work with parents is essential. Our institutions for delinquents have never yet been able to really tackle this problem. Group discussions with parents would not be an answer to the whole problem, but they would make the work of the harassed superintendent easier, give the parents a more satisfactory feeling, and complement the work done by the caseworker. I would suggest that parents be asked to come to a few meetings right after their youngster is committed to an institution. Attendance should not be compulsory, and in this way the parents who are anxious and who want to participate will be reached first. When we have worked with all of this group and have achieved better understanding on their part, we might tackle those parents who are not eager to participate.

The group discussions with parents should be as informal as possible. It is important that they do not feel that they sit there as the accused but that the group worker is helping them to become part of the treatment and rehabilitation of their children. The discussions should give them opportunity to ask questions, to express their anxieties and even their hostility, and to learn something about the way the institution works with the children. Besides this free expression of feelings and the general discussion, the meetings should have some definite focus. Minimum content covered should be:

The purpose of the institution;
The responsibilities and functions of court, probation officers, houseparents, and clinical and educational staff;
Understanding of the needs of teen-agers;
Understanding of specific problems of their own children and their relationship to family and their own age group.

These kinds of groups should be limited in time. I would suggest six to eight meetings. According to the diagnosis made

of the parents and the children, a few of them might be selected for more intensive additional therapeutic sessions to
help them understand themselves and their children. Because
of limitations of personnel the first kind of group discussions
should be introduced almost immediately as a part of institutional procedure, while the second one should be established
wherever possibilities for it are found.

Helping the parents in groups will have the dual advantage
of reaching many more at a time as well as giving them an
opportunity to see that they are not alone in their distress
and bewilderment regarding the difficulties of their children.
Mrs. C., for instance, was in the waiting room of the Juvenile
Court. Millie, her fourteen-year-old daughter, had become
pregnant a year before and Mrs. C., a warmhearted mother,
had agreed to keep the child as her own and raise him as Millie's brother. Millie was quite frightened about her experience
and not long after her confinement ran away from home. She
was picked up by the police and now the mother was waiting
to hear what would happen. The bewildered mother could not
understand why the child had run away after she had offered
assistance and actually had given it. She felt that she was the
only one in this world who had to carry such a burden. Two
other parents in the waiting room began discussing some of
their problems, and the three got into a discussion about their
children. Mrs. C. later told the caseworker, "I think what
helped me most today was that I saw that I'm not the only
one who carries a cross. Those parents in there have their difficulties too."

How much more helpful would be a guided group discussion which would add to her sense of relief and give her
greater understanding of and practical help to continue her
difficult mother role.

GROUP WORKER'S ROLE IN IN-SERVICE TRAINING

The forms of in-service training in an institution for delinquents can be the same as in the children's institution, namely, individual interviews with houseparents, staff meetings, and special training sessions. The content will be in parts the same, especially where it relates to individual and group dynamics. A large part of the in-service training will concern itself with the matter of discipline.

The juvenile delinquent is adjudicated by a court, and the institutional personnel, therefore, is responsible for his being held in detention. This fact has to be considered in addition to our aim to make this experience educational and therapeutic. The fear of not fulfilling the purpose of "security" is very great in many counselors, and it often looms greater than their desire to understand the individual youngster. It is seen in the almost compulsive way with which most institutions treat the runaway. One cannot understand the many sadistic forms of punishment for running away, such as, for instance, putting the youngster for days on bread and water, leaving him locked in a cell with nothing to do, equipping the cell with nothing but a blanket—no mattress, no other furniture— if one does not see them as expressions of the extreme fear of the institutional personnel of having failed in this primary responsibility. There is a great deal of rationalizing about these methods, but it is clear that their basis lies in the concern with security and being afraid that one might be blamed by the superior or by the court for a runaway.

In the supervision of houseparents, therefore, it will be futile to begin discussing discipline problems as such, and by arguing which is the best form for punishment, or how much punishment should be given. It is far more important to discuss first the feelings of the houseparent and let him or her explore them and become comfortable and secure in this situation. Only if he can use himself freely with a certain feeling of individual responsibility and professional competence can he act rationally. Too many workers in an institution feel just as dependent and afraid as the youngsters under their care. Fear always turns against somebody. Since the youngsters are easily available, fear will turn mostly against them in the form of punishment.

Mrs. J., for instance, kept a runaway girl in the kind of confinement that I described. In discussing it, she maintained that she herself did not really consider this a helpful method, but she was afraid of criticism from the supervising agency and that was why she did it. Though it was quite possible that this too was only putting the blame on somebody else and that she herself actually felt the need for such punishment, it showed the lack of freedom for making her own decisions. Mrs. J. must be helped to accept responsibility for methods of handling the youngsters within a framework of limitations set by the basic philosophy of treatment.

Another fear with which the supervisor will have to deal is that of unknown forces in the youngsters themselves. Delinquency seems to many something foreign, and all of us are afraid of what we cannot comprehend. It will be important to help the houseparent see how delinquent behavior is not as different from normal behavior as he thinks. A housefather who is very disturbed by the apparent "laziness" and resistance to learning on the part of a boy will be much better able to deal with it when he learns that he too sometimes resists learning and does not want to move into something that demands a great deal of effort on his part. When he understands this he will see that the boy's resistance is not a "play of the devil," but a form of common human behavior. By losing his fear he will be able to deal with this rationally and firmly.

Supervision cannot help the houseparent who himself

shows disturbed behavior and who has strong sadistic tendencies. This is an area for psychiatry and such personnel should not be employed in our institutions. We must realize, though, that often behavior which looks like this is actually not deeply rooted but has come from insecurity and misunderstanding of function. In an institute with houseparents of a State Training School, several housefathers demanded angrily to know why they were forbidden to use corporal punishment. If the workshop leader had concluded immediately that these were cruel and inhuman men, he would have either given up the discussion or entered into a fruitless quarrel with them. "Assuming from the first that they were not seriously disturbed people, only confused because of the difficult task before them and suddenly deprived of a tool that they had used for many years and that had made it possible for them to keep difficult problems under control, he decided to help them with their fear and confusion.

Mr. J (the institute leader) asked the men what they wanted to achieve in their work with the youngsters. They said they wanted to help them to be good and capable citizens. Mr. J asked whether they were sure that they wanted this or whether they wanted them to be kids who made no trouble in the institution. There was quite a discussion regarding the fact that one would not exclude the other but that they all knew youngsters who had behaved well in the institution because they were afraid, but had started their delinquent behavior the moment they had left the institution. They all agreed after some deliberation that the first goal they named was the important one. Mr. J then wondered what was achieved by the beating. They said that it frightened them but that they also learned that one was not allowed to do certain things. Mr. J agreed to this, and led the discussion towards some consideration of what the background and experiences of most of the boys were before coming to their institution. It became clear that most of those youngsters had experienced harsh treatment and corporal punishment before they came to the institution but had obviously indulged in delinquent behavior in spite of this. Mr. J then asked them what they expected the superintendent to do if they themselves made mistakes. Did they avoid their mistakes best if they got a heavy dressing-down or did it help them more if the mistake was discussed with them and they were expected not to repeat it? Several of them gave an amused account about how mad they were when one of the supervisors had treated them quite harshly. Mr. J used this account by showing how hostility rises if one is treated harshly and how inner control is not established this way. Mr. J admitted that it "usually worked" in the sense that the behavior was not repeated while the powerful person was around. This brought the discussion back to the attitude of the boys. It was agreed that inner control would not be established through corporal punishment. It was interesting that at this point the discussion began to revolve around the question what could one do if one did not use corporal punishment. It had moved away from the original idea that this was the only method.

We see here that those who were pleading for corporal punishment were not sadists who had a need to use this, but bewildered adults who were afraid because the only method they knew had been taken away from them and they didn't know how to handle the youngster who made work difficult for them. The institute leader, by giving them recognition that they had had a method that worked for certain purposes and then in letting them understand the real purpose towards which they were working, helped them not to feel resentful, but to look for new ways of approaching the youngsters.

The zealous reformer sometimes overlooks the human attributes of those who have for many years worked with difficult problems without any help. We cannot take away from people all their former methods and their way of dealing with others without replacing it with something with which they can feel just as secure.

In supervising the young and inexperienced worker in an institution for delinquents, we will have to help them to accept the reality, for instance, of failure. I have met over and over people in institutions who had been known as progressive pioneers in the work with delinquents and who later became punishing and cynical. In one of the institutions a superintendent told me, "I also once believed in all that stuff about understanding the youngster. You soon learn that the only thing that helps is an iron hand. I advise all my attendants to never let them out of sight and never for one moment let them be idle. I have learned that this is the only way to deal with them." In all his dealings with the youngsters he showed a deep disdain for them. A young housefather in another institution said to me, "You know we all come with quite sentimental ideas about the youngsters. We soon find out how mean they are." It is frightening to see that reality is leading those workers into the extreme of cynicism.

Supervision, therefore, from the beginning has to stress reality and to make it clear that we must expect failure but that that must not prevent us from continuing to learn about the youngsters, to individualize them, and to continue giving our best to them. It is important, for instance, to be prepared for the youngsters' trying out the worker in various ways, even if trust was given to them. They have to run away, for instance, to see whether they will be accepted and treated again like a human being or whether all the kind attitudes were only pretense. In all our work with sickness or with delinquency, we have to accept the fact that it can occur again and it is important not to become cynical because of this.

One of the most difficult skills is to help houseparents or attendants in institutions for delinquents to do *recording* that will be of help in making decisions regarding treatment plans for the youngster. Most summary recordings coming from houseparents are very meager and do not give the information that is necessary, such as a recording that simply says, "She does not get along," or "She is no trouble in the cottage." What is needed is the same kind of information that we felt was necessary in children's institutions. A short daily log should be required of the houseparent in such an institution and it should include the same information suggested in the chapter on children's institutions. The individual report, too, could be written according to the outline given there. It is sufficient that the houseparent report the obvious behavior. Interpretation should emerge in the clinical staff meeting. An interesting example of how this can be achieved is seen in the following record.

The housemother's comments were:

She has only one friend at a time to whom she clings tightly. She confides in her. She is agreeable with adults and a good worker. She is well liked by everyone on the staff. She sometimes tells only part of the truth.

This short comment was very helpful for treatment purposes.

The caseworker recorded:

She expresses fears about being abnormal and crazy. She needs much reassurance. She begins to trust the caseworker. An attachment to one friend is probably a real major step in her development and should not be discouraged. She indulges in much fantasy.

The clinical discussion helped the housemother see that the tall tales that the girl was telling were a defense mechanism and that this was a youngster who badly needed to gain status among her contemporaries. The housemother's comment that she had found individual friends and that she was agreeable towards adults helped the rest of the staff to see her improvement. The recommendation at that time was to encourage her to make friends, to continue a supportive relationship with the caseworker, and to allow her in her work assignments to gain status.

We see here that the summary regarding the individual does not have to be a long one to become valuable.

In another instance the housemother described how Phyllis was extremely satisfied in her group living situation and seemed to settle down in it as if she never wanted to leave. This comment, coupled with the caseworker's note:

She is completely rejected by her family and knows of no one who is interested in what happens to her, knows of no one with whom she would like to live or with whom she could live.

leads to the recommendation that help must be given to Phyllis not to become *too* satisfied in the institutional situation because she could easily withdraw into it to get away from the lonely outside world. To provide for this girl's future, plans must include companionship and real acceptance outside the institution.

Short recording done by the houseparents must become an integral part of the work assignment. Only this way can the valuable observations of day-by-day living become effective for diagnosis and treatment.

Far too many of our institutions are overcrowded and the houseparents have to work with much too large a number of residents. It will be important to help the houseparents not to feel too frustrated if they cannot always do what they consider best practice. They may be convinced that individualized service is important, but if we ask of them to take care of sixty or eighty youngsters at a time, we only make them extremely guilty and unhappy by putting demands on them that simply cannot be fulfilled. When this is the case, training and supervision should give reassurance and acceptance of the fact that many of the best practices cannot be carried through. The group worker can help the houseparent make use of a few helpful devices, such as dividing the group into smaller units and trying to supply him with volunteer help, and in addition to this can make him feel secure in the knowledge that not too much is expected of him in terms of individualization. What can be expected of him is the use of the situation to create an accepting and healthy group climate.

All this points up the necessity of improving personnel in our institutions. I want to stress, though, that improvement does not come exclusively by employing *more* personnel but that hand in hand with additional staff must go an improvement in their quality, through selection as well as through training and supervision.

In the beginning of this chapter we spelled out the different functions of the social group worker:

1. Supervision and training of houseparents.
2. Direct group leading of therapeutic groups and formed clubs and councils.
3. Being responsible for activity group programs.
4. Supervision of volunteers.
5. Work with parents' groups.

As a member of the clinical staff, the group worker is responsible with others on the team for diagnosis and for recommendations regarding release or treatment.

The group worker should not be part of an outside service but should be part of the institutional staff because of his relationship to the life blood of the institution, the group living.

His ability to diagnose people, especially in relationship to their group experience, is vital in institutions for delinquents, because we are dealing with an age group to whom group experience is extremely important. This diagnostic ability should be of special help also in reception centers, such as those organized by Youth Commissions in several states, and in short-term detention homes.

7. SOCIAL GROUP WORK IN PRISONS

Social group workers have practiced in children's institutions and institutions for delinquents and in recent years also in mental hospitals. There is little experience of social group work in prisons. There have been a few interesting attempts in group therapy conducted by psychologists and psychiatrists. The whole field of prison reform is in a state of great flux. Many new programs are very much in an experimental stage. In the opinion of several persons interested in prison reform, the vital contribution of the social group work method should not be overlooked.

We are in a period of changing attitudes regarding the adult offender. It would be presumptuous to assume that until recently nobody cared about prison reform. Actually, there has been a great deal of thinking about the purposes of prisons and for a long time men have fought for improvement, each time using the best knowledge of their time. The names of Enoch Wines and Zebulon Brockway stand out in the nineteenth century as great reformers who made an outstanding effort to make prisons into real centers of rehabilitation.

The silence system and the individual caged cells, which seem to us today like cruel torture methods, actually were progress in their time and represented idealistic efforts based on existing knowledge. It was thought, for instance, that silence would enhance meditation and allow the prisoner to take counsel with himself. The difficult and complicated mechanisms of human emotions and the vital importance of communication were not known. The Quakers, especially, who had experienced the benefits of silence in their own congregation, could not have understood at this time how differently the disturbed human being reacts than the one who is comparatively at peace with himself. Individual cells were certainly an improvement compared with the overcrowded jails where everybody from the murderer to the pocket thief were pressed together in a sweating, cursing, and dirty mass. If today we could build and staff a prison according to the best present-day knowledge, later centuries would probably look at it as only a feeble attempt towards perfection.

Problems of prison reform are of immense magnitude because of public apathy or hostility toward the adult offender and because of the way an earlier century has expressed its thinking by establishing huge buildings which withstand time and perpetuate its approach. Public misinformation about prisons has led to too little financial support of them and too poor personnel in them. We have some outstanding wardens in this country who, because of their courage and their persistence in fighting against inhuman treatment, should deserve the homage of a whole nation. Myrl E. Alexander, while Assistant Director of the United States Bureau of Prisons, said in a recent article:

We might quite properly conclude that the jail is the most retarded of all the agencies established to deal with the complicated social and behavior problems in a community.[1]

Warden Walter M. Wallack expressed in a very simple manner his criticism of the treatment of the adult offender:

[1] "Let's Look at Our Jails," *Federal Probation*, September, 1952, p. 15.

Our first mistake is that we forget that prisoners are people.[2]

Realizing the difficulty arising from the many differences among individuals in our prisons, the different behavior patterns as well as dynamics, the different mental abilities and offenses, any method that is considered to make a contribution has to be presented with all humility. It must be conceded that any single method can be only a small part of the whole effort to treat and to rehabilitate. If I present here the necessity for adding the group work method to our program for helping prisoners, I am doing this mainly because all of us realize that the criminal's breakdown has occurred somehow in relation to other people, and that it is necessary for him to recover the ability to get along with society, whatever his antisocial behavior was.

ELEMENTS OF TREATMENT

Usually in adult life, groups do not have the same vital importance that they have for adolescents. They do not represent a whole way of life to the adult. For the healthy adult, the group supplies an opportunity for association with others when he needs to reverse his desire to be alone. The group gives him an opportunity to see himself in relation to others, and it makes it possible for him to act more effectively than he acts when he is by himself. In many adult groups, the group bond is not as strong emotionally as it is in adolescence. Yet people in prison are forced to live together in spite of the fact that as individuals they often are at different stages of personal development.

[2] "Stone Walls Do a Prison Make," *Federal Probation*, September, 1952, p. 7.

In many offenders, some of the natural group feeling is lacking or has been twisted or arrested in an earlier stage of development. To one, group associations might mean as much dependency as to the adolescent and he will find himself in the grip of anybody who is able to exploit this juvenile need. To another, group association means only dissatisfaction and annoyance and every contact with another person arouses in him anger and resentment and leads to a fight; to a third one, group associations intensify his feeling of inadequacy and he withdraws into fantasies or finds relief in some act that will make him feel that he has outwitted someone else.

Yet as adults the demand is laid upon us to get along with others and to be responsible in our associations with them. The middle-aged woman before the parole board who tries to explain some unacceptable behavior in the institution by saying that everybody else did the same thing is still in the stage of the young child who does not take responsibility for her own behavior. She is in danger of always using this as an excuse for her own actions. The forty-year-old man who says, "From now on I will always do what I am told," is like a small child and will continue getting into difficulties because he does not accept responsibility for himself.

If our goal is to help the prisoner become a self-respecting citizen who will contribute in a positive way to society, we must be sure that we are giving him a basis for this while he is in our hands. I am aware of the fact that with a few adult offenders we do not know yet how we can help them, but the number is comparatively small. There is an appalling lack of knowledge among the public of the great variation among the prison population. Many offenders are willing and capable to lead a law-abiding and useful life if we do not destroy them while they are behind walls or through our prejudices after they are out.

The group worker's contribution to the rehabilitation process will lie mainly in diagnosis and treatment as part of a clinical team. I recently visited a small women's reformatory. There was regular work for the women as well as recreational outlet and a general attitude of treating them as human beings. Yet, in spite of all this, the superintendent would be the first one to admit that there is a great need for diagnostic and treatment services. Decisions regarding release or stay of a prisoner are hard to make because of the lack of such services. Psychological testing, group work and casework services, and psychiatric consultation should be introduced in such institutions to help answer the following questions:

1. *What is the deeper motivation for committing the crime?* A housewife and mother of several children has forged several checks. Her husband charges her with extravagance. She says she did it because there was sickness in the family. Both husband and wife may be perfectly honest in thinking that what they say is true. Yet a better knowledge of the home situation and an increased observation of the woman's behavior show a somewhat different picture. The husband is an exacting and rather demanding person who has to have his food prepared perfectly, who wants to have his children looking always neat, who insists on a well-kept home. The woman feels inadequate in regard to such demands and does not know exactly how to live up to them. She is anxious to please her husband, in fact, is quite afraid of him. The easy way to live up to such demands is to put more money into the household than is available. In understanding this, we realize that the woman needs assistance in gaining self-confidence, some direct teaching in homemaker skills, and some insight into her own feelings of fear in relation to her husband. The caseworker in individual interviews and the group worker in group discussions should help the husband to understand his part in his wife's behavior and help him reduce some of his demands. This will be an

important contribution to rehabilitation of the woman after her return to her own home.

2. *What is the motivation for changed behavior?* Is it a feeling of genuine guilt? Is it fear of further reprisal? Is the person unhappy with himself? Is change occurring because of a good relationship with someone whom one wants to please through better behavior? If the motivation is, for instance, only fear of reprisal, longer and more intensive work is necessary to help the person internalize some of the demands of society. If it is unhappiness with oneself, it will be important to find the points of strength in the prisoner and help him put those into a balance with his shortcomings. Each time a better diagnostic understanding of motivation will give invaluable help for treatment.

3. *What is his or her basic attitude towards other people?* Is it mainly a deep sense of hostility? Is it a paranoic attitude of feeling persecuted and singled out from all others, and therefore, a deep bitterness towards everybody, or is it fear of others combined with a withdrawal that breaks out in delinquent behavior? Or is it a relationship of submission to the demands of everybody stronger or more clever and, therefore, a compulsion to be domineering and never to submit to anybody else's suggestions or demands?

An answer to these questions can mainly be found in observing relationships in the group.

4. *What is the capacity of accepting reasonable limitations?* Is this a person who cannot accept limitations at all or someone who will accept limitations from his or her equals but never from authority? Or is he just the opposite, somebody who will accept limitations from authority only, but never if they come from somebody on an equal level? It was important to observe this, for instance, in the case of a young offender who superficially seemed to make an excellent adjustment in prison. He was courteous and very willing in all the relations

he had with the guards. Only in observing him during leisure time in the yard was it seen that he actually was extremely unconforming, would not accept anybody else's rights besides his own, and would fly into a rage when other prisoners got in his way and abuse them verbally and physically. It became important in the treatment of this prisoner to help him gain greater insight into his feelings towards a person in authority, not because he was defying them but because he was too conforming to them and, therefore, channeled all his hostility against equals.

5. *What is his attitude towards himself?* Is he depreciating himself and feeling that he is not worth anything? Has he a completely unrealistic idea of his capacities? Does he feel that he is so bad that he almost wants to destroy himself? Does he begin to see that he can use help in relation to his own inner conflicts? All these will be important questions to answer.

The answers to these five questions will help parole boards as well as those who are in daily contact with the prisoner. They will be found in individual interviews, in observations at work places, and in observations of daily group life.

The group worker is not an entertainer, though recreational activities are important to break the monotony of prison life. Some of these activities are better carried on by a person trained in physical education who can teach sports and help with the physical workout. The group worker's task will be a sensitive listening to outspoken or unspoken needs, determining some leisure-time programs according to them, and observing and helping with interpersonal relationships. His function will be observation at the time where there is free intermingling, such as in the prison yards, helping to institute activities which will fulfill particular needs, and leading of therapeutic group discussions.

DISCUSSION GROUPS

The guiding principles for a discussion group will be the same as described in the chapter on delinquents.[3] Group therapy can be conducted in this form with some highly intellectual prisoners who can understand interpretations of complicated psychological phenomena. Other group discussions in prisons might relate to those same questions, but must be conducted in a simple language. In addition to this, everyday questions of life will have to be discussed. In a recent interview with the warden of one of the large State Reformatories he emphasized the need to prepare inmates for everyday life. He gave examples of how important it would be to discuss before release how to keep some household accounts, even how to write out a check legally. In many group discussions it was found that simple facts of sex were unknown, even though prisoners were boasting a great deal about their experiences. Many of these group discussions will be the same as any group worker knows them to be in adult groups in the community.

One of the questions which has been raised frequently is whether the person who conducts these kinds of therapeutic discussions should be completely divorced from the authoritarian setting. It is often felt that free group discussions are not possible if the therapist is identified in any way with authority. I myself do not agree with this point of view for several reasons: (1) It is not realistic and somewhat deceptive. Actually, anybody doing this kind of work must at least take on the role of diagnostician as well as therapist. In the form of diagnosis, therefore, he has an influence on the inmate's fate and can never be completely neutral. (2) Therapeutically

[3] An excellent article regarding guided group interaction in prisons is Lloyd W. McCorkle's "Group Therapy in the Treatment of Offenders," *Federal Probation*, December, 1952, p. 22.

I think it unsound to create another dichotomy in the prisoner's mind about the "bad" authority and the "good" therapist. He has to come to terms with authority and emphasizing that the one with whom he can speak freely is not part of the authoritarian system will only increase his resentment towards the demands placed on him by the reformatory. It is dangerous to make out of the clinical service the "fairy godmother" as opposed to all the other efforts in the prison. It is important to let the prisoners know that they can be frank and open in a discussion with the person who at the same time carries responsibility in relation to decisions made about them.

As an example I am quoting from a discussion with six young inmates (offense mostly burglarly) of a reformatory.

Harry then brought out the fact that if he had had a gun and if he were on escape from a correctional institution and the law enforcement officers were attempting to pick him up, he would not hesitate to use a gun on them. This remark dropped pretty much like a bomb-shell in the group. Joe challenged him and said, "Do you mean to say that you would use the gun?" Most of the group members were incredulous but it seemed very clear that Harry was sincere enough in indicating that he would impulsively act in this way. Harry stated that he really didn't care because life in any sort of correctional setting wasn't too good and he felt he didn't have too much to lose. . . . At just about this point the members of the group mentioned the fact that all this was being discussed in my presence and that for all we know this was being taken down. Harry was a little bothered by this and he said that he supposed now this would immediately go right back to the parole board. The worker then placed before the group the question as to how this material should be used. Should we keep this completely confidential and away from the parole board or should we perhaps inform it of that which had come out? The group members expressed the idea that it was the worker's responsibility, if he knew this, to make a record of this and bring it to the attention of the parole board. The worker said that above all the purpose of these meetings is to enable them to discuss everything freely without the fear of being reported and that he hoped that when the question of release or continuation comes up that sufficient change in attitude and personality will have taken place so that this will not be a problem.

We see here that actually the worker's being part of the authoritarian setup is helpful in bringing reality into the discussions and helping the young men themselves to understand how their attitudes relate to release. At the same time we can see that the accepting attitude of the worker allows frank discussion.

The group discussions from which the previous example was taken give a good picture of the typical subjects that will come up and need to come up in this setting. They are: gripes, family relationships, understanding oneself, questioning of rules, criteria for release, use of leisure time, work, sex. Too many inmates go through the whole period of time of confinement without doing any thinking about the motivations for their actions and they gain no outlet for the resentment they harbor.

These kind of groups have the great advantage that they usually can be quite constant because the prisoners are available for a long period of time. Some group discussions from which I want to quote give an impression of how they can serve in understanding these men better and at the same time help them to understand themselves. It is only after some period of time that they begin to make some connection between their own hostility and their family background. This group had seen the film, *Angry Boy*, which had led to a great deal of discussion.

At about this juncture Harry brought up the intense hostility that he has felt towards his father and at the same time the death wishes that he had. He brought out the fact that when he took off from X he felt that the lack of family concern was such and, particularly, that his father's hostility was such, that he just didn't care what happened to him. He stated that at that time he would not even have cared if he had killed Mr. A (the person he had assaulted). It seemed fairly clear that for the first time Harry was able to establish the connection between his feeling of isolation and distance from his parents and the hostile and delinquent acts. (This young man had tried to commit suicide several times.)

It is clear that the young man's understanding this will not yet change his attitude, but the skill of the group worker will help him move toward this.

This group discussed also how it was not enough to put the blame on parents but also necessary to understand some of the parents' difficulties. One of the members had had great difficulties with his father and was sure that he might have more after his release. The record states at one point:

Joe's thinking was that he would like to see his father receive some type of treatment and in addition would like the father to have an opportunity to see such a film as *Angry Boy* that the group saw. He felt that this would be preparatory to working out a better relationship with him.

Joe is beginning to include his father in more positive thinking.

Besides the feeling of desertion by the family, there is very often the feeling that one was not justly treated by the court. It is important that some of the bitterness come out and that unrealistic accusations be discussed instead of keeping them to oneself all during confinement:

From the discussion of lack of family support we got into the trial itself and reference was made to the fact that the Judge in Bob's case said he would merely be sent up for 30 days or so. Jack contended that he too was sent here only for a brief period of time and that he then wound up spending a surprisingly long time here. At this point the worker said that this was not the case—rather that they misconstrued what was said in the court-room. Bob and some of the others became insistent so that the worker said that could be established very easily by reference to the court transcripts.

One of the files was obtained and the disposition of the Judge was discussed with the group. We see here that the worker did not go into the feeling, but first tried to establish the basic fact and from then on he could work with them regarding their feelings and why they misconstrued the court action.

The "outside" often seems the wish fulfillment for all inmates in reformatories or prisons. Yet if release is discussed more realistically, fears will be expressed and the fact can be discussed that there is something that frightens them and that has to be mastered. They begin to see that the relationships which have made for difficulties, family, neighbors, and work, will be pressing down on them again.

Fred brought up the fact that a person is simply hounded by a "fear of going back." As he verbalized it, "you just keep trying to run away. You don't know what it is, you see the cop and get scared. . . . You don't know what you are running from—but you see jail all the time." He added that one gets kind of scared to go back out. Harry and Lenny agreed too that they felt a little scared about the prospect of going out. Harry added that his father had told him, "You'll be back," and that sort of observation by his father certainly didn't make him feel any better. Fred at this time apologized to the group because he felt they would resent his monopolizing the meeting. However, the group reassured him that they did not mind his bringing out his feelings. He went on to say that he knew that even when his sister misplaced money she couldn't help but suspect him. It made him feel extremely discouraged and uncomfortable. Jerry verbalized the idea that "I was always dodging people when I was on the outside."

We see here how these rather "tough young men" feel free to admit that they are scared and how they give acceptance to each other. No individual help could be quite as effective as, for instance, letting Fred see that the other guys do not mind his bringing out feelings and allowing him to talk about his fears. At this point the discussion is quite discouraging. Help comes from one of the group members when it continues.

Harry at this point interjected with the thought, "I don't think your life is wrecked." It was his idea that fellows could make good and that the situation isn't entirely bleak.

To work this out and come to a more positive feeling is not easy, and the group falls for a while back to the gloomy part of being out on parole.

Fred pointed out that this might be true if a fellow can stay out, but that is an extremely difficult situation. Jim introduced the point that "I have had that hopeless feeling when I was out too." Jerry remarked that he has had it in the past but that he didn't have it now. He went on to say that "A lot of guys make it on parole." Harry then introduced the thought that the best way to make good on parole and keep out of difficulty is to go out to the woods, get a little cabin and hide out there for the balance of the parole period.

The latter sentence is almost a gem in helping us to understand how very unrealistic a person can be in relation to his situation. Harry is the same who had expressed great hostility against his father and who also had said that he would shoot it out with the law enforcement officer. This latter remark shows how very unsure he is of himself. All this put together gives a diagnosis and makes it clear that Harry is not ready for parole but that he needs help in his struggle with his own aggressive drives.

The interaction of the group is especially helpful when a member becomes discouraged and begins to lose all incentive for change. In group work we have found over and over that the critical power of the members is usually not only better accepted but more effective than criticism coming from the person who represents authority, even if this is the most accepting person. We have an excellent example of this with the same group in a later meeting.

Jerry went on to explain that he doesn't mind spending his life in the institution since nothing in particular awaits him on the outside. After all he works only two hours a day. And then, during his relative free time, he can amuse himself and be happy waiting and watching visitors as they go through the institution. The group, particularly Fred, was very amused by this and Fred asked, "Do you know what he reminds me of when he stands there staring over the galley at people going through? A sex criminal." Jerry just laughed at this as did most of the other members of the group and then Fred went on to ask, "What are you going to do when you get out?"

One member of the group is beginning to criticize Jerry but in a friendly way. His next step is to bring him back to some real thinking about the "outside."

Jerry replied that, "I am going West." Fred asked, "How are you going west and get clothing for it?" As far as getting clothing and money first Jerry said that he would work for it, but when the other group members asked what type of work he would be prepared to do, Jerry had no adequate answer. As far as going west is concerned, he said that he would hitchhike, and the group members were amused by this and asked where he would get money to live on. Jerry replied that he would receive some money that is being held in trust for him when he turns 21. (Jerry was 18 years of age at this time.) The group asked whether he would just wait for that. Jerry went on to say, "Maybe I'll be a bum." This again was amusing and somewhat disquieting to the group members. Paul asked, "Why not try to make something of yourself here?" Bob put in that a fellow should show that he knows how to work first and make something of himself, then he could be considered for release. Jerry replied, "I am in here to do time—not work." Tom commented with, "I am in here to do time, also, but I would go nuts sitting around a cell. I am glad that I have a seven day a week job." Jerry answered that "I don't put in more than four hours in a cell."

It is interesting to see that at this point Jerry begins to change. He got out a great deal of his resentment, but now group pressure has mounted and he begins to feel that he cannot be completely resistant in the face of this. It is at this point that the group worker enters the discussion and asks a question about the level of maturity this type of thinking reflects. The group members agree that this was the thinking of a kid rather than that of an adult. It is following this reaction that Jerry begins to talk more about his feelings and dreams when he is alone in the cell and the discussion turns to his more inner conflicts.

GROUP BOND

It has been discussed often whether friendships starting in a prison should be allowed or discouraged. Realistically we know that they *are* starting in prisons and that a common experience usually does create a bond. Since this is happening without our wish, it will be important to keep it at least as constructive as possible. The bond that develops under guidance will be more helpful in rehabilitation than the bond that develops through resentment and hatred. In this group, for instance, individuals express from time to time what the group means to them.

Fred went on to add something which seemed to be quite sincere and personal. He said that it was his intention not to say anything about it until group meetings would break up, but he couldn't really hold it back. He said he has come to look upon these meetings as something very important. This opportunity to get together with the other fellows and talk about things of interest to them, he felt was something that had become very meaningful to him and something which made him feel deprived if for some reason no meeting was held. He agreed, and one of the other group members pointed out, that without the meeting they went around with nails bitten down and feeling pretty low. . . . Significantly after the meeting concluded, Paul asked whether there was any possibility of continuing these types of meetings on the outside. He said that he felt that, if released, such contacts might again do him some good.

The members of the group wanted to keep in contact with those members who were put on probation and kept up some correspondence through the group discussion leader. The two following letters, written by the discussion leader to a member on parole, show the bond that developed and the help that the members of the group want to give to each other.

Dear Tom,

The members of the group were sorry that you missed the meeting. In fact Fred said, "Why did he sneak off like that?"

Most of the group members want to know what your plans are. First, they want to know what kind of a job you are going to have and where you will be working. Jerry asked particularly to know whether this place and these meetings have helped you any for what you are going to do on the outside. At this point, Fred feels very strongly that we should let you know that we think you are a pretty good Joe and we hope that you will be very successful on the outside.

Please let us hear how you are getting along at your early convenience. Fred adds to this that if you run into any difficulties, "Think before you do something." Jerry also wants to know if there are any problems that come up that you have to face whether you wouldn't write to us and let us know because we have to face the very same problems when the rest of us get out.

With best regards, we are,

Yours truly,

The Group.

We see how the group takes part in the problems of the other one and how they identify with him. Here is a second letter to the same parolee.

Dear Tom,

We received your very welcome letter and were glad to hear from you and also that everything is well. Fred understands why you left in such a rush. He said that if he were paroled, he would probably go right out too, without stopping for a group meeting.

Johnny said to tell you that we did a little acting out about your biggest problem: "Saying 'no' to the boys." Paul took your place and all of us tried real hard to get him to "go along on some wild times." He refused, and we think that you will be able to do the same. It could mean the difference between staying out and joining the group again.

All of us would like to see you personally and talk with you. We would be glad if you have the time and can afford it to drop in again for a visit. Before coming though, be sure to write to check with us whether the date you have in mind is okay and whether there will be a meeting when you come. Best wishes from all of us.

Yours truly,

The Group.

The bond which develops this way might become the force that will keep the men from falling back into criminal behavior. We have no proof yet for this, but from our general knowledge of people we know that the feeling of belonging often overcomes a great deal of hostility. There is room for a long-time research project in this area.

CONTRIBUTIONS OF SOCIAL GROUP WORKER

I want to make a special point here about the use of both men and women on the clinical team in prisons and reformatories for both sexes. I am perfectly aware of the fact that it has seldom been tried out yet, but the few attempts that have been made have proved exceedingly helpful. There is no question that many men need a therapeutic relationship with a mother figure and that many women need to learn that there are kind fathers and not only the stern or abusing males whose images they carry with them. In one of the prisons which deals mainly with young men offenders, a woman was introduced as the group worker against the protest and skepticism of many in authority. In the two years in which she has worked there the climate has improved considerably and the prison authorities insist they would never want to work without a woman in this position again. I am sure that— if we find the right people—the same will apply in a woman's prison if a man is introduced on the clinical team.

In an unpublished paper written in 1953, Paul H. Engstrom (member of the Minnesota Parole Board) summarized his thinking regarding the needs of a social group worker in prisons:

The social group worker is becoming more and more recognized as an invaluable member of the psychiatric team. Casework is not enough, especially in a setting like this . . . where group pressure is felt so strongly, where group loyalties are so extreme, and where there are so many men who need help. . . .

The group worker will be a member of the total rehabilitation team with responsibility for the social group work aspects of the rehabilitation program. . . .

Description of functions

A. In re: the institution

1. Participate in classification procedure. Attend classification board hearings and contribute to its determinations by diagnosing such questions as whether or not inmate could profit from group therapy.

2. Interpret the philosophy and function of group work and group therapy to professional staff members and to other institutional personnel and officials, seeking to gain unity of cooperation and support.

3. Contribute to the desperately needed cross fertilization of ideas by sharing of problems, solutions, and plans. The ultimate success of this program of rehabilitation depends upon mutual understanding and acceptance all the way to the top of the institution and the administration and the state government and the uttermost parts of our commonwealth.

B. In re: the inmates

1. Intake

a. Hold orientation meetings with inmates, properly grouped, after admission interviews by psychiatrist or caseworker, and after initial classification conferences (or possibly before).

b. Interpret prison functions, purposes, rules, routine, with possible consideration of rationale behind these things. Also possible consideration of infractions and their meaning to the welfare of the prison population.

c. Give opportunity for discussing problems of adjustment to the prison experience.

d. Help the men to recognize that they have common problems.

e. Lay groundwork for continued group therapy.

f. Allow expression of feelings or resentment at being incarcerated. Accept negative feelings. Accept resistance to help. Enable inmates to see opportunities for learning and growing in the prison experience.

g. Make tentative groupings for further diagnosis and treatment.

2. Diagnosis

a. Observe and interpret behavior of inmates in group therapy meetings, during recreation periods, in relationships with other inmates, guards, shop instructors, etc.

b. Contribute observations and interpretations at classification board meetings and later staff meetings, and to the parole board.

c. Form groupings which are proper in size and content for therapeutic purposes.

3. Treatment

a. Apply all knowledge and professional skill as a social group worker toward the goal of fitting as many inmates as possible for better adjustment on their return to their community.

b. Carefully form groups and work with them at a rate and intensity determined by the specific needs of the individual group members, and in relation to their total personalities.

c. Help the inmates in each group to work out better relationships with each other. Build a sense of responsibility for the conduct and morale of the entire group and ultimately for the entire prison population.

d. Help the group members to gain the satisfactions of friendship, recognition, status, and creative expression.

e. Channel discussions and interests toward worthwhile goals.

f. Experiment with the idea of forming groups around various foci like common vocational interests, common avocational interests, and common symptomathology (exs: forgery, abandonment, alcohol, narcotics).

g. Form groups and, with the help of consultants, work on such physical and neurological problems as epilepsy, speech difficulty, arthritis, etc.

h. Gain the acceptance of the group by relating self to it on a warm, positive, professional basis.

i. Participate with the inmates on an equal level rather than from a higher and authoritarian position.

j. Understand the dynamics of emotional illness and skillfully meet the need of inmates to release anxiety and hostility recognizing that this must be done before constructive progress can be made.

k. Include in discussions consideration of such matters as: dynamics of criminal behavior; causation of crime; the structure and meaning of emotions and how to deal with them; home and family problems; laws and why we have them; the place of values in life, etc. etc.

4. Release and Follow up

a. Help with orientation for parole or discharge by discussion of problems involved in return to the community and inmates feelings about them. This would include problems of family adjustment, employment (getting and keeping a job), acceptance of community attitudes, etc.

b. Arrange discussions centering around parole philosophy and procedure including such matters as parole rules, relationship with agent, monthly reports, etc. It is especially important to get inmate's fears, resentments, and other feelings about these things.

c. Stimulate continued participation in group activity such as church and YMCA groups; hobby, social and service groups, A.A., etc.

To the functions outlined by Mr. Engstrom I like to add two more:

Responsibility for Staff Training

In most larger prisons individual supervision of guards (they are now often better called "security officers") would be impossible. Group training sessions at regular intervals will be necessary. The group worker's role must be not to make those training sessions only content-dominated classroom sessions, but to help the guards feel like members of a team in a common endeavor. This can only be established through free give-and-take and an informal atmosphere. It will be necessary to subdivide the staff so as to make the groups not larger than twenty participants at one time.

All discussions must be related to the direct practice of the guard. They also must allow him to express and to understand his own feelings. It will be important to him to see that he, Guard A., reacts differently to prisoner S. than Guard B. reacts to the same prisoner. While he thinks that prisoner S. is a "shifty little runt," Guard B. sees him as a "skinny under-nourished fellow." In expressing this, both will learn how their feelings towards the same person arise out of their own different experiences. In learning this they will become more objective about their own observations. This will make for a more complete and true picture of each of the prisoners.

Morale among prison personnel is very often quite low and due not only to the poor pay we unfortunately give to those men and women who carry such an essential task in our society but to a feeling of inferiority. Morale will be improved through group discussions which allow for more interchange with each other, for participation in decisions about prisoners (without the final authority), and through a developing bond. (I am aware of the fact that today there often exists a strong bond among prison personnel. Yet it is mostly created, unfortunately, by the need of holding together against the inmate.)

Work with Relatives of the Prisoner

We talked about the anxiety of parents in institutions for delinquents and how group discussion can help with relief of such feelings and can help towards better care of the youngster when he returns. In dealing with relatives of prisoners we have to relate to increased anxiety, often increased hostility either towards the prisoner or towards the court, sometimes outright rejection of the prisoner, and at other times an unrealistic shielding of him. The group discussion leader will have to deal with all these different feelings at the same time. Though this is a difficult task, it opens up an opportunity for more realistic thinking, since the relatives see others and will recognize the biased view more easily in others than in themselves. These groups will by necessity be heterogeneous and have constantly changing membership. About five meetings should be offered to every relative at the time of the inmate's entering the institution. After this time the group worker should make a diagnosis regarding the need of individual members to continue or their ability to go on without those sessions.

Clinical services for people in prison are *not* a luxury item but an essential. A member of a parole board said to me that we are acting today in prisons as if we had hospitals with nothing but beds. We throw the patients in without knowing what their sickness is, put them all together, the one with tuberculosis, the one with a broken leg, and the one with a head injury, and give them no care, just feed them. After a while we look at them and say, "Well, they look all right," and send them out. Social workers, who, as Charlotte Towle once said, should be "the conscience of society," have sadly neglected the men and women in prison. They have often been discouraged because of the political implications of prison appointments, or are afraid of dealing within the legal structure which has to be authoritarian and cannot allow the client to come for help on his own free will. We have to accept political realities and influence them, the way Dorothea Dix in the mid-nineteenth century stood before the legislature and fought for the cause of the mentally sick. We have to be able to work with people who do not come to us because they want to but because they are forced to and still help them to accept us after we have let them see that we really have something to offer to them. We ourselves have to come to terms with the problem of authority, realizing that it is not something that is bad in itself, but only if it is misused in a punishing way.

We will have to realize that work in prisons, jails, and reformatories and work with the adult offender is an open field for those young people who can combine warmth with a capacity to accept hostility, intelligence and clinical astuteness with a capacity to translate it into practical work. Both specializations in social work, casework and group work, must become an indispensable part of prison treatment.

8. SOCIAL GROUP WORK IN INSTITUTIONS FOR THE AGED

In recent years there has been a flood of literature about the aged in this country and public attention has been called to their plight. In a competitive society such as ours is, where a premium is paid for being able to stand on one's own feet and to be independent of everyone else, old age becomes a problem. This is still a young and pioneering country and, therefore, the able-bodied person is the important one and not the sick and the aged. At the same time medical science has prolonged life and we are faced with an increased aging population. It is inhuman to let people live and yet not allow them a purpose for living.

A young social worker was working with an older person who had been severely sick but had recovered through medical care with its most modern and latest achievements. After release from the hospital the man stood alone with no purpose in life and no one interested in him. He expressed his intention of throwing himself under a train because life was not worth living. The young social worker said to me, "Somebody must sit in heaven and laugh at us. We are putting them together, limb by limb, but we are not really giving them life." Man cannot accept just vegetating. He needs a purpose in life and recognition and companionship.[1]

[1] Others have written intensively about the needs of older people and about

We know that a great deal of work is needed with all older people, whether they live alone or in institutions. One would assume that homes for the aged fulfill the need for companionship. This unfortunately is not true in many cases. A large number of public or private boarding homes and institutions offer nothing but a place to live. Only the very alert aged person will find satisfaction in the kind of solitary activity he can pursue in his own room or will be able to initiate contacts with others. Most of the residents cannot take this initiative. In a report submitted to the National Mental Health Authorities on the use of Federal Health Grants for an activity project in commercial boarding homes for older persons, Mrs. Ida Davis said:

It is our impression that the residents are more handicapped than the average older person—physically, mentally and emotionally, and that they have fewer than average family, personal and community ties.[2]

Another group worker who started a project in an institution for the aged told about the fact that even two people living in the same room did not know each other's name and that they hardly spoke to each other. The word LONELINESS is written in big letters even in the congregation of communal living, and it is unfortunately combined with the deep feeling of loss of self-respect. It is clear that this cannot be overcome through "entertainment." Far too often old age institutions have been made the target for charity projects of youth groups or other community groups who visited them, sang a few songs to them, served them some food, and then left. This whole

community efforts to help them. Two such publications are: Jerome Kaplan, *A Social Program for Older People* (Minneapolis: University of Minnesota Press, 1953); and *Community Services for Older People, The Chicago Plan* (Chicago: Community Project for the Aged of the Welfare Council of Metropolitan Chicago, 1952).

[2] Mimeographed report (Minneapolis: Family and Children's Service, 1952).

procedure is actually degrading and leaves a taste of bitterness. It makes the older persons feel even more that they are "objects" and that they are considered unable to do anything for themselves. They have no opportunity to participate at such occasions and no interaction is occurring between them to get better acquainted with each other.

The group worker's work in institutions for the aged will, therefore, be direct work with groups. If it is a larger program comprising several institutions or an unusually large institution, he will work with volunteers who do the group leading. In both cases it is the establishment of special groups or clubs that will make a contribution to group living. The purpose of these clubs is clear-cut and fourfold:

1. To raise the self esteem in those participating.
2. To give an opportunity for planning.
3. To become a part of their own small community and, if possible, a part of a larger community.
4. To establish a group bond that may replace the warmth of family relationships.

These are the general purposes. The group will mean something different to every individual in this larger framework. I am quoting from the individual summaries given by a group worker which shows some of these differences.

Mr. Z is proud and cantankerous, rejecting friendships until the friendly intentions of the other persons become overwhelmingly clear to him; then seemingly unsure of their loyalty, testing those friendships again and again. He does love deeply the friends who can successfully be put to the test.

The group relations were helping Mr. Z. over his suspicious attitude towards people. He was described as a man who had been deeply in love with his wife who had died several years before. He was actually crying for such friendships, but he was unable to reach out to them by himself. The group worker needed to combine the offer of group relationships with intensive individual attention before he could really be drawn into the group. She records:

Mr. Z refused to sit with the group, said he could never be a part of it because he is "too nervous." The effort of the group worker had been to talk with him, getting what interesting information he would give about travel especially and to bring this information back to the group thus trying to bridge the gap. Early in the period of group sessions he seemed to have a close relationship only with S whom he pitied, and with Mr. J. After Mr. J's death he seemed to reject all relationships in the group except for the one with the group worker, until recently when he re-established his relationship with S and did form new ties to Mr. G and Mr. H. Much of this progress had been accomplished through Mr. G's tireless efforts which were encouraged by the group worker.

We see how the group worker is working with the individual and with other members in the group to help him over a difficult and lonely period after the death of the one friend he had acquired. We must realize that the loss of beloved people is very frequent at this age, and adds to the feeling of loneliness and in many cases of anxiety, because of the end being so close.

We see the help which the group can give to a completely different personality in the following summary.

Mrs. B is younger than all the others. She has severe palsy, is scarcely able to speak and unable to move unaided but her mind is perfectly clear and her memory good. She has need for recognition and acceptance other than pity. This is shown by her pride in carrying details in her memory to help the group progress. She appreciates on-the-level kidding and joking and contributes jokes. She has a need to be a part of group decisions and plans as shown by her part in planning a party and in selecting a group name.

She loves pretty things and gets satisfaction out of understanding the processes involved in making things. We know this from the fact that she occasionally indicates her desire to be shown articles in the process of being made.

We see here an extremely handicapped person who is gaining a great deal from the group by knowing that she is valuable to it and not just somebody who is tolerated. She is unable to do many things that the group is doing but she can participate in the more intellectual endeavors. Any kind of program that would be handed down to her without her being able to participate would only increase her feelings of inability.

It must be a sad experience to have worked all one's life and then suddenly realize that this capacity has gone. The person who has practically been a "work horse" with few outside interests has the hardest time to adjusting to imposed leisure. Mrs. L. is an example of this specific difficulty:

Mrs. L has attended all group sessions though with much reluctance. . . . She does, however, always enjoy group sessions. She is 77 years old, "with a lean and hungry look," somewhat untidy and always insisting how ill she is and that she has a right to rest. She worked hard as a maid all her life until her retirement. She loved the work and was evidently a loyal and devoted employee. . . . She has been in this boarding home for three years and has not made a completely good adjustment. She has worked so hard physically all her life that she has never learned how to enjoy leisure or any of the pursuits such as fine handwork that can go with leisure. She misses the recognition she received when employed. In the group we have come to realize that her needs are best fulfilled by short time handwork projects requiring little skill but producing articles that look good and for which she can receive some of the recognition she needs. Her interest in travel was brought out in our map project, her eyes shining with pleasure as she was encouraged to tell about the one trip she had (on the

Great Lakes). To build on this interest, she has, at the group worker's suggestion, been coloring a map to send to her son.

We see that the group must help Mrs. L. to adjust to a completely changed mode of life. Since interests besides work were not cultivated in younger life, one has to discover which ones can have some meaning to her. It is also important to help her with her obvious feelings of guilt about doing nothing which she expresses by insisting how ill she is to justify her "life of leisure." If she is helped to overcome her guilt feelings, she will have less need to complain and will allow herself to enjoy this period of life.

The group worker is dealing in these groups with people who have achieved a certain life pattern and who do not want to change a great deal. While we are helping in youth groups and in children's groups with the growing-up process, we are working in older groups with people with established personalities. There is an ability to change, but it is less strong and in many cases not as necessary. In group relations this makes for some special aspects in the way members accept or reject each other. Helping a rejected member being accepted in a group seems to be harder in old age groups than in others because the attitudes are quite definite and often well rationalized.

An example of this is the situation in a boarding home in which the women had formed a special club. A man who had previously lived in another boarding home and had been very active in a club there had expressed the wish to be part of the club in the new home. This was discussed with the club members, who first objected to his membership. The group worker explained to the club that this new resident would be very much hurt if he could not join the group and after some discussion they agreed that they would accept him. Nevertheless, the group worker knew that this might not change their attitude when he actually arrived. The record states:

I arrived early because I anticipated there might be some difficulty in regard to Mr. A joining the group. We brought in two tables making a long table at which to work instead of the small table at which we had previously worked. I thought if we were not quite so crowded and physical contact was not quite so close there might be less rejection of Mr. A in the group. Mr. A immediately expressed himself as willing to help sew clowns for the service project. His sewing was rather poor but it was not the poor quality of sewing that bothered the group. Mrs. P and Mrs. Q and Mrs. L were obviously very disapproving of a man sewing at all and also of his admission to the group. Mrs. P became so hostile about it that she stayed but a minute and then left with quite an angry look on her face. I followed her unobtrusively and discussed the matter with her. She apologized and said that she felt she had acted hastily and would return to the group. She did return and acted with considerable self-control, although it was clear she did not approve of a man sewing.

This incident shows how help is needed to establish relationships and how it cannot be left completely to the initiative of one or another of the members in the boarding home.

It is even more difficult if a member has a personality that interferes with the pleasure of the others. In this case the group worker needs to help this member to work on some change in herself. In a training session of volunteers one of the volunteers brought up her most difficult problem.

Mrs. E was extremely bossy with the other members of the group. She knew that they did not like it but could not seem to keep herself from being bossy and telling them what to do. Her bossiness and tactless manner had finally hurt one man's feelings so that he had risen in the group and made a speech about the fact that he had thought the group was a place where friendship should flourish, but that it seemed that it was not so and that he, therefore, was leaving.

It will be the task of the group worker to help Mrs. E. to see how she is spoiling her own chances in the group and how she needs to relate differently to other members. At an age where one has lived a long time with oneself such demand for change is hard. It will be necessary for the group worker to be understanding of this and not expect either complete nor fast change. In a summary of this group, after a longer period of work with it, the same volunteer reports:

Mrs. E tries to curb her tongue though she will never be able to get it completely under control, but the others seem to be growing to understand her better and not be so resentful of her occasional sharp cracks. She has very good qualities too, which I think the others are coming to recognize so that they can overlook her worst shortcoming. Having the club has provided the means for the various members to become well acquainted with each other and some fine friendships between the members of the household have developed as a result. There seems to be an increasing "family" feeling between them. We have warm happy times on club days.

The volunteer working with the group is realistic about how far change can go. The club itself had to learn to accept a more difficult member and in doing so developed a feeling of bond. Friendship and acceptance, which are badly needed at this age, had been achieved by the efforts of the particular member herself and by the other members stimulated by the group worker.

Activities in the group will have to be related to the capacities and handicaps of the members, but they can be as varied as any other club program. In an institution for the aged with many European immigrants one of the residents complained that club programs were too often conducted with a certain form of condescension even if the person conducting it was not consciously aware of this. The young worker did not realize that she was dealing with a group of people who had read a great deal and traveled much. They were polite in letting her introduce handicrafts, but among themselves they talked about how childish this activity seemed to them. When the worker learned to understand this she began to listen more attentively to the wishes expressed by the older people themselves. Very soon a history course was established. With the introduction of some experts and the help of some residents who prepared themselves in the history of their particular countries, a stimulating program was developed. Out of such an undertaking a whole project might emerge in which the older people can make a real contribution to the historical understanding of immigration waves into the United States. They could either write or tell about their memories and they might gain a great deal of satisfaction out of knowing that they are part of an important historical development and that they now become part of recording it. We are wasting an enormous amount of historical source material by not making more use of the specific interest of our older citizens in talking and thinking about their pasts.

In institutions for the aged the function of the social group worker is direct work with specific groups. Many institutions for the aged will not be able to afford a full-time social group worker on their staff. Several institutions may join together in one project and the group worker will either lead several groups in different homes or will establish a project that will give volunteers a satisfying activity. If the actual group meetings are conducted by volunteers, individual interviews and general training sessions will be necessary. They will help the volunteers with program planning, group work principles, and a better understanding of the aged. One volunteer said:

Since she had worked at three different boarding home groups that she had found that all three groups were very different, that she might have acquired stereotypes from working with one group that would be different from those she would acquire working with another group. She felt there was too much generalization about an age group including teen-agers, etc. She said she had come across a line in a paper which said, "We are inclined to think of older age as irritable, but actually the seeming irritability is due to insecurity and ill health."

In actual work with the older people we realize that they too are each one a distinct individual with liabilities but also with great capacities. The more positive we are approaching people, the more surprised we will be at their capacity for warmth, acceptance, and real human friendship. We have generally pushed the older person into a cold and lonely world and they have reacted by being disagreeable and whining and asking for a great deal of physical attention. In supplying them with self-respect and the right to be part of the community, we discover often their capacity to be giving and to make real contributions. It is important that they feel that they are truly "senior citizens" in a community which accepts them as capable human beings. The social group worker's contribution to the institutionalized aged is to enhance this possibility by offering opportunities for making such contributions and to relate the older person more satisfactorily to the group which has taken on the vital replacement of the family.

9. DEDICATED TO HELPING PEOPLE

But the things with which we have been charged are difficult, almost everything serious is difficult, and everything is serious.[1]

And now we have come to the end of this book. It is a sober and practical book. Yet behind the soberness and the sometimes trivial-sounding examples lies work with the most important fabric of which life is woven: the relationship between man and man in its deepest meaning. And we are concerned with this relationship in settings which are somewhat apart from everyday normal life and with people, young and old, who have experienced some breakdown. This breakdown has occurred either in themselves or in their environment. Sometimes they will get over it quickly, and sometimes the road to recovery and change will be long and involved. Sometimes we do not even know whether they will succeed.

People, all people, need some help along the way. People in institutions need this help especially. We have developed many professional skills for fulfilling this task. The medical profession, teachers, psychologists, social workers, and many vocational services work together. Inside the institution daily life takes on large proportions and means the difference between a "marking time" to get out or a beginning capacity for recovery. Group living, therefore, is the vital treatment area. We have developed a profession, social group work,

[1] Rainer Maria Rilke, *Letters to a Young Poet* (London: Langley, 1943), p. 16.

which can be helpful with this. This book was dedicated to this task and to the task of those who do the daily job with the group worker, the houseparents, the group counselors, the guards. We have pointed out the function of the group worker as

1. Supervision of houseparents, counselors, or guards.
2. Direct group work with formed therapeutic groups inside the institution.
3. Supervision and coordination of special recreational services.
4. Responsibility for referral to resources for group association in the community.
5. Work with volunteers.
6. Work with relatives of residents in the institution.
7. Giving help with diagnosis as a responsible member of the treatment team.

Depending on the kind of institution, some of these functions will be more important than others. In some institutions the social group worker will have to add responsibility for group life of the institutional personnel itself.

Supervision does not consist in just watching what the other person is doing, but in giving understanding help through individual sessions as well as through stimulating in-service training.

The houseparent, the guard, and the group counselor will begin playing a more professional role. Their learning will come through the social group worker in the institution as well as through outside institutes and further education.

The goal of all education and treatment is to help men and women to free themselves and to become capable of making the most of what is in them while considering the rights of others. The goal is the same for all people in institutions. Their capacities will differ and their point of departure in relation to others will be different from individual to individual, but basically the goal is unchanged and our main task is to help them keep their heads high and learn to love and want to be part of humanity.

We have realized that the more we know about human beings, the better we will be able to work with them. Even with the best of intentions we will make great mistakes if we do not accept this truth. On the other hand, all scientific knowledge will not be used helpfully if we do not want to use it that way. Deepest insight into human beings can be used in a punishing and diabolic way if it is not combined with our own warmth and love and respect for the people with whom we work. Science has been able to harness atomic power. Only our values will determine whether we use it constructively or for destruction only. Knowledge about people is as dangerous or as beneficial as atomic knowledge. With greater knowledge, increasing power over human beings is put into our hands. It will be up to us whether we use it *for* those dependent on us or *against* them.

Residents in institutions will find their way to each other somehow, but it is the task of the group worker to help them do this so that warmth begins to flow instead of hatred. Hate breeds only despair or new defiance.

In institutions those responsible for daily living take on a greater importance than any human being in other life situations. They hold in their hands every minute of the day. This Godlike position can easily tempt us to feel like little Gods and to want to make the resident or inmate over in our own image and guide every step of his way the way *we* want it. Insight into ourselves and a constant and repeated probing regarding our motives will be indispensable in this kind of work. Sometimes we start with kind feelings and high idealism, but the temptation of running somebody else's life who is completely in our hands is very great. We have to remind ourselves that we are each and every one different from each other and have the right to be so.

While I am writing this, young Joan is staying at my house. She had a short stay in an institution for delinquents. I asked her what we should do to make this a more helpful experience. The first answer was a vehement, "Do away with Miss X. She treats us like dirt." And then came another comment: "It is still a reformatory if you have to scrub floors every day on hands and knees while other equipment is available and if you are never supposed to speak unless you are spoken to." Joan is not complaining about physical abuse, but what has been abused is the power over another human being. Unnecessary humiliation was added to an already troubled and resentful human soul.

We are *not* talking about sugar-coating institutional life. We are *not* talking about "frills" to make life "soft" compared to what it is on the outside. We are not sentimentalists. As group workers we are putting demands on human beings wherever they are by asking them not to simply do what we tell them but to learn to live in situations which demand responsible behavior. To many people this is a hard demand, harder than conforming. Yet—besides the effort—it gives the reward of deep satisfaction.

In our work with people we must learn to combine scientific knowledge with great warmth, understanding of their failure, weakness, and hate with recognition of their capacity to find also strength and ability to love. We must combine seriousness with laughter, humility with the conviction of the importance of our work.

We will have to learn to help people, but we will also need to catch ourselves each time when we become too protective. I earlier quoted some of the wise words of Mrs. Macauley, and I would like to end with her wonderful wisdom in talking to her boy.

Schools are only to keep children off the streets, but sooner or later they've got to go out into the streets, whether they like it or not. It's natural for fathers and mothers to be afraid of the world for their children but there's nothing for them to be afraid of. . . .[2]

It is not only the person in the institution we must help to become free. It is we, ourselves, who are dealing with them who have to free ourselves of our own fears and our own distrust.

Only then will we be able to use knowledge, skill and method truly for the re-establishment of sound human relations and help tortured and unhappy human beings become part of the community of men.

[2] William Saroyan, *The Human Comedy* (New York: Harcourt, Brace, 1943).

SELECTED READINGS

Aichorn, August, *Wayward Youth*. New York: The Viking Press, 1935.

Alexander, Myrl E., "Let's Look at Our Jails," *Federal Probation*, September, 1952.

Asp, Julian, "Children in Institutions," *Minnesota Welfare*, January, 1952.

Bardwell, Blanche, *A Study of Holland Hall, An Institution for Adolescent Girls*. Master's Thesis, University of Denver, School of Social Work, 1947.

Bennett, James V., "Prisons in Turmoil," *Federal Probation*, September, 1952.

Bettelheim, Bruno, *Love Is Not Enough*. Glencoe, Ill.: The Free Press, 1950.

"Building Asset Citizens," National Child Welfare Division, *The American Legion*, Indianapolis, 1941-43.

Burmeister, Eva, *Forty-five in the Family*. New York: Columbia University Press, 1949.

Clendenen, Richard, "To Synchronize the Training-Social Program with Life in the Community," *The Child*, November, 1949.

―――― "After Training School, What?" Federal Security Agency, US Children's Bureau, 1950.

Clinard, Marshall B., Review of *Delinquents in the Making: Paths to Prevention* by Sheldon and Eleanor Glueck, *Federal Probation*, March, 1953.

Cohen, A. Alfred, "Use of Group Process in an Institution," *Social Work*, Vol. I, No. 4 (October 1956), 57-61.

Cohen, Frank J., *Children in Trouble*. New York: W. W. Norton & Co., 1952.

Community Services for Older People, The Chicago Plan. Chicago: Community Project for the Aged of the Welfare Council of Metropolitan Chicago, 1952.

Coyle, Grace, *Group Work with American Youth*. New York: Harper & Bros., 1948.

——— "Social Group Work," in *Social Work Year Book, 1951*. New York: American Association of Social Workers, 1951.

Deutsch, Albert, *Our Rejected Children*. Boston: Little, Brown and Co., 1950.

——— *The Mentally Ill in America*. New York: Columbia University Press, 1949.

Eliot, Martha M., "A New Start on an Old Problem," *Federal Probation*, March, 1953.

Ellingston, John R., *Protecting Our Children from Criminal Careers*. New York: Prentice-Hall, Inc., 1948.

Emma Pendleton Bradley Home, Annual Report for 1952. Riverside, Rhode Island.

Erikson, Erik H., *Childhood and Society*. New York: W. W. Norton & Co., 1950.

Fairman, Phyllis Dickinson, *An Application of Principles of Clinical Group Work to the Recreational Program in a Temporary Study Home for Children Referred for Foster Home Placement*. Master's Thesis, Wayne University, School of Social Work.

Farrar, Marcella and Nelida Ferrari, "Casework and Group Work in a Home for the Aged," *Social Work*, Vol. 5, No. 2 (April 1960), pp. 58-62.

Felix, R. H., M.D., "The Responsibility of the Community for the Juvenile Delinquent," Proceedings of the National Conference of Social Work. New York: Columbia University Press, 1947.

"A Few Facts About Juvenile Delinquency," *Federal Probation*, March, 1953.

Fogel, David, "Use of Groups in a Juvenile Hall," *Correction Psychiatry and Journal of Social Therapy*, Vol. X, No. 5 (September 1964).

Foster, Sybil, "Mental Health Needs in Children's Institutions," *Mental Hygiene, January,* 1938.

Gault, Robert H., "Highlights of 40 Years in the Correctional Field—and Looking Ahead," *Federal Probation,* March, 1953.

Gibran, Kahlil, *The Prophet.* New York: Alfred A. Knopf, Inc., 1923.

Gula, Martin, "Study and Treatment Homes for Troubled Children," Proceedings of the National Conference of Social Work. New York: Columbia University Press, 1947.

Harmon, Maurice A., "The Importance of Staff Team Work in a Training School," *Selected Papers in Group Work and Community Organization.* Columbus, Ohio: National Conference of Social Work, 1952.

——— "The Receptive Process in a State Training School," *Focus,* November, 1950.

Institute of Children's Institutions (Mimeographed Report). Chicago, March, 1949.

Jocelyn, Irene, *The Adolescent and His World.* New York: Family Service Association of America, 1952.

Kaplan, Jerome, *A Social Program for Older People.* Minneapolis: University of Minnesota Press, 1953.

Keane, Sister M. Charles, R.S.M., *The House Mother,* Washington, D.C.: National Conference of Catholic Charities, 1954.

Kephardt, Newell G., "Group Autonomy in a Children's Institution," *Mental Hygiene*, October, 1938.

Konopka, Gisela, *The Adolescent Girl in Conflict*, Englewood Cliffs, New Jersey: Prentice-Hall, 1966.

—— *Social Group Work: A Helping Process*, Englewood Cliffs, New Jersey, Prentice-Hall, 1963.

—— "Social Group Work Method: Its Use in the Correctional Field," *Federal Probation*, Vol. XLV, No. 1 (March 1950).

—— "What Houseparents Should Know," *Children*, Vol. III, No. 2 (March-April 1956), pp. 49-54.

—— "Implications of a Changing Residential Treatment Program," *American Journal of Orthopsychiatry*, Vol. XXXI, No. 1 (January 1961), pp. 17-39.

Lippman, Hyman S., "Preventing Delinquency," *Federal Probation*, March, 1953.

—— "Treatment of the Juvenile Delinquent," *Proceedings of the National Conference of Social Work*. New York: Columbia University Press, 1945.

Lourie, Norman V., and Rena Schulman, "The Role of the Residential Staff in Residential Treatment," *American Journal of Orthopsychiatry*, Vol. XXII (October 1952), No. 4.

Maier, Henry, ed., *Group Work as Part of Residential Treatment*, New York: National Association of Social Workers, 1965.

Maxwell, Jean M., "Group Services—Well-being for Older People, *Social Work with Groups*, 1960, New York: N.A.S.W., 1960, pp. 74-85.

McCorkle, Lloyd W., "Group Therapy in the Treatment of Offenders," *Federal Probation*, December, 1952.

McCullers, Carson S., *The Member of the Wedding* (Play).

McKelvey, Blake, *American Prisons*. Chicago: University of Chicago Press, 1936.

Milner, John G., "Personal Factors in Correctional Work," *Federal Probation*, September, 1952.

Minnesota State Training School for Boys. General Report, Division of Public Institutions, St. Paul, Minnesota.

Nash, Bernard R., *A Study of the Time Distribution, Leisure Time Program Content and Available Leisure Time Facilities in Eight Minnesota Child Caring Institutions*. Master's Thesis, University of Minnesota, School of Social Work, 1953.

National Conference on Prevention and Control of Juvenile Delinquents, Reports. Washington, D.C., November, 1946.

National Council on Crime and Delinquency, *Standards and Guides for the Detention of Children and Youth* (2nd ed.), New York, 1961.

Norman, Sherwood and Helen, *Detention for the Juvenile Court*. New York: National Probation Association, 1946.

Redl, Fritz, and George V. Sheviakoff, *Discipline for Today's Children and Youth*. Washington, D.C.: Department of Supervision and Curriculum Development, N.E.A., 1944.

Redl, Fritz and David Wineman, *The Aggressive Child*, New York: Free Press of Glencoe, 1957.

Residential Treatment Centers for Emotionally Disturbed Children, a listing. Washington, D.C.: Federal Security Agency, Social Security Administration, Children's Bureau, 1952.

Rilke, Rainer Maria, *Letters to a Young Poet* (Translation). London: Langley & Sons, The Euston Press, 1943.

Saroyan, William, *The Human Comedy*. New York: Harcourt, Brace & Co., Pocket Book Edition, 1945.

Schrout, Florence, *Some Aspects of a Group Work Program in a Children's Institution*. Master's Thesis, Columbia University, School of Social Work, 1949.

Schulze, Susanne, Ed., *Creative Group Living in a Children's Institution*. New York: Association Press, 1951.

——— and Morris F. Mayer, *Training House Parents*. Washington, D. C.: Federal Security Agency, Social Security Administration, Children's Bureau (Mimeographed Report).

Simos, Jack, *Manual for Houseparents*. St. Paul: Division of Social Welfare, Minnesota Department of Social Security, 1952.

Slavson, S. R., *An Introduction to Group Therapy*. New York: Commonwealth Fund, 1943.

Smith, Barbara L., *Programming in a Treatment Home for Disturbed Children*. Master's Thesis, Wayne University, School of Social Work.

Stapf, Marjorie, *Group Work Service in a Home for Unmarried Mothers*. Master's Thesis, University of Minnesota, School of Social Work, 1951.

Story, Sally, *Group Work in a Shelter for Unmarried Mothers*. Master's Thesis, Columbia University, School of Social Work, 1951.

Strang, Ruth, "Facts to Tell Young People about Juvenile Delinquency," *Federal Probation*, December, 1952.

Tine, Sebastian, Katherine Hastings, and Paul Deutschberger, "Generic and Specific in Social Group Work Practice with the Aging," *Social Work with Groups*, 1960, New York: N.A.S.W., 1960, pp. 86-99.

Trecker, Harleigh, *Social Group Work*. New York: Association Press, 1955.

U.S. Department of Health, Education and Welfare. *Institutions Serving Delinquent Children—Guides and Goals*, Children's Bureau Publication No. 360, Revised Edition, 1962.

Van Der Wart, Esther, *The Use of Limitations in Two Groups in a Children's Treatment Home*. Master's

Thesis, University of Minnesota, School of Social Work, 1953.

Wallack, Walter M., "Stone Walls Do a Prison Make," *Federal Probation*, September, 1952.

Whittaker, James and A. Trieschmann, *The Other 23 Hours*, Aldine Publishing Co., Chicago, 1969.

Wilson, Gertrude, and Gladys Ryland, *Social Group Work Practice*, Boston: Houghton Mifflin Co., 1949.

Witmer, Helen Leland, and Ruth Kotinsky, Eds., *Personality in the Making*. New York: Harper & Bros., 1952.

——— *We Call Them Delinquents*. New York School of Social Work (Mimeographed paper).

INDEX